S0-CFE-983

THE METAPHYSICS OF EVERYDAY LIFE

In *The Metaphysics of Everyday Life* Lynne Rudder Baker presents and defends a unique account of the material world: the Constitution View. In contrast to leading metaphysical views that take everyday things to be either nonexistent or reducible to micro-objects, the Constitution View construes familiar things as irreducible parts of reality. Although they are ultimately constituted by microphysical particles, everyday objects are neither identical to, nor reducible to, the aggregates of microphysical particles that constitute them. The result is genuine ontological diversity: people, bacteria, donkeys, mountains, and microscopes are fundamentally different kinds of things – all constituted by, but not identical to, aggregates of particles. Baker supports her account with discussions of nonreductive causation, vagueness, mereology, artifacts, three-dimensionalism, ontological novelty, ontological levels and emergence. The upshot is a unified ontological theory of the entire material world that irreducibly contains people, as well as nonhuman living things and inanimate objects.

LYNNE RUDDER BAKER is Distinguished Professor of Philosophy at the University of Massachusetts, Amherst. Her publications include *Persons and Bodies: A Constitution View* (2000) and *Explaining Attitudes: A Practical Approach to the Mind* (1995).

CAMBRIDGE STUDIES IN PHILOSOPHY

General Editors

JONATHAN LOWE (University of Durham)
WALTER SINNOTT-ARMSTRONG (Dartmouth College)

Advisory Editors:

JONATHAN DANCY (University of Texas, Austin)
JOHN HALDANE (University of St Andrews)
GILBERT HARMAN (Princeton University)
FRANK JACKSON (Australian National University)
WILLIAM G. LYCAN (University of North Carolina at Chapel Hill)
SYDNEY SHOEMAKER (Cornell University)
JUDITH J. THOMSON (Massachusetts Institute of Technology)

RECENT TITLES:

RAYMOND MARTIN *Self-Concern*
ANNETTE BARNES *Seeing Through Self-Deception*
MICHAEL BRATMAN *Faces of Intention*
AMIE THOMASSON *Fiction and Metaphysics*
DAVID LEWIS *Papers on Ethics and Social Philosophy*
FRED DRETSKE *Perception, Knowledge, and Belief*
LYNNE RUDDER BAKER *Persons and Bodies*
ROSANNA KEEFE *Theories of Vagueness*
JOHN GRECO *Putting Skeptics in Their Place*
RUTH GARRETT MILLIKAN *On Clear and Confused Ideas*
DERK PEREBOOM *Living Without Free Will*
BRIAN ELLIS *Scientific Essentialism*
ALAN H. GOLDMAN *Practical Rules: When We Need Them and When We Don't*
CHRISTOPHER HILL *Thought and World*
ANDREW NEWMAN *The Correspondence Theory of Truth*
ISHTIYAQUE HAJI *Deontic Morality and Control*
WAYNE A. DAVIS *Meaning, Expression and Thought*
PETER RAILTON *Facts, Values, and Norms*
JANE HEAL *Mind, Reason and Imagination*
JONATHAN KVANVIG *The Value of Knowledge and the Pursuit of Understanding*
ANDREW MELNYK *A Physicalist Manifesto*
WILLIAM S. ROBINSON *Understanding Phenomenal Consciousness*
D. M. ARMSTRONG *Truth and Truthmakers*
KEITH FRANKISH *Mind and Supermind*
MICHAEL SMITH *Ethics and the A Priori*
NOAH LEMOS *Common Sense*

JOSHUA GERT *Brute Rationality*
ALEXANDER R. PRUSS *The Principle of Sufficient Reason*
FOLKE TERSMAN *Moral Disagreement*
JOSEPH MENDOLA *Goodness and Justice*
DAVID COPP *Morality in a Natural World*

The Metaphysics of
Everyday Life

An Essay in Practical Realism

LYNNE RUDDER BAKER

University of Massachusetts, Amherst

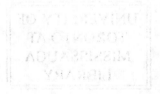

CAMBRIDGE
UNIVERSITY PRESS

CAMBRIDGE UNIVERSITY PRESS
Cambridge, New York, Melbourne, Madrid, Cape Town, Singapore, São Paulo, Delhi

Cambridge University Press
The Edinburgh Building, Cambridge CB2 8RU, UK

Published in the United States of America by Cambridge University Press, New York

www.cambridge.org
Information on this title: www.cambridge.org/9780521880497

© Lynne Rudder Baker 2007

This publication is in copyright. Subject to statutory exception
and to the provisions of relevant collective licensing agreements,
no reproduction of any part may take place without
the written permission of Cambridge University Press.

First published 2007

Printed in the United Kingdom at the University Press, Cambridge

A catalogue record for this publication is available from the British Library

ISBN 978-0-521-88049-7 hardback

Cambridge University Press has no responsibility for
the persistence or accuracy of URLs for external or
third-party internet websites referred to in this book,
and does not guarantee that any content on such
websites is, or will remain, accurate or appropriate.

UNIVERSITY OF
TORONTO AT
MISSISSAUGA
LIBRARY

For my dear friend and colleague,
Gareth B. Matthews,
with gratitude and affection

Contents

Preface   *page* xiii

INTRODUCTION   1

1   Beginning in the middle   3
Why do we need a metaphysics of ordinary things?   6
ID phenomena   11
Philosophy in the middle of things   13
Practical realism   15
What lies ahead   21

PART I   EVERYDAY THINGS   23

2   The reality of ordinary things   25
Motivation for nonreduction   25
The idea of constitution   32
Is the idea of constitution plausible?   39
Thinking things into existence?   43
Conclusion   47

3   Artifacts   49
Aggregates and artifacts   49
Conditions for being an artifact   51
A Constitution View of artifacts   53
The significance of malfunction   55
The ontological status of artifacts   59
Conclusion   66

4   Human persons   67
The Constitution View of human persons   67
Coming into existence: human organisms
      and human persons   72

ix

Contents

Life and death | 82
Quasi-naturalism and the ontological uniqueness
of persons | 85
Three approaches contrasted | 90
Conclusion | 93

PART II   THE EVERYDAY WORLD | 95

5   Commonsense causation | 97
Jaegwon Kim's arguments against nonreductive
mental causation | 99
Does Kim's key argument generalize
to all macrocausation? | 104
Response to Kim's key argument | 106
An account of nonreductive causation | 111
Saving nonreductive materialism | 116
Conclusion | 119

6   Metaphysical vagueness | 121
Arguments for metaphysical vagueness | 123
Where in the world is vagueness? | 127
Spatial and temporal boundaries | 128
The vagueness of the constitution relation | 132
Sorites arguments | 135

7   Time | 142
The A-series and the B-series | 143
The indispensability of both A- and B-series | 145
A theory of time | 149
Metaphysical implications | 152
Beyond Presentism and Eternalism | 154
Conclusion | 155

PART III   METAPHYSICAL UNDERPINNINGS | 157

8   Constitution revisited | 159
Definition of "x constitutes y at t" | 160
Unity without identity | 166
The same F | 169
Objections and replies | 172

Contents

9   Mereology and constitution   181
    Sums and constitution   182
    A Constitution View of parts   187
    Are parts more basic than wholes?   190
    The ontological status of sums   191
    Some philosophical puzzles   194
    Conclusion   197

10 Three-dimensionalism defended   199
    Three-dimensionalism vs. four-dimensionalism   199
    The argument from vagueness   201
    Count indeterminacy?   208
    "Paradoxes of coincidence"   208
    Reasons to prefer three-dimensionalism   213
    Conclusion   217

11 Five ontological issues   218
    An account of ontological significance   218
    Time and existence   226
    Ontological novelty   234
    Ontological levels   234
    Emergence   237
    Conclusion   239

Select bibliography   241
Index   250

Preface

Nonphilosophers, if they think of philosophy at all, may wonder why people work in metaphysics. After all, metaphysics, as Auden once said of poetry, makes nothing happen.[1] Yet some very intelligent people are driven to spend their lives formulating and arguing for metaphysical claims. Part of what motivates metaphysicians is the appeal of grizzly puzzles (like the paradox of the heap or the puzzle of the ship of Theseus). But the main reason to work in metaphysics, for me at least, is to understand the shared world that we all encounter and interact with.

The title of this book, *The Metaphysics of Everyday Life*, may bring to mind the title of Freud's lively book, *The Psychopathology of Everyday Life*, published in 1904. Although scientifically obsolete, Freud's little volume aptly describes numerous kinds of familiar phenomena. In *The Psychopathology of Everyday Life*, Freud focused on ordinary mistakes that go unnoticed: forgetting proper names, mistakes in reading, mislaying things, forgetting to do things, and so on. These banal errors appear to be random but, according to Freud, are products of subconscious desires. Putting aside Freud's own explanations, we can applaud Freud's seeing significance in occurrences that are usually overlooked as haphazard and purposeless. Whereas Freud saw *psychological* significance in ordinary things and our interactions with them, I see *ontological* significance in ordinary things and our interactions with them.

In addition to responding to critics and expanding my earlier work – work that appeared in *Persons and Bodies: A Constitution View* (Cambridge University Press, 2000) and in *Explaining Attitudes: A Practical Approach to the Mind* (Cambridge University Press, 1995) – *The Metaphysics of Everyday Life* offers detailed treatments of some of the most important issues in metaphysics: nonreductive causation, vagueness, mereology, artifacts, three-dimensionalism, time, ontological novelty, ontological levels, and

---

[1] W. H. Auden, "In Memory of W. B. Yeats."

emergence. On each of these topics, I present a fresh account in line with my overall view of Practical Realism. The result is a unified ontological theory of the whole material world that contains people, as well as non-human living things and inanimate objects.

A number of people have generously helped me, whether they have found my views congenial or not – in particular, Phillip Bricker, Roberta De Monticelli, Edmund Gettier, David B. Hershenov, Frank Hindriks, Ralph Kennedy, Hilary Kornblith, Menno Lievers, Gareth B. Matthews, Anthonie Meijers, Derk Pereboom, Jonathan Schaffer, Stephen P. Schwartz, Theodore Sider, Marc Slors, Katherine Sonderegger, Robert A. Wilson, and Dean Zimmerman. I have benefited from correspondence with Tomasz Kakol at the Nicholas Copernicus University in Poland. I also thank the participants in my Metaphysics Seminar at the University of Massachusetts, Fall 2004.

Although none of the chapters of *The Metaphysics of Everyday Life* has been published before in its current form, parts of chapters have ancestors that appear in the following publications: "First-Person Knowledge," and "Third-Person Understanding" in *The Nature and Limits of Human Understanding: The 2001 Gifford Lectures at the University of Glasgow*, ed. Anthony J. Sanford, (London: T&T Clark, 2003) (ch. 1, ch. 4); "Philosophy *in Mediis Rebus*," *Metaphilosophy* 32 (2001): 378–394 (ch. 1); "Everyday Concepts as a Guide to Reality," *The Monist* (2007) (ch. 2; ch. 8); "The Ontology of Artefacts," *Philosophical Explorations* 7 (2004): 99–111 (ch. 3); "The Ontological Status of Persons," *Philosophy and Phenomenological Research* 65 (2002): 370–388 (ch. 4, ch. 11); "When Does a Person Begin?" *Social Philosophy and Policy* 22 (2005): 25–48 (ch. 4); "Persons and the Natural Order," *Persons: Human and Divine*, ed. Dean Zimmerman and Peter van Inwagen (Oxford: Oxford University Press, 2007) (ch. 4); "Moral Responsibility Without Libertarianism," *Noûs* 40 (2006): 307–330 (ch. 4); "Nonreductive Materialism," *The Oxford Handbook for the Philosophy of Mind*, ed. Brian McLaughlin and Ansgar Beckermann (Oxford: Oxford University Press, forthcoming) (ch. 5); "Temporal Reality," *Time and Identity: Topics in Contemporary Philosophy*, Vol. 6, ed. Michael O'Rourke, Joseph Campbell, and Harry Silverstein (Cambridge, MA: MIT Press, forthcoming) (ch. 7, ch. 11); "On Making Things Up: Constitution and its Critics," *Philosophical Topics* 30 (2002): 31–51 (ch. 8); "Why Constitution is Not Identity," *Journal of Philosophy* 94 (1997): 599–621 (ch. 11).

Many of the arguments here have descended from papers that I have presented at conferences and universities. Audiences to whom I owe thanks for helpful criticism include those at presentations at the following: Notre Dame University (2005); the Inland Northwest Philosophy Conference at the University of Idaho (2005) (read in absentia; discussion recorded); Conference on Artefacts in Philosophy, Technical University of Delft (Holland) (2004); the Werkmeister Conference on Folk Concepts (2004); the Philosophy Working Group (Erasmus University, Technical University of Delft, Technical University of Eindhoven, Nijmegen University, Utrecht University) (2004); Canisius College (2004); the Philosophical Workshop on Individuality and Person, University of Geneva (2004); Conference on Dimensions of Personhood, University of Jyväskylä (Finland) (2004), Utrecht University (Holland) (2004); the Conference on Personal Identity, Social Philosophy and Policy Center, Bowling Green State University (2004); the Seminar on Persons and Artifacts, Technical University of Delft (Holland) (2003); Book Symposium on Theodore Sider's *Four-Dimensionalism*, American Philosophical Association, Pacific Division (2003); Spring Symposium on *Persons and Bodies*, Ohio University (2003); SUNY at Buffalo (2003); Erasmus University of Rotterdam (2003), Connecticut College (2003); The Chapel Hill Colloquium (2001); The Gifford Lectures, Glasgow University (2001); Conference on Reasons of One's Own, University of Utrecht (Holland) (2001), Leiden University (Holland) (2001); Conference on Self-Consciousness, University of Fribourg (Switzerland) (2000); Memorial Conference for Roderick M. Chisholm at Brown University (2000); Washington University (St. Louis) (1999), the University of Missouri (Columbia) (1999), the University of Toronto (1999); the Australasian Association of Philosophers, Annual Meeting, Melbourne AU (1999); the Australian National University, Research School of Social Sciences (1999) and Yale University (1998).

I continue to be grateful for the support and help of my husband, Tom Baker, and of my friend, Kate Sonderegger.

Introduction

1

Beginning in the middle

Reality comprises everything there is. It is not the province solely of specialists, but is well known to all. Everything is part of it: the gardener and her tulips, the prisoner and his chains, the cook and his food processor are all real things that should be included in a complete account of what there is.[1] The aim of *The Metaphysics of Everyday Life* is to present a theory that focuses on the familiar objects that we encounter every day – flowers, people, houses, and so on – and locates them irreducibly in reality.

Let us begin with a distinction between manifest objects of everyday life (roses, chairs, dollar bills, etc.) and the underlying objects that we can hope that physics will tell us about. Suppose that the underlying objects are collections of particles. I want to defend a metaphysics that gives onto-logical weight to the manifest objects of everyday life. This view is an alternative to contemporary metaphysical theories that take ordinary things to be "really" just collections of particles. Such theories then have to answer the question – How do we account for the fact that, if your lover and your prize roses, say, are "really" just collections of particles, they seem to be a person and and a plant, and do not seem like just collections of particles? One attempted answer is that we simply choose to employ concepts like "person" and "plant" to refer to certain collections of particles. In contrast to such a "conceptual" account of ordinary things, I want to provide an "ontological" account that is nonreductive with respect to the manifest objects of everyday life.

By saying that I want to provide an "ontological" account of ordinary things, I mean that I include in ontology – the complete inventory of what exists – the objects that we daily encounter (passports, fish, etc.). The words "fish" and "passport" are not merely predicates; they express properties.

---

[1] As I shall explain, things are included in a complete account of what there is in virtue of being of one primary kind or another. (See chapter 2.) The gardener, the prisoner, and the cook are all members of the primary kind *person*.

A fish or a passport has the property – essentially, as I'll explain in chapter 2 – of being a fish or a passport. *Fish* and *passport* are primary kinds. Ontology includes not just physical particles and their sums, but also fish and passports. Moreover, I take everyday discourse about ordinary things not only to be largely true, but also to mean what speakers think it means. Unless there is some reason to do otherwise, I take what we commonly say (e.g., "It's time to get your passport renewed," or "The fish today is fresh") at face value. I do not systematically reinterpret ordinary discourse in unfamiliar terms, nor do I suppose that ordinary discourse is defective or inferior to some other (imagined) regimented language. Sentences about ordinary things mean what ordinary speakers think they mean, and such sentences are often true. If I am correct, then the ordinary things that we commonly talk about are irreducibly real, and a complete inventory of what exists will have to include persons, artifacts, artworks, and other medium-sized objects along with physical particles.

Let me make two terminological points. (a) I shall use the term "irreducibly real" and its variants to refer to objects that belong in ontology: objects that exist and are not reducible to anything "else." So, in my usage, someone who says, "Sure, there are tables, but a table is just a bunch of particles," takes tables to be reducible to particles and hence takes particles, but not tables, to be irreducibly real. A complete ontology – comprising everything that is irreducibly real – on my view will include manifest objects like tables.

(b) I shall use the term "the everyday world" and its variants as labels for the target of my investigation. The everyday world is populated by all the things that we talk about, encounter, and interact with: inanimate objects, other people, activities, processes, and so on. It is the world that we live and die in, the world where our plans succeed or fail, the world we do or do not find love and happiness in – in short, the world that matters to us. My aim, again, is to give an ontological account of the shared world that we encounter and to argue that a complete inventory of all the objects that (ever) exist must mention the medium-sized objects that we are familiar with: manifest objects of the everyday world belong to irreducible reality.

Many contemporary metaphysicians reject this project at the outset: Why bother, they ask? There is a longstanding tradition in philosophy that downgrades manifest things. Although that tradition may be traced back at least to Plato, it is influential today. Some contemporary metaphysicians reject ordinary things because they take irreducible reality to be exhausted by a completed physics; some reject ordinary things because they take commonsense objects to be too sloppy – they gain and lose parts; they have no fixed boundaries – to be irreducibly real. Many of today's philosophers take concrete reality to be nothing but fundamental particles and their fusions, or instantaneous temporal parts, and/or a few universals, and see no ontological significance in ordinary things like trees and tables.[2]

There is an important respect in which today's anti-commonsense metaphysicians differ from Plato. Plato used the idea of the Forms to answer questions that arose in the everyday world: What makes this person just or that painting beautiful was its participation in Justice Itself or Beauty Itself. The Forms, though in a timeless realm inaccessible to the senses, were not entirely cut off from the world that we encounter. Indeed, they were used to explain how the everyday world appeared the way that it did. Today's anti-commonsense metaphysicians, by contrast, have no truck metaphysically with the everyday world: What they say about the underlying objects sheds no light on manifest objects, or explains why they appear as they do. Manifest objects are to be understood in terms of concepts and language, not in terms of irreducible reality.

Opposing the anti-commonsense tradition (both its Platonic and contemporary versions) is another one – a tradition that treats manifest things as irreducibly real. Again, by saying that manifest things are "irreducibly real," I mean that ordinary things are not reducible to, or eliminable in favor of, anything else and hence that medium-sized objects must be included in any complete ontology. With roots in Aristotle, the tradition that takes ordinary things to be irreducibly real has included such recent philosophers as the classical American pragmatists and G. E. Moore. However, this "commonsense" tradition is far from dominant today.[3] As I have already suggested, I want to carry this commonsense tradition

---

[2] I have in mind philosophers like David Lewis, David Armstrong, Theodore Sider, and Peter van Inwagen. (I count Van Inwagen in this group because, although he countenances organisms, he takes organisms to be fusions of particles; indeed, on his restricted view of fusions, any fusion of particles is an organism.)

[3] There have been recent signs of resurgence, however. See, for example, Crawford L. Elder, *Real Natures and Familiar Objects* (Cambridge, MA: MIT Press, 2004); Amie L. Thomasson, *Fiction and Metaphysics* (Cambridge: Cambridge University Press, 1999) and *Ordinary Objects* (Oxford: Oxford University Press, 2007); and Michael C. Rea, "Sameness Without Identity: An Aristotelian Solution to the Problem of Material Constitution," *Ratio* 11 (new series) (1998): 316–328. Some aspects of his *Naming and Necessity* (Cambridge, MA: Harvard University Press, 1972) suggest that Saul Kripke would also be sympathetic, but he is so cautious in his commitments that I hesitate to claim him as an ally.

forward by presenting and defending a comprehensive metaphysics of the things that we daily encounter. But why? Why do we need a meta-physics that takes ordinary things to be part of irreducible reality? Why not stay with the prevailing anti-commonsense tradition in analytic metaphysics?

WHY DO WE NEED A METAPHYSICS OF ORDINARY THINGS?

There are several answers to this question. Recall the distinction between manifest objects and underlying entities, conceived of as collections of particles. We have reasonably serviceable criteria of identity, both syn-chronic and diachronic, for most manifest objects of everyday life. Of course, there are problems (e.g., with the ship of Theseus). But fairly well understood practices, backed up by tort law, enable us to get along with our everyday attitudes toward manifest objects. However, we do not, in general, have comparably serviceable criteria of identity, either synchronic or diachronic, for the collections of particles that might be thought to coincide with these manifest objects.

The identity conditions of the underlying objects – various collections of particles – depend on the identity conditions of the manifest objects. We have no idea about the identity of the underlying entities independently of the manifest objects with which they presumably coincide. If manifest objects are "really" just collections of particles, this deficiency in our grasp of identity conditions for the underlying objects threatens the rationality of our everyday attitudes and practices.

Our attitudes and practices concern manifest objects to which the attitudes and practices are directed. If A borrows B's chair, A's obligation is to return the chair, a manifest object for which we have identity conditions. B wants *it* (the chair) back – regardless of the fact that it is now made up of a different collection of particles after A scratched it. The rationality of our attitudes and practices requires that we identify objects over time, and the only objects that we can identify are manifest objects, not collections of particles. So, holding that manifest objects are just collections of particles puts our everyday attitudes and practices concern-ing them at risk of irrationality.

A promising way to remove this threat of irrationality is to come up with a way to correlate the manifest objects with their corresponding underlying objects that respects their coincidence, as well as their distinct-ness, and allows the underlying objects to piggyback on the manifest objects for their (rough) identity conditions.[4] And this is just what my metaphysical theory of ordinary objects attempts to do.

This basic motivation for a metaphysics of ordinary things suggests further reasons to take ordinary objects to be irreducibly real: Taking manifest objects to be irreducibly real provides the most straightforward explanation of experience and its probative value. If ordinary objects are irreducibly real, we can straightforwardly explain the reliability of our sensory evidence; descriptions directly based on experience may be metaphysically (maximally) accurate. Anti-commonsense metaphysicians who deny that ordinary objects are irreducibly real, by contrast, must also deny that descriptions of reality based on experience are ever metaphysically (maximally) accurate. Indeed, according to the anti-commonsense tradition, the metaphysically most accurate descriptions of what we actually experience are unrecognizable to most of us. For example, in the anti-commonsense tradition, the most metaphysically accurate description of someone's being hit head-on by an oncoming car in the wrong lane may well be in terms of intersecting trajectories of two combinations of particles arranged carwise[5] – combinations for which we have no identity conditions except in terms of manifest objects like cars. The commonsense tradition, by contrast, allows us to understand the everyday world without reinterpreting ordinary experience in alien ways.

Another reason to take ordinary objects to be irreducibly real is that the everyday world, populated by ordinary things, is the locus of human interests and concerns. If we want to have rational debate about moral, political, social, and legal issues, we have reason to pursue a metaphysics of ordinary things. It would be useful to have reasons grounded in irreducible reality, and not just in our concepts, to back our moral positions. For example, I do not want to appeal just to our concepts to decide one way or the other whether destroying pre-implantation human embryos in stem-cell research is tantamount to murder. (And fortunately, the view that I propose does ground an answer to this question in irreducible reality. See chapter 4.) Similarly for moral debates generally: for example, debates about animal rights, assisted suicide, and treatment of prisoners.

---

[4] This way of putting the point was suggested to me by Gary Matthews, who notes that the suggestion is just Aristotle's in modern dress.

[5] The anti-commonsense philosophers help themselves to terms like "carwise" – terms that presuppose the ordinary things whose existence they reduce to something else or deny altogether.

This book is not a book on ethics, still less on public policy. I am not claiming that a metaphysics of ordinary objects will settle any moral debate, but it does open up ontological space to consider ethical issues in light of what is irreducibly real in the world around us. The whole arena of human concerns is completely invisible to anti-commonsense metaphysics, which relegates issues of human concern to concepts of little moment to metaphysics. If reality is to bear on *any* moral, social, political, or legal issues, then it will have to include ordinary objects like persons. So, anyone who considers irreducible reality relevant to issues of human concern has a good reason to pursue a metaphysics of ordinary objects.

Finally, we also have reason to take ordinary objects to be irreducibly real because they figure ineliminably in successful common causal explanations of everyday phenomena. Here is an argument:

Premise (1): Any objects and properties that are needed for causal explanations should be recognized in ontology.

Premise (2): Appeal to ordinary objects and properties is indispensable in causal explanation.

Conclusion: Ordinary objects should be recognized in ontology.

Premise (1) is supported by the general principle that anything that has effects is real. This is a converse of "Alexander's Dictum," according to which "to be real is to have causal powers."[6] (See chapter 5.) Premise (1) is relatively uncontroversial.

Premise (2) is justified by countless examples from ordinary life as well as from the social sciences. The evidence that ordinary things have causal powers rests on the success and reliability of a huge class of causal explanations that appeal to properties of ordinary things. For example: Use of stamps with too little postage caused a letter to be returned to the sender. A slump in automobile sales caused the automakers to lose money. The riots caused a conservative reaction. All these are legitimate causal explanations: They are instances of counterfactual-supporting generalizations. They could well be cited in research papers in economics, political science, or sociology. And they all appeal to ordinary things and ordinary properties as being causally efficacious.

---

[6] Jaegwon Kim, "The Nonreductivist's Troubles With Mental Causation," in *Supervenience and Mind: Selected Philosophical Essays* (Cambridge: Cambridge University Press, 1993): 336–357. Kim endorses Alexander's Dictum.

Finally, there are no other explanations in terms of molecules or atoms that better explain the phenomena (a letter's being returned to sender, carmakers' losing money, a conservative reaction). So, rather than getting better explanations of such phenomena from underlying objects and properties, we would simply lose sight of what we wanted to understand. Causal explanations in terms of ordinary objects and properties explain phenomena that we want to explain. Ordinary things figure indispensably in causal explanations and hence belong in the ontology. (For a detailed account of nonreductive intentional causation by ordinary things, see chapter 5.)

In sum, we have overwhelmingly greater reason to believe in the irreducible reality of ordinary objects and properties than to believe in any theory that denies that they are irreducibly real.[7] The evidence of our senses, of which the commonsense tradition avails itself, trumps arcane arguments leading to anti-commonsense conclusions cut off from anything we can confirm in experience. We know about ordinary things first-hand: we encounter them, we manufacture them, we interact with them.[8] Our knowledge of collections of simples or fundamental particles is much more meager, and much more distant, than is our knowledge of ordinary things.[9] So, we have many reasons to pursue a metaphysics that takes ordinary objects to be irreducibly real.

These reasons to take ordinary objects to be irreducibly real do not contravene physics. Quite the contrary. As we shall see, the idea of constitution allows stable ordinary objects to be ultimately constituted by constantly changing sums of particles, without being reducible to the sums that constitute them. (See especially chapter 9.) Persistence at the level of ordinary objects is consistent with fluctuation at the level of atoms or subatomic particles. Nor is it anti-scientific to suppose that we need

---

[7] This point is familiar from G. E. Moore.

[8] This is not to deny that there are illusions and hallucinations; it is only to say that irreducibly real objects can be experienced (under conditions that epistemologists specify). Even if a Cartesian Evil Genius were logically possible, we would have no reason whatever to affirm his existence, and much reason to deny it. I discuss this in "First-Person Externalism," *The Modern Schoolman*, forthcoming (2007). Also, see my "Social Externalism and First-Person Authority," *Erkenntnis*, forthcoming.

[9] For example, Theodore Sider takes the irreducible existents to be instantaneous temporal parts. An instantaneous temporal part physically cannot be experienced. The closest we can get to this reality is to a nondenumerable infinity of instantaneous temporal parts. See Theodore Sider, *Four-Dimensionalism: An Ontology of Persistence and Time* (Oxford: Clarendon Press, 2001).

9

causal explanations beyond those offered by natural science.[10] Our ordinary experience generates questions whose answers cannot be given in the language of natural science. Consider, for example, causal explanation of soldiers' being deployed inside a wooden horse. Homer had a causal explanation using terms that referred to manifest objects. We have no better explanation today; we would not even think to look to physics to explain the soldiers' deployment in the Trojan Horse. We might look to (macro-level) physics to explain how the horse was built, but not why it was built or how it was used.

Finally, let me address a commonly heard argument against a metaphysics of ordinary things – an argument from parsimony. The premise is that recognizing ordinary things needlessly bloats ontology. We can do just as well, it is said, with an ontology that contains only particles and their sums (and perhaps sets). So, parsimony dictates that recognizable ordinary things not be in the ontology.

But parsimony is not the correct virtue to appeal to unless one *already* has a coherent and comprehensive view. I shall try to show that the most coherent and comprehensive view of the everyday world countenances the irreducible reality of ordinary things. The basic reason to pursue a metaphysics of ordinary things is that appeal to ordinary things is needed for a coherent and comprehensive metaphysics that secures the rationality of our practices and attitudes toward the things we encounter. Thus, we have good reason not to take manifest objects "really" to be just collections of particles. That would be to take manifest objects, which we encounter first-hand, to be "really" we know not what.

Some philosophers may be unmoved by such considerations. So let me leave it at this: Parsimony is not the only intellectual virtue. A metaphysical theory should help us understand reality and our experience of it. It is difficult to see how understanding is served by the suggestion, for example, that it is never the case that, ontologically speaking, there is exactly one cat in the room. It is even more mysterious to add that we shouldn't worry about this since we still may truly say that there is exactly one cat in the room.[11] Reality as experienced is strange enough; metaphysics should not make it even more so. The ultimate test of a metaphysical theory, after

---

[10] The domain of my view here is the natural world – the world of ordinary things. This view is neutral about the existence of anything supernatural. I do not take this neutrality to be in any way anti-scientific, just "anti-scientistic."

[11] Cf. David Lewis, "Many, But Almost One," in *Papers in Metaphysics and Epistemology* (Cambridge: Cambridge University Press, 1999): 164–182.

coherence and clarity, is a pragmatic one: What are its consequences? Does it make sense of what it set out to illuminate? This is the bar at which I shall rest my case.

ID PHENOMENA

One prominent feature of the everyday world is that it is populated by things – such as pianos, pacemakers, and paychecks – whose existence depends on the existence of persons with propositional attitudes. I call any object that could not exist in a world lacking beings with beliefs, desires, and intentions an "intention-dependent object," or an "ID object."[12] ID objects that we are familiar with include kitchen utensils, precision instruments, credit cards, and so on. ID properties are properties that cannot be instantiated in the absence of beings with beliefs, desires, and intentions; and similarly, for ID events and ID phenomena generally.

Many, if not most, social, economic, political, and legal phenomena are ID phenomena. For example, the event of writing a check is an ID event, because there would be no such thing as writing a check in a world lacking the social and economic conventions that presuppose that people have beliefs, desires, and intentions. (Writing a check is a fundamentally different kind of phenomenon from moving one's hand, and still more different from one's hand's moving.) Most human activities are ID phenomena – both individual (getting a job, going out to dinner, designing a house) and collective (manufacturing automobiles, changing the government, etc.). They could not exist or occur in a world without beliefs, desires, and intentions.

Other communities may be familiar with other kinds of ID phenomena; but all communities recognize many kinds of ID phenomena – e.g., conventions and obligations.[13] ID properties stand in contrast to nonID properties – e.g., being a promise as opposed to being an audible emission, being a signature as opposed to being a mark on paper, being a dance step as opposed to being a foot motion. The audible emission, the mark on paper, the foot motion could all exist or occur in a world lacking beings

---

[12] Gary Matthews suggested the term "ID phenomena" for phenomena whose occurrence or existence depends on there being entities with propositional attitudes.

[13] In earlier writings, I used the expression "intentional object" to refer to ID objects. Although I characterized what I meant by "intentional object" carefully, I am now using the technical term "ID object" (or "intention-dependent object") in order to avoid confusion with uses of "intentional object" associated with Brentano and Meinong.

with propositional attitudes, but the promise, the signature, and the dance step could not.[14]

The dependence of ID phenomena on beings with intentions is not merely causal, but is ontological. As an example of merely causal dependence on intentional agents, consider uranium fission. Uranium fission could not exist in our world without the causal intervention of beings with beliefs, desires, and intentions. The radioactive isotope of uranium is rare in nature, and it seems that no natural process could bring enough of it together to yield a critical mass. But in another very different world, uranium fission could obtain without the intervention of intentional agents. So, uranium fission is not an ID phenomenon.

By contrast, the dependence of an automobile on intentional agents is ontological. Consider the physical particles that make up your automobile. In a world in which those particles were the only existing things, there would be no automobile – no matter how the particles were arranged. If in outer space, particles spontaneously coalesced into something that looked like an automobile, there would be no automobile. It is not just that the aggregate of particles would not be called an "automobile." It really would not be an automobile. An automobile is essentially a kind of vehicle designed for transportation. The property of being an automobile is not just a contingent property of some otherwise nonvehicular thing. As we shall see in chapter 3, a world without intentional agents ontologically has no room for automobiles.

Although my interest here primarily concerns material objects, the range of ID phenomena is enormous. ID phenomena include: events (e.g., a baseball game), objects (e.g., a driver's license), actions (e.g., voting), dispositions (e.g., being honest), activities (e.g., reading your mail), institutions (e.g., a national bank), medical procedures (e.g., a heart transplant), business dealings (e.g., manufacturing new medications and marketing them) – all these are ID phenomena.[15] All artworks and artifacts are ID phenomena. Intentional language contains terms (e.g., "wants to buy milk," "was elected president," "paid her taxes") whose application presupposes that there are beings with beliefs, desires, and intentions. So, actions – like buying a car,

---

[14] As we shall see, a promise is essentially a promise. Whatever is a promise could not exist in another world and fail to be a promise, but the associated audible emission that constitutes the promise could exist in another world and not constitute a promise. The relation between the promise and the audible emission is constitution, not identity.

[15] Amie L. Thomasson discusses varieties of existential dependence in her *Fiction and Metaphysics*.

sending an email, or washing the dishes – are ID events whose occurrence entails that there are beings with beliefs, desires, and intentions. ID phenomena, then, are not just mental phenomena, but encompass a huge range of nonmental phenomena (like being in debt or being a delegate) that characterize the world as we know it.

However, not all things in the everyday world are ID objects. For example, planets and dinosaurs could – and presumably did – exist in a world without beliefs, desires, and intentions. In the everyday world, whether an object is an ID object or not is often insignificant: It is usually irrelevant whether what constitutes a ball is a piece of natural rubber (i.e., not an ID object) or a piece of artificial rubber (i.e., an ID object). My theory of the world as encountered allows for the distinction between ID objects and others, but does not highlight it. My main contribution here is to recognize, and to draw attention to, the existence of ID phenomena.

PHILOSOPHY IN THE MIDDLE OF THINGS

To philosophize about the everyday world is to begin in the middle of things in three ways. The first way is semantic: We cannot philosophize without a language, and any language that we have embeds a picture of the world. To learn a language is to learn the way the world is (or might be). When a child learns what "brother" means, she learns what brothers are. We cannot distil our knowledge of language from our knowledge of the world. So, we must begin in the middle with the language that we have on hand.

The second way that philosophy begins in the middle is epistemological: The Cartesian ideal of finding an absolute starting point without any presuppositions is illusory. The most that we can do is to be aware of our presuppositions; we cannot eliminate them. Wherever we choose to start, we are in the middle of things, epistemologically speaking.

The third way that philosophy begins in the middle of things is ontological: The objects of interest at least initially are medium-sized things – primarily people, but also nonhuman organisms and other natural objects, and artifacts, and artworks. These are the kinds of things that populate the world that we all unavoidably contend with and care about. And it is that world – the everyday world – that I am ultimately interested in understanding.

These three ways in which philosophy begins in the middle of things are interrelated. The reason that there is no presuppositionless starting point is that one cannot do philosophy unless one has a natural language, and any natural language has countless presuppositions about the way the world is. And all natural languages, to my knowledge, recognize medium-sized objects, some of which have intentional states. It is medium-sized objects that we have sensory contact with; it is medium-sized objects whose presence or absence we can confirm by observation; it is medium-sized objects that we can manipulate for our own purposes. The advent of nanotechnology does not diminish the importance of medium-sized objects. Indeed, the pay-off of nanotechnology will be in the arena of medium-sized objects.

It is not surprising that natural languages recognize medium-sized objects since survival depends on relations to such things. We are no more able to do philosophy by stepping outside of our language than we are by stepping outside of our evolutionary history. So, it is an inescapable fact that we begin with a body of substantive presuppositions. Moreover, we have reason to have confidence in the truth of these presuppositions. Since natural languages have been forged by eons of successful use, the built-in worldview of medium-sized objects is more likely to be correct, to quote J. L. Austin, than "any that you or I are likely to think up in our armchairs of an afternoon."[16]

A philosopher who begins in the middle of things is not barred from technical pursuits in philosophy, as we shall see. Unlike those who take philosophy to be a priori, however, I want my metaphysical claims to be motivated by something other than rational intuition or self-evidence. For example, I have felt pushed to endorse essentialism – roughly, the view that things have properties without which they could not exist. (If x has F essentially, then there is no possible world or time at which x exists and lacks F.) I certainly do not take essentialism to be self-evident. Rather, for me, essentialism is motivated by such down-to-earth considerations as the fact that there are conditions under which a particular manor house, say, would cease to exist.[17] Essentialism is not justified by appeal to pure reason, but by appeal to reflection on ordinary things that we antecedently care about and by the theoretical work that essentialism does once postulated. This version of essentialism, stemming as it does

[16] "A Plea for Excuses," *Philosophical Papers* (Oxford: Oxford University Press, 1961): 123–152 (quote, p. 130).
[17] See my *Persons and Bodies: A Constitution View* (Cambridge: Cambridge University Press, 2000): 35–39.

from reflection on the everyday world, seems fully compatible with a basically pragmatic outlook.

PRACTICAL REALISM

The kind of pragmatic outlook that I endorse is called "Practical Realism."[18] On this approach, metaphysics should not swing free of the rest of human inquiry. Metaphysics should be responsive to reflection on successful cognitive practices, scientific and nonscientific. In particular, there is no requirement that all knowledge be vindicated by science.

To argue that not all knowledge requires vindication by science, I want to distinguish three grades of empirical involvement. The first, and most fundamental, grade of empirical involvement comprises what is confirmable or disconfirmable by ordinary observation. The second grade of empirical involvement comprises what is confirmable or disconfirmable by systematic experimental inquiry. The third grade of empirical involvement comprises what is confirmable or disconfirmable by integratability into the physical sciences.

(1) The first grade of empirical involvement recognizes phenomena to be empirical when they are confirmable or disconfirmable by ordinary observation. Here I include observation from everyday life. Anyone can confirm that fire burns, or that a person's nose will bleed if struck sharply, or that traffic is heavy on Friday afternoons before holiday weekends. Such generalizations are continually being confirmed by all of us, scientists and nonscientists alike. Generalizations that are empirical in this sense are confirmed and disconfirmed in the course of ordinary life, and are warranted as long as they reliably enable us to accomplish our aims – regardless of the ultimate outcome of any science. When David went out to slay Goliath, he did not need to wait for a mature physics to be justified in selecting stones instead of twigs for his slingshot. The justification available to David for selecting stones was as complete as it would be today: knowledge of quantum mechanics would neither add to his grounds nor undermine them. Concerning the first grade of empirical involvement, we are all empiricists without any special scientific training. This is the grade at which what is empirical underwrites our know-how about getting along in everyday life. Our knowledge of language is empirical in this

---

[18] I discussed Practical Realism in *Explaining Attitudes: A Practical Approach to the Mind* (Cambridge University Press, 1995), and in *Persons and Bodies*.

sense: it is on the basis of experience that we know what to say when, and that we know, for example, that water is the stuff that falls from the sky and fills the oceans, etc. Call what is empirical at this first grade of empirical involvement the "ordinary-empirical."

(2) The second grade of empirical involvement recognizes phenomena as empirical when they are subject to experimental tests which yield replicable results. Consider, for example, a study that used videotapes of unstructured social interactions, from which sixty-two behaviors were coded.[19] The researchers asked college students how they would use the sixty-two behaviors to judge the degree of each of five personality traits (extroversion, agreeableness, conscientiousness, emotional stability, and openness). This yielded the college-student subjects' explicit theory of traits. The researchers compared the subjects' explicit theory with how the subjects actually judged the five personality traits on the basis of what they actually observed on the videotape (this yielded the subjects' implicit theory of behavior). Then, they compared both explicit and implicit theories with the actual trait-behavior associations from friends. The researchers drew conclusions about what behaviors subjects explicitly believe they use as an indication of particular personality traits, about what behaviors subjects actually use in making specific trait judgments, and about correlations between the behaviors exhibited on the videotapes and the personality descriptions provided by friends. The results, as you may expect, were complicated. If the results stand up under replication, then the experiment yields empirical knowledge at the second grade. When standard social-science research uncovers something that we did not already know by ordinary-empirical means, then it is empirical at the second grade of empirical involvement, the "experimental-empirical."

(3) The third grade of empirical involvement recognizes phenomena as empirical when they can be integrated into the physical sciences. There is no consensus as to what counts as integration into the physical sciences, but part of the idea is this: The categories in terms of which we classify phenomena (that are empirical at the third grade) must be explicable solely in terms of the categories of the physical sciences. So, if the social sciences, which paradigmatically are experimental-empirical, are themselves

---

[19] D. Funder and C. Sneed, "Behavioral Manifestations of Personality: An Ecological Approach to Judgmental Accuracy," *Journal of Personality and Social Psychology* 64 (1993): 479–490. This study was discussed by Barbara von Eckhardt in "The Empirical Naivete of the Current Philosophical Conception of Folk Psychology," given at the Central Division meeting of the APA in 1995.

deemed to be empirical at the third grade, then their legitimacy depends on whether or not their categories of, say, intentionality can be reduced to categories taxonomic in the physical sciences. If so, they are empirical at the third grade of empirical involvement, the "physical-science-empirical."

The three grades of empirical involvement help locate Practical Realism with respect to other philosophical positions. Robust scientific realists like Paul Churchland consider the empirical to be exhausted by what I called the "physical-science-empirical."[20] All truths must be integratable into the physical sciences. A broader scientific naturalist like Hilary Kornblith takes the empirical to be exhausted by the experimental-empirical together with the physical-science-empirical.[21] A Practical Realist, by contrast, has a still broader notion of "empirical." What is empirical includes not only what is physical-science-empirical and what is experimental-empirical, but also what is ordinary-empirical. Although it would be foolhardy to fly in the face of established scientific results, philosophical results are not confirmed or disconfirmed on the basis of assimilability into science.

Phenomena involving everyday behavior of ordinary things – medium-sized objects (artifacts as well as natural objects), animals, and people – are ordinary-empirical; our knowledge of the behavior of ordinary things is neither a priori nor in need of validation by science. A Practical Realist may be thought of as an apostate scientific pragmatist who takes the field of truth to extend beyond the physical sciences – and even beyond the sciences altogether – to commonsensical claims that are reliable and indispensable for getting along in the world. Knowledge of the everyday world is mostly ordinary-empirical. Knowledge of everyday phenomena is confirmed by everyone who buys groceries or applies for a job. Such knowledge cannot be dispensed with in favor of scientific-theoretical knowledge. Without the knowledge acquired by ordinary-empircal means, a scientist could not even make it to the lab.

Our everyday knowledge of the world is empirical (albeit what I have called "ordinary-empirical"). If people stopped slowing down at Yield signs, we would revise our belief that people generally slow down at Yield signs. Revisability of belief on the basis of experience is a hallmark of the empirical – regardless of whether or not the belief is integratable into

---

[20] For example, see his *A Neurocomputational Perspective: The Nature of Mind and the Structure of Science* (Cambridge, MA: MIT/Bradford, 1989).

[21] For example, see his *Inductive Inference and Its Natural Ground: An Essay in Naturalistic Epistemology* (Cambridge, MA: MIT Press, 1993).

physical science. We can count on such homely generalizations as "rumors can cause harm," or "a sharp rap on the nose causes it to bleed," or "driving while drunk is dangerous." Our everyday knowledge of the world has epistemic, as well as prudential, virtues: Everyday knowledge, though revisable, is remarkably reliable. We depend on it; we cannot help depending on it, and our use of it enables us to act successfully and to satisfy our desires.

In light of these virtues, it is difficult to take seriously those who pretend that our knowledge of the everyday world is just a folk theory that must be cast aside if it is not vindicated by science. Indeed, among the medium-sized objects are the precision instruments vital to vindicating science. We can't very well doubt the reality of gauges or telescopes if we depend on them to verify scientific hypotheses. We live in a world of medium-sized objects that behave in largely predictable ways. It is not that science tells us *what* exists; science tells us what *else* exists.

This Practical Realist emphasis on the everyday world, with its ID phenomena, calls into question the foundational role that some philosophers give to a distinction between what is mind-independent and what is mind-dependent. For example, Ernest Sosa has reported:

What the metaphysical realist is committed to holding is that there is an in-itself reality independent of our minds and even of our existence, and that we can talk about such reality and its constituents by virtue of correspondence relations between our language (and/or our minds), on the one hand, and things-in-themselves and their intrinsic properties (including their relations), on the other.[22]

How should one understand this distinction? If one took what is mind-dependent to be subjective or private (as "qualia" are supposed to be), then the mind-independent/mind-dependent distinction would not be exhaustive. Artifacts, for instance, would be neither mind-independent nor subjective. Hence, a mind-independent/mind-dependent distinction that equated mind-dependence with subjectivity would not be a suitable basis for metaphysics. But before turning to the usefulness (or lack of it) of the mind-independent/mind-dependent distinction as a basis for metaphysics, let me expose an incoherent way to make the distinction.

The mind-independent/mind-dependent distinction is often taken to be a distinction between what is "up to nature" and what is "up to us."

---

[22] Ernest Sosa, "Putnam's Pragmatic Realism," *Journal of Philosophy* 90 (1993): 605–626. Reprinted in *Metaphysics: An Anthology*, ed. Jaegwon Kim and Ernest Sosa (Oxford: Blackwell, 1999): 607–619. The quotation is on p. 609.

Such an equation is untenable if "up to us" means "what is optional for us" or "what is under the control of human decision." A distinction between what is mind-independent and what is optional for us is neither exclusive nor exhaustive. It is not exclusive: Almost all the states of affairs that are optional for us have mind-independent components: e.g., building a highway is optional for us, but requires all kinds of mind-independent materials. Nor is a distinction between what is mind-independent and what is optional for us exhaustive: Much of the world as encountered is neither mind-independent nor optional for us. Our interest in taking care of our children is not mind-independent, nor is it an interest that we could simply decide to change. Our being language users is neither mind-independent, nor "up to us." A biologically given interest is not optional, and in the example of taking care of children or of being a language user, not mind-independent either. So, if we take "mind-dependent" to mean "what is optional for us" or "what is up to us," then a distinction between what is mind-independent and what is mind-dependent is neither exclusive nor exhaustive. Such a distinction cannot be a basis for metaphysics.

I suspect that "mind-independent" is an example of what J. L. Austin called a "trouser word": It wears the pants in the family, and "mind-dependent" must be defined in terms of it – as what is not mind-independent. Other construals of the distinction (e.g., as what is optional for us as opposed to what is "up to nature") are unsatisfactory as a basis for metaphysics, as we have just seen. It is coherent to take "mind-independent" to apply to anything that is part of "in-itself reality independent of our minds and even of our existence," and to take "mind-dependent" to apply to anything that is not mind-independent. But the line drawn by this distinction sheds little light – at least not on the world as we encounter it.

For example, artifacts – like all ID objects – turn out to be mind-dependent on the coherent construal of the mind-independent/mind-dependent distinction. This is so because artifacts are not part of in-itself reality independent of our minds and even of our existence. Nothing would be a carburetor in a world without intentional activity.[23] So restricting irreducible reality to what is mind-independent will not only eliminate everything whose existence depends on language, but also artifacts.

The portion of reality that is *excluded* from the "in-itself reality independent of our minds and even of our existence" contains much of what

---

[23] See a lengthy discussion of artifacts (specifically, of carburetors) in my *Explaining Attitudes*.

19

we interact with: e.g., artifacts, artworks, economic items (certificates of deposit, credit cards), consumer goods, documents. It also excludes such varied properties as being philanthropic, being in debt, being employed, being drunk, being conscientious, having a banking system, breaking a treaty, suspending habeas corpus, and on and on. Moreover, on the coherent construal of the mind-independent/mind-dependent distinction (which takes everything that is "independent of our minds and even of our existence" to be mind-independent and everything else to be mind-dependent), carburetors and dreams come out on the same side of the ontological divide. I am confident that it is basically wrong-headed to put artifacts and after-images in the same ontological category, and hence I am also confident that the mind-independence/mind-dependence distinction is itself misguided as a basis for metaphysics.

To reject the mind-independence/mind-dependence distinction as the basis of metaphysics is to reject the idea that there is a sharp division between language and "the world." But, of course, language is not isolable from the world. As David Wiggins put it, "Let us forget once and for all the very idea of some knowledge of language or meaning that is not knowledge of the world itself."[24] Language is infected with the world, and the world as we know it is infected with language through and through.

The significance of downplaying the mind-independence/mind-dependence distinction is this: What is in the ontology need not be wholly independent of us. That is, ontology need not be wholly independent of our language, our activities, our conventions and practices. This book is evidence that we need not think in terms of a dichotomy of mind-independence vs. mind-dependence. Of course, there is such a distinction. What I am calling into question is its philosophical significance.

Hence, I do not call myself a Metaphysical Realist, but a Practical Realist: Realist because I believe that there may exist objects and properties beyond our ability to recognize them; Practical because I believe that the everyday world – that part of reality that includes us, our language, and the things that we interact with – is no less ontologically significant than the microphysical parts of reality. We shall make no headway on a philosophical understanding of the everyday world if we frame our investigation globally in terms of mind-independence vs. mind-dependence.

---

[24] David Wiggins, *Sameness and Substance Renewed* (Cambridge: Cambridge University Press, 2001): 12.

WHAT LIES AHEAD

I shall present and defend a metaphysical view that respects the irreducible variety of kinds of things and properties in the world. On this view, there is a deep ontological difference between a world with people and a world without people, between a world with nuclear weapons and a world without nuclear weapons, between a world with satellite TV and a world without satellite TV. The contrasts are not merely superficial: A world with people has in it objects of fundamentally different kinds from worlds without people. The differences between a world with people (or cows or space ships or sarcaphogi or electron microscopes or . . .) and a world without them are not just differences in what concepts are deployed. The differences are ontological, not just "conceptual."

Ontology, as I have noted, is an inventory of what exists. Since contingent, concrete objects exist at some times but not at other times, we are in no position to provide a complete ontology before the end of time. Nevertheless, modulo new developments, we can make an inventory as of now. Rather than itemize what exists (a hopeless task), I will present a schema for the ontology of the material world.

The Metaphysics of Everyday Life is divided into three parts. Part I gives an ontological account of everyday objects. Part II discusses basic features of the everyday world. Part III provides the technical apparatus that backs up the account. In part I, I first set the stage with the present chapter (ch. 1), and then present a metaphysical picture of ordinary things in terms of what I call the "Constitution View" (ch. 2). Then, I show how the Constitution View applies to two of the most significant kinds of things we encounter and interact with: artifacts (ch. 3) and persons (ch. 4).

In part II, I critically discuss Jaegwon Kim's reductive view of causation, and provide an alternative to do justice to commonsense causation (ch. 5). Next, I argue that there is vagueness in the world – in spatial and temporal boundaries of ordinary objects and in the constitution relation itself (ch. 6). Finally, I present an account of time that is adequate both to physics and to human experience (ch. 7).

In part III, I provide a hard-core defense of a number of controversial ideas and underlying assumptions. I begin part III with a technical discussion of the notion of constitution – the leading idea of the Constitution View – and other ideas used to understand the everyday world (ch. 8). Then, I show that although constitution is not a mereological relation (i.e., constitution is not a relation between parts and wholes), the Constitution

View does have a place for mereology; I give an account of parthood that is consonant with the Constitution View (ch. 9). Then, since I assume three-dimensionalism throughout, I defend three-dimensionalism against an important argument for four-dimensionalism (ch. 10). This is followed by a chapter on five ontological issues, including ontological commitment and ontological novelty, two of the distinctive features of my view; I defend an nonreductive conception of levels of reality along with an account of emergence. These accounts are bolstered by a discussion of time and existence (ch. 11).

PART I

Everyday things

2

The reality of ordinary things

Are ordinary things irreducibly real? Are the medium-sized objects that we interact with daily (automobiles, people, trees) really the diverse entities that we take them to be; or are they really something else – perhaps homogeneous things like four-dimensional "spacetime worms" or collections of three-dimensional "simples"? I shall argue that ordinary things are irreducibly real, three-dimensional objects (I'll argue for three-dimensionalism in chapter 10) and that they really are of vastly different kinds. The variety of things is not merely conceptual: variety is not just a matter of different concepts being applied to things that are basically of the same sort. Rather, the differences among ordinary things are ontological: a screwdriver is a thing of a fundamentally different kind from a walnut, and both belong in a complete inventory of what exists. To vindicate such beliefs, I shall propose a nonreductive view of reality that makes sense of the world as it is encountered in ontological – and not just conceptual – terms.

In this chapter, I shall set out, and begin to defend, the particular brand of nonreductionism that I favor – I call it the "Constitution View." If the Constitution View is correct, then ordinary things are as real as the fundamental entities of physics; ordinary things are irreducible objects, distinct from collections of microphysical entities. My aim is to offer a metaphysical theory that acknowledges the genuine reality of what our everyday concepts (as well as our scientific concepts) are concepts *of*.

MOTIVATION FOR NONREDUCTION

On September 11, 2001, as everyone knows, the towers of the World Trade Center in New York were attacked. Ontologically speaking, how should we understand this horrific event? Did anything really go out of existence when the towers collapsed, or did we just stop applying the word "tower" to what, ontologically speaking, existed both before and after the attack? I want to discuss the attack on the World Trade Center in order

25

to motivate a nonreductionist view of ordinary things: When the towers collapsed, entities that had existed ceased to exist altogether.

Ontologically speaking, what happened when the towers came down? Here are three possibilities:

(1) Eliminativism: Strictly speaking, no towers ever existed: the word "tower" is not a referring word. All that existed were simples arranged towerwise. Sentences like "The towers fell" are to be rephrased with plural quantification and the predicate "are arranged towerwise." When the towers fell (as we say), the only change was in the arrangement of the particles. But nothing went out of existence.[1]

(2) Reductionism: There were towers, but the towers were really just the matter that occupied spacetime points arranged towerwise. The towers were, in other words, mereological sums of particles at those spacetime points. Any matter-filled spacetime points have sums; we have names for some of the sums that are arranged in certain ways (e.g., "towers"). All that really exist are matter at spacetime points and their sums arranged in various ways. "Tower" is just a name we give to sums in a certain arrangement. Concepts like *tower* reflect our interests, and reality is independent of our interests.[2]

(3) Nonreductionism: The apparent towers really existed in their own right, so to speak. Particles made up the towers, but the towers were not just identical to particles – or to mereological sums of particles – arranged towerwise. I associate this last view with a number of philosophers. It is my view.

Philosophers may hold different of these views for different domains. (For example, Peter van Inwagen is an eliminativist with respect to towers and other inanimate complex objects, but not with respect to organisms.) Focusing on inanimate complex objects like the towers, I shall briefly compare and contrast the three views (or types of views), then turn to a more detailed elaboration of my version of nonreductionism. For convenience, I'll use the term "particles" as a dummy word for physical particles, matter at spacetime points, or simples, depending on the view in question.

---

[1] I associate eliminativism with respect to the towers with Peter van Inwagen (*Material Beings* [Ithaca, NY: Cornell University Press, 1990]).

[2] I associate reductionism with David Lewis (*Parts of Classes* [Oxford: Basil Blackwell, 1991]). However, Lewis was a four-dimensionalist, and I do not argue against four-dimensionalism until chapter 10.

First, consider an ontological comparison-and-contrast: On all three views, there were particles arranged towerwise at 8:30 a.m., and those particles still existed at 10:00, but they were no longer arranged towerwise at 10:00. On the three-dimensionalist reductionist views and on eliminativist views, ontologically speaking, nothing literally went out of existence between 8:30 and 10:00; there was only a change in the arrangement of particles. On eliminativist views, ontologically speaking, there were no towers in the first place. So, it is easy to see that on eliminativist views, nothing literally went out of existence between 8:30 and 10:00. The reductionist case may not be as easy to see.

Let's start with three-dimensional reductionism. A three-dimensionalist cannot consistently hold that there are towers and that each tower is identical to a collection of three-dimensional particles (or sums of particles). A tower can survive being chipped and hence losing a few particles. But the collection of three-dimensional particles to which the tower is (putatively) identical cannot survive losing a few particles. If a reductionist considers three-dimensional simples and sums of three-dimensional simples to be the basic entities, then nothing that gains or loses simple parts over time can be identified with any basic entities. Ordinary objects gain and lose their three-dimensional simple parts over time. So, a three-dimensionalist of that sort cannot be a reductionist about ordinary objects.[3]

A three-dimensionalist reductionist may object that a tower is not to be identified with a bunch of particles, but with particles-arranged-in-a-certain-way; and, she may claim, particles-arranged-towerwise and the same particles-arranged-rubblewise are different objects. But what exists in both the case of the tower (= particles-arranged-towerwise) and the case of the rubble (= particles-arranged-rubblewise) are just the particles. Arrangements are not items in the ontology; they are not objects at all.[4] For a three-dimensionalist reductionist, the difference between the towers and the rubble is like the difference between ten marbles arranged in a circle and the same marbles arranged in a row: there is no ontological

---

[3] Phillip Bricker was helpful in discussing three- and four-dimensionalism.

[4] So, a three-dimensionalist who rejects nonreductionism should turn to eliminativism, and say that there are no towers, just particles-arranged-towerwise. By contrast, four-dimensionalists can say that there are towers, and that a tower is identical to particles-arranged-towerwise. On four dimensionalism, particles-arranged-in-way1 and particles-arranged-in-way2 are distinct objects, because difference in arrangement implies difference in time. And on four-dimensionalism, particles existing at different times (i.e., particles that are parts of the same spacetime worm) are different objects (different temporal parts).

difference. The difference is rather that our concept *tower* (or *circle*) applies to one but not to the other.

Unsurprisingly, most reductionists are four-dimensionalists. According to standard four-dimensionalism, concrete objects are spacetime worms that come into existence at their earliest stage (or part) and go out of existence at their latest stage (or part).[5] There are countless, nameless spacetime worms coming into existence and going out of existence everywhere all the time. With the superabundance of worms beginning and ending at every spacetime point, it is not difficult to suppose that two of them are the towers. The worms that we name (e.g., "tower," "rubble") are the ones that we have interest in. The temporal parts that made up the tower at 8:30 were also parts of unbelievably many different worms, many of which continued after 10:00; some of those worms included *both* the parts that we call "tower" and parts that we call "rubble." Ontologically speaking, there are myriads of spacetime worms that share all the temporal parts of the towers and that continue to exist after 10:00. For a four-dimensionalist to say that a tower went out of existence before 10:00 is for her to pick out a worm that had no more temporal parts by 10:00. But there is nothing ontologically distinctive about such a spacetime worm, as opposed to a spacetime worm that has some temporal parts that we call "tower" and other temporal parts that we call "rubble."

Ontologically, on four-dimensionalism, there is no more difference between a tower and a quantity of rubble than the difference between the first half of the tower's life and the second half of the tower's life. Of course, the tower and the rubble are different (but connected) spacetime worms; so are the first and second halves of the tower's life. What distinguishes the difference between the tower and the rubble from the difference between the first and second halves of the tower's existence is largely conceptual[6]: we apply the same concept to the first and second half of the tower's existence, but we apply different concepts to the tower and the rubble. When a four-dimensionalist says that the towers went out of existence, she is using "goes out of existence" in a way that applies equally to the first half of the towers' life that goes out of existence before the second half begins. From a four-dimensionalist's point of view, the towers'

---

[5] For a detailed discussion of four-dimensionalism, see chapter 10.

[6] There was also a greater change in the distribution of qualities over spacetime when the tower went out of existence than when the first half of the tower's life went out of existence; but change in the distribution of qualities is not an ontological change.

collapse was no more loss to reality than the end of the first half of the towers' life.

So, on eliminativism and reductionism, the significance of the difference between what existed before and after the collapse of the towers should be understood in conceptual or semantic terms, not in ontological terms. All the objects (or, in the case of Van Inwagen, nonliving objects) that exist, according to both eliminativism and reductionism, are particles (matter at spacetime points or simples) arranged in certain ways. On the eliminativist and three-dimensionalist reductionist views, there is no *ontological* difference at all between the towers and the rubble, and on four-dimensionalism there is no *more ontological* difference between the towers and the rubble than there is between the first and second halves of a tower's life.[7]

By contrast, on the nonreductionist view, the collapse of the towers was a loss to reality, ontologically speaking. The change between 8:30 and 10:00 was more than a change in the arrangement of particles. Indeed, the eliminativist and reductionist may be right to insist that particles and their sums continued to exist but were rearranged. But according to the nonreductionist, there were objects that were not identical with sums of particles and that went out of existence altogether when the towers collapsed. At the time of the collapse, the things that were towers literally went out of existence; they did not just lose the property of being towers and acquire the property of being rubble. The towers were not just sums or particles that changed shape; they were objects that once existed and then ceased to exist. The contents of the world changed between 8:30 and 10:00; on the nonreductionist view, complete inventories of the world would include different objects at 8:30 and at 10:00. Only a nonreductionist approach allows the extensions of everyday concepts like *tower* to be ontologically significant.[8]

Now turn to the semantic comparison-and-contrast: The difference between eliminativism on the one hand and reductionism and nonreductionism on the other seems to be semantic: the reductionist and nonreductionist take "tower" to be a referring word, but the eliminativist does not.[9] The eliminativist, as well as the reductionist and nonreductionist, can take

[7] Now I return to assuming three-dimensionalism until chapter 10, where I'll argue for it.
[8] See chapter 11 for a detailed discussion of ontological significance.
[9] There is no ontological difference on (one interpretation of) the assumption that mereology is, as Lewis says, "ontologically innocent." It is reasonable to interpret the assertion that mereology is ontologically innocent to imply that the existence of parts is wholly sufficient for the existence of their sums. *Parts of Classes*: 81.

the sentence, "There are towers" to be true.[10] The eliminativist takes that sentence to be true in virtue of having a paraphrase that does not mention towers: "There are some simples arranged towerwise."[11] The paraphrase (putatively) expresses the same fact as the original sentence, "There are towers." When we say, "The towers collapsed," eliminativist metaphysicians must supply a paraphrase: e.g., "The simples that had one arrangement (towerwise) now have another arrangement (rubblewise)." The eliminativist cannot suppose that the sentence "the towers collapsed" is both true and literally an expression of the proposition that the towers collapsed. For the eliminativist, common nouns in everyday discourse disappear under analysis. So, although the eliminativist can take everyday discourse at face value, he requires odd paraphrases of much of everyday talk; speakers do not mean what they think that they mean.

By contrast, the reductionist and nonreductionist take the sentence "There are towers" to be true as expressed; they need no paraphrase that does not mention towers. The reductionist and nonreductionist can agree that "there were towers that collapsed between 8:30 and 10:00" is true and means that there were towers at 8:30 (without paraphrasing "towers" away) and that they went out of existence before 10:00. But according to reductionism, talk about the collapse of the towers is really just talk about the rearrangement of particles. Reductionist and nonreductionist differ on what the tower is: On the reductionist view, a tower is identical to a sum of particles (or simples) arranged in a certain way.[12]

Both reductionists and eliminativists in effect say, "The world is nothing like the way you think it is," and many add, "but that does not matter because you may still say everything that you want to say." So you may rightly *say* "The towers collapsed," but nothing went out of existence in the robust sense that a nonreductionist intends. From a three-dimensionalist reductionist's point of view, what "went out of existence" was only an arrangement of still-existing three-dimensional particles (as if arrangements were objects); from a four-dimensionalist reductionist's point of view, what went out of existence was only a temporal part – just as the temporal part that was the second week of the tower's career went out of

---

[10] Some eliminativists would not even take the sentence "there are towers" to be true. E.g., Trenton Merricks takes "chairs exist" to be false, but introduces the term "nearly as good as true" for false statements that Fs exist if there are things arranged F-wise. Trenton Merricks, *Objects and Persons* (Oxford: Clarendon Press, 2001): 170–171.
[11] Cf. Van Inwagen, *Material Beings*: 109.   [12] Cf. Lewis, *Parts of Classes*: 87.

existence at the beginning of the third week of the tower's career.[13] Only nonreductionism takes our everyday discourse to be true on a face-value reading, according to which "the towers collapsed" implies that something important went out of existence altogether.

There is a straightforward contrast among the three approaches that is made apparent by the existential quantifier, $\exists$:

According to Eliminativism about towers, every instance of $\exists x (x$ *is a tower)* is false.

According to Reductionism about towers, instances of $\exists x (x$ *is a tower)* are true but redundant. That is, our ontology need not mention towers. If we quantify over the items to which towers are reducible, we need not quantify additionally over towers. The existence of towers is taken care of by mentioning the items to which towers are reducible.

According to Nonreductionism about towers, instances of $\exists x (x$ *is a tower)* are both true and nonredundant. If we did not mention towers in our ontology, we would be missing some things that really exist.

The semantic and ontological differences among the three views, I believe, give us prima facie reason to be nonreductionists about towers, and hence to be nonreductionists about the extensions of everyday concepts like *tower*. Only nonreductionism takes objects themselves to have gone out of existence[14] when the towers collapsed, and only nonreductionism takes our everyday discourse at face value. Let us now turn to the task of formulating a nonreductionist view that allows ordinary objects – not just particles and their sums – to be a distinct part of reality.

The World Trade Center towers were part of the everyday world – the world that includes the things that we talk about and interact with: material objects, other people, activities, processes, and so on. Indeed, the towers were intention-dependent, or ID, objects: The objects that are towers could not have existed in a world without entities with attitudes. Towers are artifacts (see chapter 3) that have ID properties (properties that cannot be instantiated in a world without entities with attitudes) and relational properties essentially. They are the objects that they are because they were designed for certain purposes.

If, as I claim, the towers were not just identical to arrangements of particles, what *was* the relation between the twin towers and the aggregates of particles that made them up? My answer is: constitution. Constitution is

---

[13] See, e.g., David Lewis and Theodore Sider (reductionists); Peter van Inwagen and Trenton Merricks (eliminativists about inanimate objects).

[14] Where "goes out of existence" is more robust than what happened to the first half of the tower's life during the second half.

a single comprehensive metaphysical relation that unites items at different levels of reality into the objects that we experience in everyday life: the trees, the automobiles, the credit cards, and the people. These objects are irreducible to the aggregates of particles that make them up.

THE IDEA OF CONSTITUTION

Constitution is a very general relation, ubiquitous in the world. It is a relation that may hold between granite slabs and war memorials, between pieces of metal and traffic signs, between DNA molecules and genes, between pieces of paper and dollar bills – things of basically different kinds that are spatially coincident.[15] The fundamental idea of constitution is this: when a thing of one primary kind is in certain circumstances, a thing of another primary kind – a new thing, with new causal powers – comes to exist.[16] When an octagonal piece of metal is in circumstances of being painted red with white marks of the shape S-T-O-P, and is in an environment that has certain conventions and laws, a new thing – a traffic sign – comes into existence. A traffic sign is a different kind of thing, with different causal powers, from a scrap piece of metal that you find in your garage. Yet the traffic sign does not exist separately from the constituting piece of metal. Constitution is a relation of unity – unity without identity.

My thesis is this: All concrete objects found in the world that we encounter are constituted objects. Sometimes an ordinary object is constituted by another ordinary object – as when a mallet is constituted by a piece of wood – but ultimately all ordinary material objects are constituted by aggregates of subatomic particles.[17] As I construe it, constitution is not a part/whole relation: If x constitutes y at t, x is not part of y at t.[18] The identity of a constituted object is independent of the identity of its parts,

---

[15] For a discussion of whether or not spatial coincidence, when joined with the causal efficacy of ordinary things, leads to intolerable causal overdetermination, see chapter 5.

[16] Since I shall formulate and discuss in detail the definition of "x constitutes y at t" in chapter 8, I shall only describe constitution informally here.

[17] I say "aggregates of subatomic particles," rather than just "subatomic particles," because I take constitution to be a relation between x and y at a time. If plural quantification is otherwise satisfactory, I could take ordinary objects to be ultimately constituted simply by particles. I think that the difference would be merely verbal.

[18] So, "constitutes" is not a synonym of "composes" as mereologists use it. As we shall see in chapter 9, I take mereological summation to be aggregation. And constitution is a very different relation from aggregation.

which may change. Nor are the persistence conditions of a constituted object given by its parts or by the persistence conditions of its parts. Constituted objects have different causal powers from their lower-level constituters. E.g., a menu signed by Picasso has different causal powers from the aggregate of particles that constitutes the menu and the ink. (See chapter 5.) And constituted objects have different essential properties (and different persistence conditions). E.g., my socks and the pieces of cloth that constitute them have different persistence conditions: A piece of cloth could survive being cut into a flat piece; my sock could not.

Several features of the idea of constitution are important here. First, the relation of constitution, which I have discussed in elaborate detail elsewhere,[19] is in some ways like identity. However, constitution is not identity. If you wonder how a relation could be *like* identity, but not *be* identity, think of what philosophers have called "contingent identity." By "identity," I mean strict identity: $x = y \rightarrow \Box \, (x = y)$.[20] The idea of constitution plays the role in my view that the idea of various forms of "contingent identity" (e.g., relative identity, temporal identity) plays in others' views. (Indeed, my view has the advantage of achieving [by means of constitution] what other philosophers want to achieve when they invoke ersatz "identity." My view does not weaken the traditional idea of identity.) Identity is necessary; constitution is contingent. Hence, constitution is not identity.

Behind the idea of constitution is an Aristotelian assumption. For any x, we can ask: What most fundamentally is x? The answer will be what I call x's "primary kind." Everything that exists is of exactly one primary kind – e.g., a horse or a passport or a cabbage.[21] An object's primary kind goes hand in hand with its persistence conditions. Since a thing has the same persistence conditions in every possible world and time at which it exists, it has its persistence conditions essentially. And since an object's

---

[19] See my *Persons and Bodies: A Constitution View* (Cambridge: Cambridge University Press, 2000). For a preliminary discussion of the notion of constitution, see "Unity Without Identity: A New Look at Material Constitution," in *New Directions in Philosophy: Midwest Studies in Philosophy* 23, ed. Peter A. French and Howard K. Wettstein (Malden, MA: Blackwell Publishers, 1999): 144–165.

[20] Thus, I neither need nor want to countenance counterparts.

[21] An object can have a primary-kind property that is not *its* primary-kind property contingently. I spell this out with the idea of "having properties derivatively": A piece of marble can have the property of being a statue derivatively. See chapter 8 for details.

primary-kind property determines what it most fundamentally is, an object has its primary-kind property essentially: An object could not exist without having its primary-kind property.[22]

Although the idea of primary kinds is inspired by Aristotle, I differ from Aristotle in several ways: First, according to the Constitution View, there are primary kinds of artifacts, as well as of natural objects. Second, according to the Constitution View, a primary kind may be just a kind of thing; it does not have to be a kind of a broader kind (like a kind of furniture). In particular, although on my view, *person* is a primary kind, I need not say that a person is a kind *of* some further kind (such as a kind of animal).[23] Third, as we shall see in the discussion of having properties derivatively, something may have a primary-kind property without having that property as *its* primary-kind property. There are two ways to fall under a primary kind: to be essentially of that kind or to be contingently related by constitution to something that is essentially of that kind.[24] So, something may have a primary-kind property contingently when suitably related to something that has it essentially.[25]

Every object has its primary kind essentially, but not every kind is a primary kind. E.g., *teacher* is not a primary kind; nor is *puppy*. Teachers may cease to be teachers without ceasing to exist (e.g., they may retire); so may puppies cease to be puppies without ceasing to exist (e.g., they may grow up). Constitution is a relation between things of different primary kinds. So, a person may acquire the property of being a teacher; but a person does not constitute a teacher since *teacher* is not a primary kind.

Of course, there is no exhaustive list of primary kinds. Indeed, there could not be a complete list of primary kinds until the end of the world. New inventions create new primary kinds. (See chapter 11.) But there is

---

[22] To borrow some paraphrases about essential properties from Chisholm, if x has the property of being a horse essentially, then "x is such that, if it were not a horse, it would not exist"; or "God couldn't have created x without making it such that it is a horse"; or "x is such that in every possible world in which it exists it is a horse." Roderick Chisholm, *Person and Object* (LaSalle, IL: Open Court Publishing Company, 1976): 25–26.

[23] Gareth B. Matthews has made me realize how different my view is from Aristotle's.

[24] See Ryan Wasserman's "The Constitution Question," *Noûs* 38 (2004): 693–710.

[25] Many properties (unrelated to this discussion) may be had essentially by some things and nonessentially by other things. A planet has the property of having a closed orbit essentially; a comet that has a closed orbit has that property nonessentially. (This assumes that planets are planets essentially; otherwise it is only a de dicto necessity that planets have closed orbits.)

a test for a kind's being a primary kind: A primary kind is a kind in virtue of which a thing has its persistence conditions. An object x has K as its primary kind only if: x is of kind K every moment of its existence and could not fail to be of kind K and continue to exist. Something that has K as its primary kind cannot lose the property of being a K without going out of existence altogether.[26] When Gutenberg invented the printing press, I believe that he created a new primary kind – a kind that changed the course of history. Printing presses go out of existence when barbarians smash them to bits; they do not just lose the property of being printing presses, and become something else: they go out of existence altogether.

Objects related by constitution are of different primary kinds. The primary kind of a constituted thing, as I mentioned, contributes to the thing's persistence conditions. Flags and pieces of cloth are primary kinds with different persistence conditions: Tear off the edges of a piece of cloth and you have a different piece of cloth; tear off the edges of a flag and you still have the same flag. A flag, as it is shot and tattered and repaired in battle, is constituted by different pieces of cloth at different times. The flag is constituted by one piece of cloth at time t and by a different piece of cloth at a later time after a few hours of battle. Nevertheless, the same flag continues to wave even though it is constituted by a different piece of cloth. The flag persists through changes of the piece of cloth that constitutes it. This illustrates a general feature of constitution: If x constitutes y at t, it is possible that y exist at t but x not exist at t. So, again, constitution is not identity.

The piece of cloth that constituted the tattered flag is in turn constituted by an aggregate of molecules, and so on down to the constituting aggregate of subatomic particles. If we descend down any chain of constitution relations, sooner or later we will come to aggregates as constituters. But since constitution is a different relation from aggregation (or mereological summation), constituted objects are distinguished from the aggregates that constitute them.[27]

---

[26] In addition to having its own primary-kind property essentially, a thing may have another primary-kind property contingently if constitutionally related to something that has it essentially: Michelangelo's David has *being a statue* as *its* primary-kind property and hence has it essentially; the constituting piece of marble has *being a statue* contingently, in virtue of its constituting something that has the property of *being a statue* essentially.

[27] See chapter 9 for further discussion of mereology.

Indeed, aggregates have different persistence conditions from constituted things.[28] Consider a river. The river persists through many different aggregates of molecules that constitute it at different times. A certain aggregate of H_2O molecules may constitute a river at one time, but that aggregate may exist at a later time without constituting the river (after a dog has splashed some water out of the river, say). The aggregate of H_2O molecules exists exactly as long as the H_2O molecules in it exist – however scattered they may be. Persistence conditions of constituted things are tied to the relevant primary kind; persistence conditions of aggregates are tied only to the existence of the items in the aggregate. The river/aggregate of molecules example also illustrates the fact that constitution, unlike identity, is a temporal relation: x may constitute y at one time but not at another.

Constitution is a relation that things have in virtue of their primary kinds. As I have suggested, when things of certain primary kinds are in certain circumstances, things of new primary kinds, with new kinds of causal powers, come into existence. For example, when a piece of marble is carved into a certain shape by a member of an artworld, a sculptor, a new thing of a new kind – a statue – comes into existence. If a piece of marble constitutes a statue, then the primary kind of the marble statue is *statue*. The piece of marble still exists, but the statue now has pre-eminence. What makes the difference between a statue and a mere piece of marble is that the existence of the statue requires an artworld or an artist's intention or whatever is required by the correct theory of statues. The distinction between ID objects (like statues) and nonID objects (like pieces of marble) lies in the sort of circumstances a constituter must be in to constitute an object of a certain kind. For example, statue-favorable circumstances are intentional: they include, e.g., artists with certain intentions; planet-favorable circumstances are not intentional: they include, e.g., a certain mass of material revolving around a star. But both statues (ID objects) and planets (nonID objects) are constituted objects.

The importance of constitution lies in the fact that it brings into being new objects of new primary kinds. For example, when a certain combination of chemicals is in a certain environment, a thing of a new kind comes

---

[28] As we shall see in chapter 3 in the discussion of artifacts, the items in aggregates have primary kinds, and the aggregates may have those primary kinds by courtesy. The primary kind of an aggregate consisting of a horse and a buggy would be *horse/buggy*. Assigning such hybrid primary kinds to aggregates is just a convenience.

into existence: an organism. That particular combination of chemicals constitutes at t that particular organism. A world with the same kinds of chemicals but a different distribution of chemicals or an environment different in other ways may lack organisms, and a world without organisms is ontologically different from a world with organisms. So, constitution makes an ontological difference.[29]

If constitution is not identity, however, we need an explanation of the fact that, if x constitutes y at t, then x and y share so many properties at t. Not only are x and y at the same places at the same times (as long as one constitutes the other), but x and y have many properties in common: weighing 200 lbs., having a toothache, sitting down – properties that do not entail the existence of anything at any other time or in any other world.

There is an explanation: Even though constitution is not identity, it is a relation of genuine unity. And because constitution is a relation of genuine unity, if x constitutes y at t, x may borrow properties at t from y and y may borrow properties at t from x. (Chisholm introduced me to the idea of borrowing properties, but I have modified his idea quite a bit for my own purposes.[30] On my view, if x constitutes y at t, then both x and y borrow properties at t from each other.) The intuitive idea of borrowing a property or of having a property derivatively is simple. If x constitutes y at t, then some of x's properties at t have their source (so to speak) in y, and some of y's properties at t have their source in x.

I have put this point less metaphorically elsewhere by defining "x has property H at t derivatively," but here I'll just illustrate the idea.[31] Consider some properties of my driver's license, which is constituted by a piece of plastic: My driver's license has the property of being rectangular only because it is constituted by something that could have been rectangular even if it had constituted nothing. And the piece of plastic has the property of impressing the policeman only because it constitutes something that would have impressed the policeman (a valid driver's license) no matter what constituted it. The driver's license has the property of being rectangular derivatively, and of impressing the policeman nonderivatively;

---

[29] For greater detail, see *Persons and Bodies*. See also the Book Symposium on *Persons and Bodies* in *Philosophy and Phenomenological Research* 64 (2002): 592–635, and my "On Making Things Up: Constitution and its Critics," *Philosophical Topics: Identity and Individuation* 30 (2002): 31–51.

[30] For an account of "one-way" borrowing, see Chisholm, *Person and Object*: 100ff.

[31] See *Persons and Bodies*, and "On Making Things Up." Also see chapter 8.

the piece of plastic that constitutes my driver's license has the property of being rectangular nonderivatively, and of impressing the policeman derivatively.

The second illustration of having a property derivatively is perhaps more controversial. *Person* is your primary kind. *Human animal* is your body's primary kind. You are a person nonderivatively and a human animal derivatively; and your body is a human animal nonderivatively and a person derivatively. Although you are a person and your body is a person, there are not two persons where you are. This is so because constitution is a unity relation. If x constitutes y at t, and x is an F at t derivatively and y is an F at t nonderivatively – or vice versa – then there are not thereby two Fs.[32]

Each object has its primary-kind property both nonderivatively and essentially. Your primary kind is *person*. Your body's primary kind is *human animal*. Even though being a person is a primary-kind property that you have nonderivatively, your body has that property derivatively – solely in virtue of constituting you (who are a person nonderivatively). Even though you are a person essentially, your body is a person contingently: When your body no longer constitutes you, it is no longer a person. Still, your body is not a separate person from you; the fact that your body is a person at t is just the fact that you are a person (nonderivatively) and your body constitutes you at t.[33]

Not all properties may be had derivatively.[34] For example, as we have seen, primary-kind properties – like being a person, or being a human

---

[32] Being a person essentially and being a person contingently are two ways of having a single property along one dimension; being a person nonderivatively and being a person derivatively are two ways of having a single property along another dimension. But if *being essentially a person* were a distinct property from *being contingently a person*, or if *being nonderivatively a person* were a distinct property from *being derivatively a person*, none of those "properties" could be borrowed. The definition of "having a property derivatively" would rule out having any of these properties derivatively. See chapter 8 and *Persons and Bodies*, ch. 2.

[33] For further discussion of this point, see *Persons and Bodies*, ch. 7, and "Materialism With a Human Face," in *Body, Soul, and Survival*, ed. Kevin Corcoran (Ithaca, NY: Cornell University Press, 2001): 159–180.

[34] The following kinds of properties cannot be had derivatively: (1) any property expressed in English by "possibly," "necessarily," "essentially," or "primary-kind property," or variants of these terms – call these "alethic properties"; (2) any property expressed in English by "is identical to," "constitutes," "derivatively," "exists," or "is an object" or variants of these terms – call these "identity/constitution/existence properties"; (3) any property such that necessarily, x has it at t only if x exists at some time other than t – call these "properties rooted outside the times that they are had"; (4) any property that is a conjunction of two or more properties that either entail or are entailed by two or more primary kind properties (e.g., being a cloth flag, being a human person) – call these "hybrid properties." In *Persons and Bodies*, I amend the definition of "having a property derivatively" to accommodate having hybrid properties derivatively.

animal – may be had derivatively: my body now is derivatively a person. However, other properties – like being a person essentially, or having *human animal* as one's primary kind – cannot be had derivatively. My body does not have the property of having *being a person as its primary-kind property* at all (not derivatively, not nonderivatively). Rather, my body has the property of being a human animal as its primary-kind property. If being an F and being a G are two primary-kind properties, x may have both – one as its primary-kind property and the other derivatively – but it does not follow from this that x is of two primary kinds.[35]

The fact that constitution is a relation of real unity has two implications for the idea of having properties derivatively: On the one hand, if x has a property derivatively, then there are not two separate exemplifications of the property: x has the property solely in virtue of its constitution-relations to something that has the property independently. On the other hand, if x has a property derivatively, x still really has it. I really am a body (derivatively); if my foot itches, then I itch. And my body is really a person (now); when I have a right to be in a certain seat, my body has a right to be in that seat. Constitution is so intimate a relation, so close to identity, that if x constitutes y at t, then – solely in virtue of the fact that x constitutes y – x has properties derivatively at t that x would not have had if x had not constituted y. (And vice versa.) The idea of having properties derivatively accounts for the otherwise strange fact that if x constitutes y at t, x and y share so many properties even though x ≠ y.

In short, although constitution is not identity, constitution is a unity-relation. The unity produced by constitution allows two-way borrowing of properties – from constituted to constituter, and from constituter to constituted. It is because constitution is a relation of unity (though not identity) that many properties are shared by both constituter and constituted.

IS THE IDEA OF CONSTITUTION PLAUSIBLE?

Some philosophers find the idea of a comprehensive relation that is neither identity nor separate existence simply to be implausible. How could there

---

[35] There may be conjunctive primary kinds. Assuming that *can-opener* is one primary kind and *corkscrew* is another, then the property of being a can-opener and a corkscrew is a primary-kind property. (I believe that Thomas Nagel is responsible for a "can-opener/corkscrew" example.)

be ontologically distinct things at the same place at the same time? In chapter 8, I shall give an explicit definition of "x constitutes y at t" in familiar terms. However, here I want to respond to the "incredulous stare" in two ways – one historical, the other metaphysical.

First, historically, the ground for a relation of unity without identity was laid by Aristotle's notion of numerical sameness without identity. Aristotle distinguished sameness in number from sameness in being, and he furnished examples of numerical sameness that are not cases of true identity. True identity is sameness in being or substance or logos. One sort of numerical sameness without true identity is Aristotle's idea of accidental sameness, discussed illuminatingly by Gareth B. Matthews.[36]

For example, when a man becomes musical, the man survives but the unmusical man does not. "When the man rises, the seated man ceases to be; when the woman awakens, the sleeping woman passes away; when the baby cries, the silent baby perishes."[37] Each of these pairs is an accidental unity. On the one hand, there are not two men, two women, or two babies; on the other hand it is "only in an accidental sense that they can be said to be the same (person or thing)."[38] Seated Socrates is an accidental unity if and only if: "there is a concrete substance, s, such that, necessarily, seated Socrates exists if and only if s is accidentally seated (or s is accidentally Socrates)."[39]

Aristotle's notion of accidental sameness should be interpreted "ontologically," not linguistically; for example, it should not be construed as part of an account of the way that singular referring expressions function in a language.[40] Nor should accidental sameness be considered a matter of contingent, rather than necessary, identity. As Matthews points out, if A and B are accidentally the same, then A and B are in a way the same and in a way different.[41] But on any customary account of contingent identity, says

---

[36] See Gareth B. Matthews, "Accidental Unities," in *Language and Logos: Studies in Ancient Greek Philosophy Presented to G. E. L. Owen*, ed. Malcolm Schofield and Martha Craven Nussbaum (Cambridge: Cambridge University Press, 1982): 223–240; "Aristotelian Essentialism," *Philosophy and Phenomenological Research* 50, Supplement, (Fall 1990): 251–262, esp. pp. 258–259; "Aristotle's Theory of Kooky Objects," ms. (1992). Also see Nicholas White, "Identity, Modal Individuation and Matter in Aristotle," *Studies in Essentialism* (Midwest Studies in Philosophy XI), ed. Peter A. French, Theodore E. Uehling, Jr., and Howard K. Wettstein (Minneapolis: University of Minnesota, 1986): 475–494.
[37] Matthews, "Accidental Unities," p. 225.   [38] Ibid., p. 226.
[39] Matthews, "Aristotle's Theory of Kooky Objects."   [40] Ibid., p. 3.
[41] Matthews, "Accidental Unities," p. 229.

Nicholas White, "if A and B are contingently identical, then they *are* identical, though it is contingent that they are so, just as someone who contingently eats beans *does* eat beans, though it is contingent that he does, and it is not thereby true, in a way, that he does not eat beans."[42] Nor should accidental sameness be interpreted as any kind of relative identity.[43]

In Topics A7, Aristotle discusses different kinds of numerical sameness, one of which is accidental sameness. So, although Coriscus is a man and the masked man is a man and Coriscus is not identical to the masked man, it does not follow that there are two men. Indeed, since Aristotle does not recognize "object" or "thing" (*pragma*) as a genuine count noun, there is *no* count noun under which Coriscus and the masked man count as two. Thus, we do not end up with more men (or anything else) than we expected.[44]

We can use Aristotle's notion of numerical sameness without identity to defuse several related kinds of resistance to the idea of constitution (another kind of numerical sameness without identity, different from accidental sameness). The first kind of resistance stems from the doubt that nonidentical things can occupy the same space at the same time.[45] Aristotle's notion of accidental sameness shows that we do not have to suppose that if A and B are nonidentical, then A and B are two things. So, we need not suppose that two things occupy the same place at the same time. (In chapter 8, I shall show how the Constitution View avoids the inference from constitution to "two things.") The second kind of resistance arises from counting. Aristotle's notion of numerical sameness without identity shows that we need not (and frequently do not) count by identity.[46] (In chapter 8, I shall explicitly address several problems for constitution that seem to arise from counting.)

---

[42] White, "Identity, Modal Individuation and Matter in Arisotle," p. 477.

[43] Matthews, "Accidental Unities," pp. 229–230.

[44] Matthews, "Aristotle's Theory of Kooky Objects," p. 6.

[45] For a sympathetic discussion of nonidentical things occupying the same place at the same time, see David Wiggins, "On Being in the Same Place at the Same Time," *Philosophical Review* 77 (1968): 90–95.

[46] For an account of counting, based on Aristotle's notion of accidental sameness, congenial to constitution-without-identity, see Jeffrey E. Brower and Michael C. Rea, "Material Constitution and the Trinity," *Faith and Philosophy* 22 (2005): 57–76. Brower and Rea's construal of constitution is significantly different from mine. They take constitution to be a mereological notion; I do not. I take sameness of parts at a time to *follow from* constitution, not to be constitutive of the idea of constitution itself. See chapter 9.

The point of this historical excursion is to show that there is strong and detailed historical precedent for the idea of a relation that is not identity but is unity, a relation neither of identity nor of separateness.[47] Constitution is one such idea. Moreover, if we need a metaphysics of ordinary objects, as I argued in chapter 1, then we have little choice but to opt for something like constitution-without-identity. So, let us turn to metaphysical reasons to endorse the idea of constitution.[48]

There are (at least) two reasons to find constitution-without-identity metaphysically plausible. First, as we saw at the beginning of this chapter, the persistence conditions of ordinary objects are strikingly different from the persistence conditions of, say, the atoms that make them up. The atoms existed before and will exist after the demise of the medium-sized thing. Moreover, the same table exists before and after being scratched, but different atoms make it up before and after it was scratched. There must be a contingent, time-bound relation between an ordinary object and the atoms that make it up. Identity, as we learned from Kripke and others, is not such a relation: Identity is necessary and not-time-bound: if a and b are identical, then neither can exist without the other, and neither can have any property (modal or otherwise) that the other lacks. If a and b are one and the same object, there can be no difference *whatever* between "them." So, we have a metaphysical call for a relation that is not one of identity, but is nonetheless one of unity.

Second, as we shall see in chapter 5, ordinary things have quite different causal powers from the atoms that make them up. For example, a search

---

[47] Also see Michael C. Rea, "Sameness Without Identity: An Aristotelian Solution to the Problem of Material Constitution," *Ratio* (new series) 11 (1998): 316–328.

[48] A number of prominent philosophers in recent years have endorsed some form of constitution-without-identity. The following are just a sample: Frederick C. Doepke, "Spatially Coinciding Objects," *Ratio* 24 (1982): 45–60; E. J. Lowe, "Instantiation, Identity and Constitution," *Philosophical Studies* 44 (1983): 45–59; Judith Jarvis Thomson, "The Statue and the Clay," *Noûs* 32 (1998): 149–173; Kathryn Koslicki, "Constitution and Similarity," *Philosophical Studies* 117 (2004): 327–364; Stephen Yablo, "Identity, Essence and Indiscernibility," *Philosophical Review* 104 (1987): 293–314; Rea, "Sameness Without Identity"; Mark Johnston, "Constitution is Not Identity," *Mind* 101 (1992): 89–105; David Oderberg, "Coincidence Under a Sortal," *Philosophical Review* 105 (1996): 145–171; Ernest Sosa, "Subjects Among Other Things," in *Material Constitution*, ed. Michael C. Rea (Lanham, MD: Rowman and Littlefield, 1997): 63–89; Michael B. Burke, "Preserving the Principle of One Object to a Place: A Novel Account of the Relations Among Objects, Sorts, Sortals and Persistence Conditions," *Philosophy and Phenomenological Research* 54 (1994): 591–624; Peter Simons, *Parts: A Study in Ontology* (Oxford: Clarendon Press, 1987); Wiggins, "On Being in the Same Place at the Same Time."

warrant, when shown to the owner of a house, has the effect of the owner's standing aside and allowing the officers to enter. The reason that the search warrant has that effect concerns the circumstances, the conventions and laws surrounding search warrants. If the search warrant had been written on papyrus, or if it had been written in a different language that the homeowner also understood, it would have had the same effect. The causal properties of an ID object are not determined by the properties of the atoms that make them up. Atoms have their effects in virtue of their physical and chemical properties (e.g., atomic numbers, valence, etc.); ID objects have their effects in virtue of their intentional properties – as well as of the physical and chemical properties that they have derivatively. In chapter 5, I defend nonreductive macrocausation, and in chapter 11, I defend a constitution-based conception of ontological levels. Here, I am just trying to cite plausible metaphysical differences between constituted things and their ultimate constituters in order to provide backing to the general idea of constitution-without-identity. The historical precedent from Aristotle, together with the intuitive differences between constituted things and their ultimate constituters, makes the idea of constitution – a relation of unity without identity – plausible.

THINKING THINGS INTO EXISTENCE?

There is a worry that my view allows us simply to think things into existence. For example, Dean Zimmerman, one of my best critics, says, "Baker thinks we sometimes bring things into existence by thinking about them." As an example, he cites "a piece of conveniently shaped driftwood [that] becomes a coffee table by being brushed off and brought into the house."[49]

Not exactly. Even on my view, that's a little too quick. The piece of driftwood comes to constitute a table only in table-favorable circumstances, which include more than "being brushed off and brought into the house." The piece of driftwood comes to constitute a table in part by coming to be used in a certain already-established way. Granted, there is no exact moment at which the piece of driftwood comes to constitute a table. (In chapter 6, I'll defend vagueness of temporal boundaries.) But our practices and conventions, as well as our intentions, are what make one

---

[49] Dean Zimmerman, "The Constitution of Persons by Bodies: A Critique of Lynne Rudder Baker's Theory of Material Constitution," *Philosophical Topics* 30 (2002): 295–338, p. 333.

piece of driftwood constitute a table, and another piece of driftwood constitute a piece of art. If I saw a piece of driftwood and made up the word "bonangle" on the spot, and thought to myself, "It would be nice if the world contained bonangles; I hereby make that piece of driftwood a bonangle," I would not have brought into existence a new thing, a bonangle; our conventions and practices do not have a place for bonangles. It is not *just* thinking that brings things into existence.

Although thinking, by itself, does not bring a new concrete thing into existence, some thought and talk, in the context of conventions and practices, can enlarge the field of an already-existing primary-kind property. E.g., *Being a sculpture* was already a primary-kind property when Duchamp produced *Fountain*. Interestingly, Zimmerman uses a reference to Duchamp's *Fountain* ("a urinal becomes a sculpture when hung on a wall in a museum and given a title")[50] as an example of how my view would allow objects to become artworks "simply by our thinking of them as such." But again, what made *Fountain* an artwork was not just "thinking of [it] as such." If it had not been presented (and as it happened, signed, "R. Mutt") by someone like Duchamp at a much earlier point in the history of art (with all its conventions), that urinal would not have constituted an artwork at all. Again: This is a case, not of bringing into existence a new primary kind, but enlarging the field of a well-established primary kind.

Now the difficulty pops up from the other side. If how we talk and interact plays a role in what exists, then – for example – how much change would be required for *being a president* to be a primary-kind property? *Being a president* is a kind property, but it is no more a *primary*-kind property than is *being a student*. But if the Constitution View allows that our conventions and intentions can help determine which properties are primary-kind properties, then perhaps we could make *president* a primary kind. "How differently would we have to talk and act," Zimmerman asks, "before G. W. Bush, the man, would come to coincide with another thing, a person (derivatively) who is (nonderivatively) commander-in-chief of the armed forces, etc., but who will outlive the man G. W. and always be president?"[51] How much change in the way that we talk would it take for *president* to be a primary kind constituted at one time by George Washington, and at another time by Abraham Lincoln?

---

[50] I take it that Zimmerman does not consider *Fountain* to be an artwork distinct from a urinal.

[51] Zimmerman, "The Constitution of Persons by Bodies," p. 334.

44

My answer is that we cannot anticipate in advance what new primary kinds there may be. However, we have good reason to suspect that no change will make *president* a primary kind. Before considering these reasons, note that it is clear that *president* is not a primary kind now, that *being president* is at this time a property that persons acquire and lose. When President Kennedy was killed, the United States had a new president – LBJ. We did not have the same president constituted by a new person. (You can find this out by reading the newspapers and political science books.) So, at this time, *president* is not a primary kind. There are two reasons why I doubt that there will be any time at which *president* is a primary kind.

In the first place, if we consider the role that thought and talk have in bringing new primary kinds into existence – e.g., figuring out how to build a machine with movable type contributed to the printing press; deciding how to document citizenship contributed to passports – we will see that it is not a matter of transforming nonprimary kinds into primary kinds. We did not start with passports as nonprimary kind and then use our talk and thought to convert them into primary kinds. The sort of talk and thought that can contribute to bringing a new primary kind into existence is not talk and thought about a kind that existed already as an old nonprimary kind (like *president*).

In the second place, it is difficult to imagine any human interest that would lead to conventions making *president* a primary kind. Our conventions are based on our interests, and I cannot imagine any human interest that would lead to conventions that would make *president* to be a primary kind. We choose what interests to have only within a limited range. We cannot just change our interests at will. I don't think that we could just decide to change our general interest in having shelter, or in being treated with dignity. I agree with the evolutionary psychologists to this extent: Our interests are not wholly malleable. So, I doubt that we could come to regard *president* as a primary kind. In that case, no change in the way that we talk would bring it about that *president* is a primary kind.

Zimmerman speaks of "powerful resistance to the idea that changes in our ways of talking about things, even coupled with simple changes in some of our nonverbal reactions to things, could by themselves bring any concrete physical object into existence."[52] I have two responses. First,

---

[52] Ibid., p. 335.

although I do hold that thought and talk make an essential contribution to the existence of certain objects, I do not hold that thought and talk alone bring into existence any physical objects: conventions, practices, and pre-existing materials are also required. So, on my view, what brings concrete things into existence is not *just* "ways of talking about things, even coupled with simple changes in some of our nonverbal reactions to things." I do not think that we just conjure up new concrete physical objects of an afternoon.

Moreover – and this is my second response – our intentional activity contributes ontologically to the existence only of ID objects, objects that could not exist in the absence of beings with propositional attitudes. Given the definition of "ID object," our role in the existence of such objects is assured. The only place for objection, I believe, lies in my assumption that there exist ID objects in the first place. But I do not see how we can make sense of our experience without ID objects like artifacts. Perhaps more significantly, intentional phenomena, including ID objects, are ineliminable from the explanatory apparatus of many of the special sciences – e.g., economics, sociology, political science, epidemiology, traffic science, and the like. It seems to me safe to affirm as real what are in the explanatory apparatus of the sciences.

Theodore Sider, like Zimmerman, firmly holds that what exists cannot depend on human activity. He remarks facetiously: "[T]he entities that exist correspond exactly with the categories for continuants in *our* conceptual scheme: trees, aggregates, statues, lumps, persons, bodies, and so on. How convenient! It would be nothing short of a miracle if reality just happened to match our conceptual scheme in this way."[53]

I reply: There need be no miracle. Reality doesn't "just happen to match our conceptual scheme." Our "conceptual scheme" is a product of our interactions in the world. We have the conceptual scheme that we have because of our actual encounters. There is simply no way that we can criticize it as a whole. (The metaphor of Neurath's ship applies here: Any rebuilding of the ship must take place while we are underway.) I join philosophers like Davidson,[54] who deny that we can step outside "our

---

[53] Theodore Sider, *Four-Dimensionalism* (Oxford: Clarendon Press, 2001): 156–157. See also Theodore Sider, Review of *Persons and Bodies: A Constitution View, Journal of Philosophy* 99 (2002): 45–48.

[54] Donald Davidson, "On the Very Idea of a Conceptual Scheme," in *Inquiries into Truth and Interpretation* (Oxford: Clarendon Press, 1984): 183–198.

conceptual scheme" and compare the scheme with reality as it is without us. The existence of trees, aggregates, statues, lumps, persons, bodies, and so on is about as well-confirmed as anything could be.

Sider continues:

> Or is it rather that the world contains the objects it does *because* of the activities of humans? This is an equally unappealing hypothesis. Everyone agrees humans have the power to select for attention a subset of the totality of objects that exist regardless of our activity. A [four-dimensionalist] worm theorist, for example, thinks that our sortal terms select ordinary continuants from a multitude of space-time worms that exist regardless of our activity. What is incredible is the claim that what there is, rather than what we select for attention, depends on human activity.[55]

I reply: This is deeply misguided. When the printing press was invented, a new kind of thing came into existence, and it changed the world. This seems to me an incontrovertible fact, not an "unappealing hypothesis." Sider's objection suggests that inventors are merely recognizers of a subset of "spacetime worms that exist regardless of our activity." Tell it to Gutenberg! A great deal of reality – though, of course, not all of it – depends on human activity. It does not follow that the only things that exist are the things that we have sortals for. There may well exist particles or biological natural kinds or future inventions that we have no sortals for.[56] The claim that what there is depends on human activity is not "incredible," nor is it an "embarrassment." It is an obvious fact.

There are many things in the world whose existence ontologically depends on intentional activity. No other view in sight begins to make metaphysical sense of the everyday world – or even to take it seriously, except as something to be explained away ontologically. On the rival views, what we take – and cannot help taking – to be real is really something else.

CONCLUSION

Instead of starting with metaphysical commitments, I prefer to approach the world with what is at hand – with what we know and cannot seriously doubt – and try to think clearly about it as unencumbered with antecedent metaphysics as we can. Rather than squeezing the world into a preconceived metaphysical straitjacket, we should let the metaphysics emerge

---

[55] Sider, *Four-Dimensionalism*, p. 157. [56] Cf. Sider, *Four-Dimensionalism*, p. 157.

from the reflection on the world as we encounter it. Using this preferred strategy, I have tried to show how the idea of constitution provides a metaphysical basis for taking ordinary objects to be real.[57]

---

[57] This chapter descended from papers read at Erasmus University (Rotterdam) in October 2003, the 2004 Werkmeister Conference at Florida State University in January 2004 (with Ronald Mallon as commentator), Canisius College in April 2004. A preliminary version was discussed by a working group of philosophers from Erasmus University, the Universities of Nijmegen Delft, Eindhoven, and Utrecht, with Theo van Willigenburg, Frank Hindriks, and Maureen Sie as commentators. Thanks to all the participants. I am also grateful to Gareth B. Matthews and Katherine Sonderegger for discussion of the matters at issue.

3

Artifacts

Artifacts are ubiquitous in the world that we encounter. Most broadly, artifacts include everything that is produced intentionally – paintings and sculptures as well as scissors and microscopes. The term "artifact" applies to many different kinds of things – tools, documents, jewelry, scientific instruments, machines, furniture, and so on. Artifacts are contrasted with natural objects like rocks, trees, dogs, that are not made by human beings (or by higher primates). Although the category of artifact includes sculptures, paintings, literary works, and performances, I shall put aside these fascinating artifacts and focus only on artifacts that have practical functions.

My concern here is with an important subclass of artifacts – technical artifacts, the material products of our endeavors to attain practical goals. Such artifacts are objects intentionally made *to serve a given purpose*. Artifacts with practical functions are everywhere. We sleep in *beds*; we are awakened by *clocks*; we eat with *knives and forks*; we drive *cars*; we write with *computers* (or with *pencils*); we manufacture *nails*. Without artifacts, there would be no recognizable human life.

Beginning with Aristotle, philosophers have taken artifacts to be ontologically deficient. By contrast, I shall use the Constitution View to develop an ontological theory of artifacts, according to which artifacts are ontologically on a par with other material objects. I shall formulate a nonreductive theory that regards artifacts as constituted by – but not identical to – aggregates of various things. After setting out the theory, I shall briefly discuss the idea of malfunction and then rebut a number of arguments that disparage the ontological status of artifacts.

AGGREGATES AND ARTIFACTS

Typically artifacts are constituted by aggregates of things. But not always: an anvil is constituted by a piece of heavy metal; a paperclip is constituted by a small piece of thin wire; and a 50 Euro note is constituted by a piece of paper. Nevertheless, the piece of thin wire and the piece of paper themselves are constituted by aggregates of molecules, which in turn are constituted by aggregates of atoms. So, even those artifacts (like paperclips) that are constituted by a single object are, at a lower level, constituted by aggregates of atoms. For purposes here, I'll consider artifacts to be constituted by aggregates of things, not by a single object. Any items whatever are an aggregate; and an aggregate is determined wholly by the items in it. The identity conditions of aggregates are simple: Aggregate x is identical to aggregate y just in case exactly the same items are in aggregate x and aggregate y. So, we have a principle governing the existence of an aggregate:[1]

(E-Agg) For any objects – call them "the xs" – there is an aggregate such that, necessarily, the aggregate exists whenever all the xs exist.

Since every x – every concrete thing – is of a primary kind essentially, we may identify the items (the xs) in an aggregate by their primary kinds. The items in an aggregate may include some items whose primary kind is F, and some whose primary kind is G, and so on. If aggregates are to constitute various kinds of artifacts, then aggregates themselves (and not just the items in them) must be of primary kinds. We may assign a primary kind to an aggregate of xs of various primary kinds. Suppose that the boat called "Boat" is constituted by a certain aggregate of planks and nails at t. The aggregate of planks and nails has a primary kind by courtesy. Aggregates of things of different kinds have a sort of surrogate primary kind consisting of all the primary kinds of the things in the aggregate. The primary kind of that aggregate is a hybrid: plank/nail. So, we have a principle governing the primary kind of an aggregate:

(PK-Agg) The primary kind of an aggregate of xs, where each of the xs is of primary kind F or of primary kind G or of primary kind H ..., is the hybrid primary kind F/G/H ...

Each of the items in the aggregate of planks and nails is itself an artifact. A plank is constituted by an aggregate of cellulose molecules and a nail is constituted by an aggregate of iron atoms. So, the aggregate of the planks and nails is itself constituted by an aggregate of natural nonartifactual things: cellulose molecules and iron atoms. And so on down to aggregates of subatomic particles. Although planks and nails (as well as the boat) are

---

[1] Given mereological theories of unrestricted composition, aggregates are just sums or fusions. See chapter 9. At this point, however, I am standing clear of mereological theories.

artifacts, the planks and nails are constituted by aggregates of natural objects. So, constitution does not distinguish between artifacts and non-artifacts (natural objects). The constitution relation holds between artifacts, between artifacts and nonartifacts, and between nonartifacts.[2]

CONDITIONS FOR BEING AN ARTIFACT

Now consider some of the distinctive features of (technical) artifacts. Most prominently, artifacts have proper functions that they are (intentionally) designed and produced to perform (whether they perform their proper functions or not).[3] Artifacts have *intended* functions, which are obviously normative. To carry out an intended function is what an artifact *is supposed to* do; to fail to carry out the function in certain circumstances is a kind of error, a malfunction. Where there is room for error or mistake, there is normativity. Normativity pervades the *Lebenswelt*: There is no intention without the possibility of its being thwarted, no desire without the possibility of its being frustrated, no function without the possibility of malfunction. We simply cannot understand the world we live in without presupposing normativity.[4] Unfortunately, like most other philosophers, I have no theory of normativity. But if we take the world as we encounter it as our starting point (as I do), then normativity is part of the price of admission. Nowhere is normativity more glaring than in the behavior of artifacts – from the trivial (people get wet when umbrellas blow inside-out) to the significant (combatants get killed when their guns jam).

What distinguishes artifactual primary kinds from other primary kinds is that artifactual primary kinds entail proper functions, where a proper function is a purpose or use intended by a producer.[5] That is, for each

---

[2] Nonartifactual constitution is illustrated by an organism and an aggregate of cells at a time.

[3] There is a lot of literature on functions. For example, see Crawford L. Elder, "A Different Kind of Natural Kind," *Australasian Journal of Philosophy* 73 (1995): 516–531. See also Pieter E. Vermaas and Wybo Houkes, "Ascribing Functions to Technical Artifacts: A Challenge to Etiological Accounts of Functions," *British Journal for the Philosophy of Science* 54 (2003): 261–289. As Vermaas and Houkes point out, some philosophers take the notion of biological function to be basic and then try to apply or transform theories of biological function (which since Darwin are non-intentionalist, reproduction theories) to artifacts. I believe that Vermaas and Houkes are entirely correct to liberate the theory of artifacts from the notion of function in biology.

[4] Nor, in my opinion, can we understand the actual world without modal ideas – like the possibility of malfunction. Hence, I reject Humean supervenience.

[5] For a thoughtful discussion of functions, see Beth Preston, "Why is a Wing Like a Spoon? A Pluralist Theory of Function, *Journal of Philosophy* 95 (1998): 215–254.

artifactual primary kind, there is a proper function such that the bearer of that artifactual primary kind necessarily has that proper function (indeed, the general term for an artifact – e.g., polisher, scraper, life preserver – often just names the proper function of the artifact). Thus, an artifact has its proper function essentially: The nature of an artifact lies in its proper function – what it was designed to do, the purpose for which it was produced.[6] An artifact's proper function is an *intended* function. Since artifacts have intended functions essentially, they are ID objects: they could not exist in a world without beings with propositional attitudes.

The proper function of a boat is to provide transportation on water. The proper function of an artifact is the intended function. An artifact may in fact never perform its proper function: Perhaps a boat is never actually put in water, or perhaps it malfunctions (sinks on launching). The aggregate of planks and nails that constitutes a boat at t inherits the proper function of a boat. But the aggregate of planks and nails only contingently has the function of providing aquatic transportation, in virtue of constituting a boat at t. The boat has its proper function essentially; the aggregate of the planks and nails that constitutes the boat at t has its proper function only contingently. After some of the planks are replaced at t', say, the aggregate that constituted the boat at t no longer constitutes it; and hence the aggregate that constituted the boat at t no longer has the proper function of providing aquatic transportation.

What proper function an artifact has determines what the artifact most fundamentally is – a boat, a jackhammer, a microscope, and so on. And what proper function an artifact has is determined by the intentions of its designer and/or producer. Here, then, are four conditions that I propose as necessary and sufficient for x's being an artifact[7]:

(A1) x has one or more makers, producers, or authors. Designers and executors of design (perhaps the same people) are authors.

---

[6] More precisely, a nonderivative artifact has its proper function essentially. The constituter of an artifact inherits the nonderivative artifact's proper function and thus has it contingently (as long as it constitutes the nonderivative artifact).

[7] In thinking about these matters, I found useful Risto Hilpinen, "Authors and Artifacts," *Proceedings of the Aristotelian Society* 93 (1993): 155–178, as well as Randall Dipert's *Artifacts, Artworks, and Agency* (Philadelphia: Temple University Press, 1993). For insightful discussions of artifacts, see Amie Thomasson's *Fiction and Metaphysics* (Cambridge: Cambridge University Press, 1999), E. J. Lowe's "On the Identity of Artifacts," *Journal of Philosophy* 80 (1983): 220–232. Also see Wybo Houkes and Anthonie Meijers, "The Ontology of Artifacts: The Hard Problem," *Studies in the History and Philosophy of Science* 37 (2006): 118–131.

(A2) x's primary kind (its essence, its proper function) is determined in part by the intentions of its authors.

(A3) x's existence depends on the intentions of its authors and the execution of those intentions.

(A4) x is constituted by an aggregate that the authors have arranged or selected[8] to serve the proper function entailed by the artifact's primary kind.

(A1)–(A4) are, I hope, an adequate account of artifacts. Now I want to fill out my characterization of constitution in chapter 2 to accommodate (A1)–(A4), and hence to accommodate artifacts. I'll illustrate with a boat and an aggregate of planks and nails. The addition is to place a twofold condition on an aggregate that can constitute, e.g., a boat:

(i) The aggregate must contain enough items of suitable structure to enable the proper function of the artifact to be performed – in the current example, the function of providing aquatic transportation (whether the proper function actually is ever performed or not); and

(ii) The items in the aggregate must be available for assembly in a way suitable for enabling the proper function of the artifact to be performed.

Call an aggregate that satisfies these two conditions "an appropriate aggregate."

A CONSTITUTION VIEW OF ARTIFACTS

According to the general definition of "constitution," if x constitutes y at t, and y's primary kind is G, then x is in what I called "G-favorable circumstances" at t. (See chapter 2 and chapter 8.) If a certain aggregate of planks and nails constitutes a boat at t, then the aggregate must be in boat-favorable circumstances at t. Consideration of artifacts suggests that we should distinguish two kinds of G-favorable circumstances for boats, say: (1) the circumstances in which a boat may come into existence; (2) the circumstances in which an existing boat continues to exist. The circumstances in which a boat comes into existence are more stringent than those for a boat's remaining in existence. So, let me spell out some features of boat-favorable circumstances for a boat's coming into existence:

---

[8] I do not want to rule out "degenerate" cases in which a natural object is appropriated without alteration. E.g., a piece of (unaltered) driftwood may be brushed off and used as a wine rack.

The boat-favorable circumstances concern the relations between an appropriate aggregate for boats, designers and/or builders. For example: (a) the aggregate must be in the presence of one or more persons who know how to build a boat from the items in the aggregate, and who either intend to build a boat from the items in the aggregate or whose activity is directed by someone who intends to have a boat built from the items in the aggregate; (b) the items in the aggregate must be manipulated by such persons (either manually or by machine) in ways that execute their productive intentions or of those directing the persons; (c) the result of the manipulation must satisfy the productive intentions of the persons.

Now with the notions of an appropriate aggregate and boat-favorable circumstances, we can adapt the general definition of "x constitutes y at t" to a boat. (See chapter 2 for a general characterization of constitution and chapter 8 for the general definition of "x constitutes y at t.") Only an aggregate that satisfies the conditions (i) and (ii) for an appropriate aggregate for boats can constitute a boat. Suppose that there is such an appropriate aggregate of planks and nails. Call it "Agg" and the boat "Boat."

Agg constitutes Boat at t if and only if: There are distinct primary kinds, boat and plank/nail, and boat-favorable circumstances such that:

(1) Agg is an appropriate aggregate of primary-kind plank/nail & Boat is of primary-kind boat; &
(2) Agg and Boat are spatially coincident at t; &
(3) Agg is in boat-favorable circumstances at t; &
(4) It is necessary that: for any aggregate that has plank/nail as its primary-kind property and is in boat-favorable circumstances at t, there exists something that is spatially coincident with the aggregate at t and has *being a boat* as its primary-kind property, and
(5) It is possible that: Agg exists at t and there exists nothing with primary-kind property *being a boat* that is spatially coincident with x at t;
(6) Agg and Boat are of the same basic kind of stuff.

When this biconditional – Agg constitutes Boat at t iff (1)–(6) – holds, (A1)–(A4) are satisfied. (A1)–(A3) are satified when Agg is in boat-favorable circumstances, and (A4) is satisfied when Agg and Boat fit the definition. Boat is nonderivatively an artifact; indeed, the boat is essentially an artifact: there is no possible world in which that boat exists and is not an artifact. Agg at t is derivatively an artifact. Agg would not be an artifact if it hadn't constituted an artifact. Even though the planks and nails in Agg are themselves artifacts, the aggregate of artifacts is not an artifact nonderivatively. (No one produces an aggregate; it comes into existence automatically, and an aggregate has no nonderivative proper function.) This completes a sketch of a theory of artifacts made up from aggregates of items.

Let me note a couple of advantages of this Constitution View of artifacts: First, it allows for novel artifacts – objects with new proper functions. An artifact's having a proper function depends in part on the author's intentions, and not on any history of selection and reproduction as proper functions in biology are. So, prototypes of innovative artifacts have proper functions.[9] Second, this account allows – as it should – that a single boat may survive various replacement of planks and nails. After replacement even of a nail, Agg would still exist (assuming that the replaced nail was not destroyed), but Agg would no longer constitute Boat; some other aggregate would. So, again, we see that Agg $\neq$ Boat.

THE SIGNIFICANCE OF MALFUNCTION

Artifacts, by definition, have intended functions. They are intentionally produced to serve practical goals. Since goals are the sorts of things that can be attained or can fail to attain, a distinction between proper performance and malfunction is built into the very idea of a (technical) artifact. Any such artifact – a hammer, a telescope, an artificial hip – may malfunction. Thus, for technical artifacts, the concepts *artifact*, *function*, and *malfunction* are conceptually linked: none is intelligible without the others. Hence, we need to discuss the idea of malfunction.

Not all cases in which something fails to perform its intended function seem to be malfunctions. For centuries, people tried to build perpetual motion machines. Of course, they all failed; a machine in perpetual motion is physically impossible. Should we say that each of the machines malfunctioned? Or: Suppose that someone had an amulet whose intended function was to protect its user and to cause harm to her enemies. (An amulet is a paradigm case of a technical artifact – "a material product of our endeavor to attain our practical goals.") The amulet was supposed to produce a desired effect when its user uttered certain incantations. It is plausible to suppose that no such causal connections are physically possible. Does the amulet malfunction? There seems to be a difference between a flaw in a design in which there was a malfunction in the mechanism (e.g., the designer had overlooked the fact that the gas would be under so

---

[9] Vermaas and Houkes take this to be a criterion of adequacy for a theory of functions.

much pressure that the device would explode when operated for more than a few seconds), and a flaw in which there was no mechanical failure, but the mechanism simply did not accomplish the intended function (e.g., a perpetual motion machine or the amulet).

The examples of the perpetual motion machine and the amulet raise questions about the concept of intended function. Can an artifact have a function that is it is physically impossible for it to perform? My suggestion is to take terms like "amulet" and "perpetual motion machine" to mean, respectively, "item intended to protect its user and to harm her enemies" and "machine intended to produce perpetual motion." Then, we can say that there are such artifacts, and that they have functions that it is physically impossible for them to perform. But I would reserve the term "malfunction" for artifacts that have functions that are physically possible to be performed. Hence, the failure of a perpetual motion machine to produce perpetual motion and the failure of the amulet to cause mishaps should not count as malfunctions.

Other cases of failure to perform the intended function that should not be considered to be malfunctions include these: A car that does not start because it is out of gas. (A car is not intended to run in conditions in which it lacks gas.) A computer that does not operate because its operator is incompetent (say, a two-year-old). In general, failure to perform an intended function is not a malfunction unless there is an attempt by a competent operator to perform the intended function in conditions for which the artifact was designed. So, here is a characterization of a malfunction[10]:

(M) x is a malfunction of an artifact A if and only if:

(a) x is a failure to perform the intended function of A, where it is physically possible that the intended function of A be performed, and
(b) x occurs when a competent operator tries to use A to perform its intended function under conditions for which A was designed.

There are a variety of sources of malfunction: the materials used may be poorly chosen (as when soft metal is used in the manufacture of a key); the materials may themselves be defective (as when too much sand is used in mortar holding up the bricks on the library); or the design may be defective (as when gas tanks in cars explode on impact); or there may be damage to the structure (as when the surface of the space shuttle *Columbia*

---

[10] Thanks to Anthonie Meijers for discussing this definition with me and making suggestions.

was punctured during take-off). Any occurrence that satisfies (M) is a malfunction.

Some malfunctions are fatal and others are not. An artifact may survive some malfunctions (the brakes can be fixed) but not others (the gas tank exploded and blew up the car). What exactly is the line, someone may ask, between having a car that is broken, and having something that is not a car at all? There is no sharp line. In the absence of a clear boundary between a malfunctioning F and a nonF, one may either take a linguistic view of vagueness or acknowledge that there is vagueness in reality. In chapter 6, I defend the latter position: there is vagueness in reality. I believe that recognition of vagueness in reality is required for a realistic view of the special sciences. I am not trying to argue for this position in this chapter. I just want to acknowledge this consequence of the Constitution View.

Let us consider an actual occurrence of a fatal malfunction, where there is no vagueness or ambiguity. On February 1, 2003, the space shuttle, *Columbia*, broke up during a seemingly routine re-entry into the Earth's atmosphere. It was a spectacular disaster, leaving myriad pieces from the shuttle scattered over several US states. (It was later determined that the malfunction was caused by damage to the left wing during launch; during the flight of the space shuttle, the damage had seemed slight.)

Contrast the Constitution View to reductionism or eliminativism about artifacts. According to eliminativism, strictly speaking, no space shuttle ever existed: the words "space shuttle" do not refer. All that existed were simples arranged space-shuttlewise; there is no object that is a space shuttle. On an eliminativist view, sentences like "The space shuttle broke up" are rephrased to eliminate the apparent reference to an object. When speaking in the "strict and philosophical sense," we may mention simples-arranged-space-shuttlewise, instead of space shuttles. When the space shuttle broke up (as we say), the only change in reality was in the arrangement of certain simples. But nothing went out of existence.[11] There exist no artifacts, though we can find true paraphrases of sentences putatively about artifacts: For "This is the house that Jack built," eliminativists may substitute "These are simples that were arranged housewise by Jack."

According to reductionism, there are space shuttles; the words "space shuttle" do refer, but what they refer to are aggregates of matter that

---

[11] I associate this view with Peter van Inwagen, according to whom the only (finite, concrete) objects that exist are simples and living organisms. See his *Material Beings* (Ithaca, NY: Cornell University Press, 1990).

occupy spacetime points arranged space-shuttlewise. The *Columbia* was nothing more or less than a mereological sum of bits of matter at those spacetime points. Indeed, every aggregate of matter-filled spacetime points have mereological sums; we have names (e.g., "space shuttle") for a few of the sums that exist, but no names for most of the sums. (Indeed, we couldn't possibly name them all; there's a nondenumerable infinity of objects.) The only concrete objects that really exist are bits of matter at spacetime points and their sums arranged in various ways.[12]

Now apply the Constitution View to the example of the space shuttle *Columbia*. The malfunction in the space-shuttle case put an end to the existence of *Columbia*. According to the Constitution View, *Columbia* really existed in its own right, so to speak. It was constituted by a vast aggregate of a complex primary kind, which itself was constituted by further aggregates, until finally there is a constituting aggregate of subatomic particles.[13] Let P be an aggregate that is a subatomic constituter of *Columbia* at t. *Columbia* was essentially a space shuttle; P was only derivatively a space shuttle at t – while P constituted *Columbia*. Recall that an aggregate exists as long as the items in it exist, no matter where they are. We cannot say, "P is identical with *Columbia* at t." We cannot say this, because we are assuming classical identity and three-dimensionalism: identity is necessary identity, not relative to time; and on three-dimensionalism, "*Columbia* at t" does not denote an entity, but an ordered pair < *Columbia*, t >. So, although P constituted *Columbia* at t, P was not identical with *Columbia* – at t or any other time.

According to the Constitution View, it is not just that we found it convenient to stop referring to P as "*Columbia*" (à la Lewis). It is rather that *Columbia* went out of existence altogether, but P did not. Nor is it just that there was no such entity as *Columbia* at all (à la van Inwagen). By contrast, on the Constitution View, the break-up of *Columbia* was a loss to reality, ontologically speaking. It is rather that there was an entity *Columbia* and there was an aggregate, P, and at the break-up, the former ceased to exist but the latter did not. The change was more than a change in the

---

[12] I associate this view with David Lewis. David Lewis, *Parts of Classes* (Oxford: Basil Blackwell, 1991). Since Lewis is a four-dimensionalist, it is more accurate to say that on his view the *Columbia* was a spacetime worm made up of a mereological sum of four-dimensional parts.

[13] I think that it is an empirical question whether there is an ultimate constituter; but if there is not, then there are still subatomic constituters. See Jonathan Schaffer, "Is There a Fundamental Level?" *Noûs* 37 (2003): 498–517.

arrangement of particles. The contents of the world changed when *Columbia* was destroyed; complete inventories of the world before and after the break-up would include different objects.[14]

The Constitution View allows us to be realists about artifacts: artifacts exist in their own right. Since part of what it is to be an artifact is to have an intended function, artifacts are always liable to malfunction. Reductionists and even eliminativists about artifacts can allow that statements about malfunction – e.g., "The space shuttle malfunctioned" – are true. But they cannot take the sentence at face value to state what it seems to state. On a reductionist or eliminativist view, such a statement is either about a change in arrangement of particles, or about no thing at all. The normativity drains away. By contrast, the Constitution View easily accepts the characterization of malfunction on its face-value interpretation, without having to reinterpret it (as van Inwagen does) or to suppose that talk about malfunction is really just talk about concepts (as Lewis does).

The Constitution View accords artifacts ontological status as artifacts. An artifact has as great a claim as a natural object to be a genuine substance. This is so because artifactual kinds are primary kinds. Their functions are their essences. Many philosophers accord to artifacts a second-class status. To such philosophers I now want to turn.

THE ONTOLOGICAL STATUS OF ARTIFACTS

Many important philosophers – from Aristotle on – hold artifacts ontologically in low regard. Some philosophers have gone so far as to argue that "artifacts such as ships, houses, hammers, and so forth, do not really exist."[15] Artifacts are thought to be lacking in some ontological way: they are considered not genuine substances. Although the notion of substance is a vexed one in philosophy, what I mean by saying that things of some kind – Fs (e.g., hammers, dogs, persons) – are genuine substances is that any full account of the furniture of the world will have to include reference to Fs. I shall argue that there is no reasonable basis for distinguishing between artifacts and natural objects in a way that renders natural objects as genuine substances and artifacts as ontologically deficient.

---

[14] For a distinction between the unrestricted domain of the existential quantifier and the ontology of the world at a given time, see chapter 11.

[15] Joshua Hoffman and Gary S. Rosenkrantz, *Substance: Its Nature and Existence* (London: Routledge, 1997): 173.

I shall consider five possible ways of distinguishing between natural objects and artifacts, all of which are mentioned or alluded to by David Wiggins.[16] On none of these, I shall argue, do natural objects, but not artifacts, turn out to be genuine substances. Let the alphabetic letter "F" be a placeholder for a name of a type of entity.

(1) Fs are genuine substances only if Fs have an internal principle of activity.
(2) Fs are genuine substances only if there are laws that apply to Fs as such, or there could be a science of Fs.
(3) Fs are genuine substances only if whether something is an F is not determined merely by an entity's satisfying a description.
(4) Fs are genuine substances only if Fs have an underlying intrinsic essence.
(5) Fs are genuine substances only if the identity and persistence of Fs is independent of any intentional activity.

Let us consider (1)–(5) one at a time.

(1) The first condition – Fs are genuine substances only if Fs have an internal principle of activity – has its source in Aristotle.[17] Aristotle took this condition to distinguish objects that come from nature (e.g., animals and plants) from objects that come from other efficient causes (e.g., beds). But it seems to me that this condition does not rule in natural objects and rule out artifacts as genuine substances. Today, we would consider a piece of gold (or any other chemical element) a natural object, but a piece of gold does not have an internal principle of change; conversely, a heat-seeking missile is an artifact that does have an internal principle of activity. So, the first condition does not distinguish artifacts from natural objects.

(2) The second condition – Fs are genuine substances only if there are laws that apply to Fs as such, or there could be a science of Fs – also

---

[16] All the conditions either follow from, or are part of, the basic distinction that Wiggins draws between natural objects and artifacts. There is a complex condition that natural objects allegedly satisfy and artifacts do not: ". . . a particular constituent x belongs to a natural kind, or is a natural thing, if and only if x has a principle of activity founded in lawlike dispositions and propensities that form the basis for extension-involving sortal identification(s) which will answer truly the question 'what is x?'" According to Wiggins, natural objects satisfy this condition and artifacts do not. David Wiggins, *Sameness and Substance Renewed* (Cambridge: Cambridge University Press, 2001): 89. I am not claiming that Wiggins denies that there exist artifacts, only that he distinguishes between natural and artifactual kinds in ways that may be taken to imply the ontological inferiority of artifacts.

[17] A substance has "within itself a principle of motion and stationariness (in respect of place, or of growth and decrease, or by way of alteration)." Aristotle, *Physics* 192b8–23.

allows artifacts to be genuine substances. Engineering fields blur the line between natural objects and artifacts. Engineering schools have courses in materials science (including advanced topics in concrete), traffic engineering, transportation science, computer science – all of which quantify over artifacts. And if we consider laws to be counterfactual-supporting generalizations, then these engineering fields are looking for laws. Even fields considered part of the natural sciences include artifactual as well as natural materials in their domains. For example, polymers are large molecules made up of repeating molecular units like beads on a string. "Natural polymers include rubber, wool, and cotton; synthetic polymers include nylon and polythene."[18] So, some instances of polymers (e.g., those made of nylon) are artifacts; others (e.g., those made of rubber) are natural objects. My university has a whole building devoted to Polymer Science. Since something's being of an artifactual kind does not preclude a science of it, the second condition does not make artifacts less than genuine substances.

(3) The third condition – Fs are genuine substances only if whether something is an F is not determined merely by an entity's satisfying a description – is semantic. Demonstrative reference is supposed to be essential to natural-kind terms.[19] The reference of natural-kind terms is determined indexically; the reference of artifactual-kind terms is determined by satisfying a description.[20] E.g., this is what Wiggins says:

---

[18] *The New York Public Library Science Desk Reference*, ed. Patricia Barnes-Svarney (New York: Macmillan, 1995: 547). Although nylon and polythene are of kinds determined by chemical composition, they are manufactured artificial human products, and their proper function is their use in various kinds of products.

[19] This claim is similar to the notion that natural-kind terms, but not artificial-kind terms, are rigid designators. (A rigid designator has the same referent in every possible world.) However, what makes the difference between "whale" and "bachelor" is not that only the former is rigid. Rather, only the former term "has its reference determined by causal contact with paradigm samples of the relevant kind." There is no reason that the terms cannot both be rigid. See Joseph LaPorte, "Rigidity and Kind," *Philosophical Studies* 97 (2000): 293–316, p. 304.

[20] Although Wiggins is an Aristotelian, this is not Aristotle's view. For Aristotle, nominal definitions are reference fixers, used to identify objects for scientific study; they contain information that a scientist has before having an account of the essence of the objects. Real definitions are discovered by scientific inquiry and give knowledge of the essences of objects identified by nominal definitions. Nominal and real definitions are not accounts of different types of entities. Rather, they are different types of accounts of the same entities. Members of a particular natural kind have the same essence (underlying structure). See Robert Bolton, "Essentialism and Semantic Theory in Aristotle: *Posterior Analytics*, II, 7–10," *Philosophical Review* 85 (1976): 514–544.

Artifacts are collected up not by reference to a theoretically hypothesized common constitution but under functional descriptions that are precisely indifferent to specific constitution and particular mode of interaction with the environment. A clock is any time-keeping device, a pen is any rigid ink-applying writing implement, and so on.[21]

Membership in a natural kind, it is thought, is not determined by satisfying a description, but by relevant similarity to stereotypes.[22] The idea is this: First, Fs are picked out by their superficial properties (e.g., quantities of water are clear liquids, good to drink, etc.). Then, anything that has the same essential properties that the stereotypes have is an F. So, natural kinds have "extension-involving sortal identifications."[23] By contrast, artifactual terms (like those I used earlier – "beds," "clocks," "knives and forks," "cars," "computers," "pencils," "nails") are said to refer by satisfying descriptions: "A clock is any time-keeping device, a pen is any rigid ink-applying writing implement and so on."[24]

I do not think that this distinction between how words refer captures the difference between natural objects and artifacts.[25] The distinction between referring indexically and referring by description, with respect to natural kind terms, is only a matter of the state of our knowledge and of our perceptual systems.[26] However gold was originally picked out (e.g., as "stuff like *this*"), now we can pick it out by (what are taken to be) its essential properties: for example, Gold is the element with atomic number 79. Not only might natural kinds satisfy descriptions, but also we may refer to artifacts in the absence of any identifying description. E.g., archaeologists may believe that two entities are both artifacts of the same kind, without having any identifying description of the kind in question. (Were they used in battle or in religious rituals?)

Thus, the third condition – Fs are genuine substances only if whether something is an F is not determined merely by an entity's satisfying a

---

[21] Wiggins, *Sameness and Substance Renewed*, p. 87.

[22] E.g., Wiggins, *Sameness and Substance Renewed*, pp. 11–12.

[23] Ibid., p. 89.   [24] Ibid., p. 87.

[25] Aristotle would agree with me on this point, I believe. His reason for downgrading artifacts ontologically is that artifacts have no natures in themselves.

[26] Moreover, indexicality should not be confused with rigidity, which does not concern how a term gets connected to a referent. For criticism of Putnam's confusion of the causal theory of reference and indexicality, see Tyler Burge, "Other Bodies," in *Thought and Object*, ed. Andrew Woodfield (Oxford: Oxford University Press, 1982): 97–120.

description – does not distinguish natural kinds from artifactual kinds, nor does it rule out artifacts as genuine objects.[27]

(4) The fourth condition – Fs are genuine substances only if Fs have an underlying intrinsic essence – does not distinguish natural from artifactual kinds. Although some familiar natural kinds – like water or gold – have underlying intrinsic essences, not all do. For example, wings (of birds and insects), mountains, and planets are all natural kinds, but none of them has an underlying intrinsic essence. Their membership in their kinds is not a matter of underlying intrinsic properties. Something is a wing, mountain, or planet not in virtue of what it is made of, but in virtue of its relational properties. For that matter, something is a bird or an insect in virtue of its relational properties – its genealogical lineage.

(5) The fifth condition – Fs are genuine substances only if the character of F is independent of any intentional activity – is the most interesting. According to some philosophers, the "character of [a] substance-kind cannot logically depend upon the beliefs or decisions of any psychological subject."[28] Unlike the first four conditions, the fifth does distinguish between artifactual and natural kinds. An artifact's being the kind of thing that it is depends on human intentions. Conceding that the necessity of intention is a difference between an artifact and a natural object, I ask: Why should this difference render artifacts deficient?

What generally underlies the claim that artifacts are not genuine substances, I believe, is an assumption that Fs are genuine substances only if conditions of membership in the substance-kind are set "by nature, and not by us."[29] But it is tendentious to claim that the existence of artifacts depends not on nature, but on us.[30] Of course, the existence of artifacts depends on us: but we are part of nature. It would be true to say that the existence of artifacts depends not on nature-as-if-we-did-not-exist, but on nature-with-us-in-it. Since nature *has* us in it, this distinction (between nature-as-if-we-did-not-exist and nature-with-us-in-it) is no satisfactory basis for ontological inferiority of artifacts.

---

[27] Joseph LaPorte also holds that some kind expressions (both natural and artifactual) designate rigidly, and some designate nonrigidly. See his "Rigidity and Kind."

[28] Hoffman and Rosenkrantz, *Substance*, p. 173.

[29] In "A Different Kind of Natural Kind," *Australasian Journal of Philosophy* 73 (1995): 516–531, Crawford L. Elder discusses this point. For an alternative that I find congenial, see Amie Thomasson, "Realism and Human Kinds," *Philosophical and Phenomenological Research*, forthcoming.

[30] In chapter 1, I argued that a distinction between what depends on nature and what depends on us is neither exclusive nor exhaustive.

There is a venerable – but, I think, theoretically misguided – distinction in philosophy between what is mind-independent and what is mind-dependent. (See chapter 1.) This distinction is theoretically misguided because it draws an ontological line in an unilluminating place. It puts insects and galaxies on one side, and afterimages and artifacts on the other. Another reason that the mind-independent/mind-dependent distinction is unhelpful is that advances in technology have blurred the difference between natural objects and artifacts. For example, so-called "digital organisms" are computer programs that (like biological organisms) can mutate, reproduce, and compete with one another.[31] Or consider "robo-rats" – rats with electrodes that direct the rats' movements.[32] Or for another example, consider what one researcher calls "a bacterial battery".[33] These are biofuel cells that use microbes to convert organic matter into electricity. Bacterial batteries are the result of a recent discovery of a micro-organism that feeds on sugar and converts it to a stream of electricity. This leads to a stable source of low power that can be used to run sensors of household devices. Finally, scientists are genetically engineering viruses that selectively infect and kill cancer cells and leave healthy cells alone. *Scientific American* referred to these viruses as "search-and-destroy missiles."[34] Are these objects – the digital organisms, robo-rats, bacterial batteries, genetically engineered viral search-and-destroy missiles – artifacts or natural objects? Does it matter? I suspect that the distinction between artifacts and natural objects will become increasingly fuzzy; and as it does, the worries about the mind-independent/mind-dependent distinction will fade away.

Let me conclude with a general argument for the ontological status of artifacts. An F has ontological status in virtue of being an F only if the F's existence depends on its being an F. For example, your bicycle has ontological status in virtue of being a bicycle because *it* would not exist at all if it were not a bicycle. By contrast, the items in your pocket do not have ontological status in virtue of being items in your pocket, but rather in virtue of being handkerchiefs, keys, coins, etc. What has ontological

---

[31] The *Chronicle of Higher Education: Daily News*, May 8, 2003.
[32] The *New York Times*, May 5, 2002.
[33] The *New York Times*, September 18, 2003. The lead researcher, Derek Lovley, who coined the term "bacterial battery," is a microbiolgist at the University of Massachusetts at Amherst.
[34] Email update from *Scientific American*, September 23, 2003.

significance in the first instance are properties – primary-kind properties.[35] (*Item in a pocket* is not a primary kind.) When a primary-kind property is instantiated, a new object comes into existence. A new bicycle is a new object in the world; instantiation of the property of being an item in a pocket brings nothing new into existence. And conversely, an item in a pocket can lose the property of being an item in a pocket without going out of existence; a bicycle cannot lose the property of being a bicycle without going out of existence. So, primary-kind properties bestow ontological significance on those things whose primary-kind properties they are.

A primary-kind property bestows ontological significance only on those things that have the property nonderivatively.[36] This is so, because if something has a primary-kind property derivatively, it may lose that property without going out of existence. E.g., the aggregate of atoms in your sofa now has the property of being a sofa derivatively. But, as we have seen, the aggregate would still exist even if it did not constitute your sofa. (If your cat scratched the sofa, the sofa would still exist but be constituted by a different aggregate from the one that constitutes it now. Yet, the old aggregate would remain in existence – even though it would no longer be a sofa derivatively.) If F is an ontologically significant property, then the addition of something that is an F nonderivatively is the addition of a new object in the world; a new (nonderivative) F is not just a change in something that already exists, but the coming-into-being of a new thing. Since there are artifactual primary kinds, and since primary-kind properties generally confer ontological status on their nonderivative bearers, it is easy to see that on the Constitution View, artifacts have ontological status.

The world after the invention of the automobile is ontologically richer than before. The addition of an automobile is an addition to what there is in the world.[37] If an automobile is destroyed – put in a crusher, say – then something goes out of existence; it is not as if the thing that was an automobile just lost the property of being an automobile and acquired the property of being a metal and plastic cube. There is not a persisting thing

---

[35] See chapter 11 for a discussion of the idea of ontological significance.

[36] For details, see chapter 11.

[37] Although I avoid the "qua" locution, the way that I have elucidated "Fs have ontological significance" suggests that an alternative to that expression might be "Fs-qua-Fs have ontological significance."

that at t_1 is (nonderivatively) an automobile, and at t_2 is (nonderivatively) a metal and plastic cube.[38] The atoms in the aggregate that constituted the automobile may still exist, but the automobile – that thing – does not. So, a complete inventory of what exists in the world must include artifacts. Therefore, on the Constitution View, artifacts – as well as natural objects – have ontological status.

CONCLUSION

When automobiles were invented, a new kind of thing came into existence: and it changed the world. It would be bizarre to suppose that such instruments of such monumental changes were not kinds of genuine substances, or lacked ontological status. Considering the world-changing *effects* of the automobile (and countless other kinds of artifacts), artifacts have as strong a claim to ontological status as natural objects.[39]

---

[38] For details about the derivative/nonderivative distinction, see chapter 2 and chapter 8.

[39] Thanks to Gareth B. Matthews for commenting on a draft. Parts of this chapter appeared as "The Ontology of Artifacts," *Philosophical Explorations* 7 (2004): 99–111; other parts will appear in *Artefacts in Philosophy*, ed. Pieter Vermaas and Wybo Houkes (in preparation).

4

Human persons

Human persons figure prominently in the everyday world. In this chapter, I shall add to the account of human persons given in *Persons and Bodies*, according to which persons are not identical to human organisms. After summarizing the Constitution View of persons, I shall consider the questions: When does a person come into existence? and When does a human organism come into existence? Then, after discussing some of the complexities of life and death, I shall show how this account of human persons satisfies a constraint that I call "quasi-naturalism." Finally, I'll contrast the Constitution View of persons with its two main rivals: Animalism and Mind–Body Dualism.

THE CONSTITUTION VIEW OF HUMAN PERSONS

According to the Constitution View, human persons are constituted by human bodies without being identical to the bodies that constitute them. Let me begin with a clarification. Several philosophers suppose that I hold that "no actual human person is identical with any actual human being."[1] That is not my view. In ordinary language, the term "human being" is used ambiguously – both to name a psychological kind and to name a purely biological kind.[2] So, I try to avoid the term. But when I use it, I am talking about human persons.

Person – like *statue* – is a primary kind, one of many irreducible onto-logical kinds.[3] Everything that exists is of some primary kind – the kind

---

[1] E.g., see Harold Noonan's contribution to an electronic symposium on *Persons and Bodies*, sponsored by the University of Rome. See *A Field Guide to the Philosophy of Mind* at: www.uniroma3.it/kant/field/bakersymp.htm.

[2] Cf. *Persons and Bodies: A Constitution View* (Cambridge: Cambridge University Press, 2000), p. 7.

[3] Since I have written a whole book developing a theory of human persons, I shall only review the theory briefly here.

that determines what the thing is most fundamentally. Things have their primary-kind properties essentially. Members of the kind *human organism* are human organisms essentially; members of the kind *person* are persons essentially. So, when a person comes into being, a new object comes into being – an object that is a person essentially.

What distinguishes *person* from other primary kinds (like *planet* or *human organism*) is that persons have first-person perspectives necessarily. When a human organism develops a first-person perspective, a new thing – a person – comes into existence. The human organism does not thereby go out of existence, any more than the piece of marble goes out of existence when it comes to constitute a statue. A human person and her body are related in exactly the same way as a marble statue and a piece of marble: the relation is one of constitution. When a piece of marble is suitably related to an artworld, a new thing – a statue – comes into existence. When a human organism comes to constitute a person, the organism has the property of being a person derivatively (in virtue of constituting something that is a person nonderivatively); and the person has the property of being a human body derivatively (in virtue of being constituted by something that is a human body nonderivatively). A human person, like a marble statue, is a unified thing.

As I have emphasized, a person is not identical to her body. But to say that a person is not identical to her body does not mean that the person is identical to the body-plus-some-other-thing (like a soul).[4] Michelangelo's *David* is not identical to a piece-of-marble-plus-some-other-thing. If x constitutes y and x is wholly material, then y is wholly material.[5] The human body (which I take to be identical to a human organism) is wholly material and the human body constitutes the human person. Therefore, the human person is wholly material. A human person is as material as Michelangelo's *David* is.

The nonidentity of a person and an organism is manifested in the fact that organisms have different persistence conditions from persons. Human organisms have third-personal persistence conditions: whether an animal continues to exist depends on continued biological functioning. Persons have first-personal persistence conditions: whether a person continues to exist depends on its having a first-person perspective.

---

[4] Someone may ask: If a human person is not identical to a body or to a soul or to a body-plus-a-soul, what is she identical to? This question is a red herring. A person is identical to herself and not another thing.

[5] For details, see chapter 8.

As far as we know, of all the beings in the world, we alone have first-personal concept of ourselves. We alone understand ourselves from "within," so to speak; we can think of ourselves without the need to identify ourselves by means of any description, name, or other third-person referring device. The human organism that constitutes my niece came into existence some months before my niece did. My niece came into existence when that human organism developed a rudimentary first-person perspective, at birth or shortly before.[6] The onset of a first-person perspective is the coming into existence of a new entity in the world. A human person essentially has a first-person perspective; a human animal does not. Your persistence conditions are first-personal: You did not exist until there was something that it is like to be you.

So, what is a first-person perspective? A first-person perspective is a very peculiar ability that all and only persons have. It is the ability to conceive of oneself as oneself, from the inside, as it were. Linguistic evidence of a robust first-person perspective comes from use of first-person pronouns embedded in sentences with linguistic or psychological verbs – e.g., "I wonder how I will die," or "I promise that I will stay with you."[7] If I wonder how I will die, or I promise that I'll stay with you, then I am thinking of myself as myself; I am not thinking of myself in any third-person way (e.g., not as Lynne Baker, nor as that woman, nor as the only person in the room) at all. Anything that can wonder how it will die ipso facto has a first-person perspective and thus is a person.

What one thinks from a first-person perspective cannot be adequately translated into third-person terms. To wonder how I will die is not the same as wondering how Lynne Baker will die, even though I am Lynne Baker. This is so, because I could wonder how I will die even if I had amnesia and didn't know who I was. A being with a first-person perspective not only can have thoughts about herself, but she can also conceive of herself as the subject of such thoughts. I not only wonder how I'll die, but I realize that I am having that thought. A first-person perspective cannot be duplicated.

A molecule-for-molecule qualitative duplicate of you would not be you, and would not have your first-person perspective. She would start out

[6] For a detailed account, see my "When Does a Person Begin?", *Social Philosophy and Policy* 22 (2005): 25–48.

[7] Hector-Neri Castañeda developed this idea in several papers. See "He: A Study in the Logic of Self-Consciousness," *Ratio* 8 (1966): 130–157, and "Indicators and Quasi-Indicators," *American Philosophical Quarterly* 4 (1967): 85–100.

with a first-person perspective that was qualitatively just like yours; but the qualitative indistinguishability would be short-lived, as you and your duplicate looked out on the room from different perspectives. Moreover, what she would know when she entertained the thought, "I wish that I felt better," is different from what you would know when you entertained the thought, "I wish that I felt better." The content of her thought-token would include the concept of herself, not yourself; and vice versa. There cannot be two persons both with your first-person perspective.

A being may be conscious without having a first-person perspective. Nonhuman primates and other higher animals are conscious, and they have psychological states like believing, fearing, and desiring. They have points of view (e.g., "danger in that direction"), but they cannot conceive of themselves as the subjects of such thoughts. They cannot *conceive of* themselves from the first-person. (We have every reason to think that they do not wonder how they will die.) So, having psychological states like beliefs and desires, and having a point of view, are necessary but not sufficient conditions for being a person. A sufficient condition for being a person – whether human, divine, ape, or silicon-based – is having a first-person perspective.[8] So, what makes something a person is not the "stuff" that it is made of. It does not matter whether something is made of DNA or silicon or, in the case of God, no material "stuff" at all. If there are Martian beings made out of green slime who had first-person perspectives, then they would be persons – Martian persons, not human persons. Any being with a first-person perspective is a person.

From the standpoint of evolution, first-person perspectives may have been "selected for" by natural selection. Alternatively, first-person perspectives (like the architectural example of spandrels) may have been a by-product of some other change. My interest in the first-person perspective is not in its origin, but in its status. First-person perspectives do not appear to be biologically significant; but whether they are biologically significant or not, first-person perspectives are ontologically significant. Only beings with inner lives are persons, and a world populated with beings with inner lives is ontologically richer than a world populated with no beings with inner lives.

---

[8] Gallup's experiments with chimpanzees suggest the possibility of a kind of intermediate stage between dogs (that have intentional states but no first-person perspectives) and human persons (that have first-person perspectives). In my opinion – for details see *Persons and Bodies*, pp. 62–64 – Gallup's chimpanzees fall short of full-blown first-person perspectives. See Gordon Gallup, Jr., "Self-Recognition in Primates: A Comparative Approach to Bidirectional Properties of Consciousness," *American Psychologist* 32 (1977): 329–338.

Biologically speaking, I'm a Darwinian: I believe that there is important continuity between the most primitive organisms and us, that we have animal natures, and that biology can uncover all there is to know about our animal natures. But there is more to us than our animal natures. I do not believe that biological knowledge suffices for understanding our nature, all things considered. Like the Substance Dualist, I think that we are ontologically special: the worth or value of a person is not measured in terms of surviving offspring. But emphatically unlike the Substance Dualist, I do not account for what makes us special in terms of having an immaterial part. What make us ontologically special are our first-person perspectives.

Let me distinguish the Constitution View of persons from Aristotle's view of form and matter. As is well known, Aristotle had a concept of a "man" – a rational animal – but no distinct idea of a person. A man is made up of matter. A man, on Aristotle's view, is a substance, but the matter that makes up a man is not itself a substance.[9] Matter alone is not a substance. On my view, a person ("a man") is a substance, but so is the human organism that constitutes the "man." (There are many other differences between the Constitution View and Aristotle's view that I cannot pursue here.)[10]

In sum: There are two important aspects of the Constitution View of human persons. On the one hand, a human person has unique first-personal persistence conditions. I continue to exist as long as my first-person perspective is exemplified; if something has my first-person perspective, then that being is a person and that person is me. Although sameness of person consists in sameness of first-person perspective, we cannot give noncircular conditions for sameness of first-person perspective over time. This is no surprise: If there were noncircular conditions, we would have a reductive account of persons in terms of nonpersonal

---

[9] If I understand her correctly, Eleonore Stump has suggested that we can construe "matter" and "form" in Aquinas, Aristotle's interpreter, as relative terms. What is formed matter at one level can be matter for something higher up the scale. On this interpretation, form both is configured and what configures other things. The matter that makes something up may itself already have form (i.e., be configured). See Eleonore Stump, "NonCartesian Substance Dualism and Materialism Without Reductionism," *Faith and Philosophy* 12 (1995): 505–531.

[10] For example, on the Constitution View, an artificial heart or an artificial hip would be a substance; but on Aristotle's view, a natural heart or a natural hip would not be a substance. (See chapter 3.) There are many issues here to be explored (elsewhere). Gail Fine and Patricia Curd have pressed upon me affinities between Aristotle and the Constitution View.

properties.[11] The conditions for the persistence of persons are absolutely unique: they are first-personal conditions that elude third-personal form-ulation. On the other hand, a human person is essentially embodied: I am a wholly material being, constituted by, but not identical to, my body.

COMING INTO EXISTENCE: HUMAN ORGANISMS AND HUMAN PERSONS

I take the question, "When does a human organism begin?" to be a biological question. This empirical question stands in contrast to the philosophical question, "When does a human person begin?" Empirical data are relevant to philosophical questions, without being conclusive.

Human organisms One frequently heard answer to the biological question is that a human organism comes into existence at the time of fertilization of a human egg by a sperm. But beware: There is not an exact moment of fertilization. Fertilization itself is a process that lasts 20+ hours.[12]

However, the view that a human organism comes into existence at – or at the end of – fertilization is logically untenable anyway, because a fertilized egg may split and produce twins. If it is physically possible for a fertilized egg to produce twins (whether it actually does so or not), a fertilized egg cannot be *identical* to an organism. As long as it is possible to twin, a zygote is not *a* human anything, but a cell cluster.[13] In the case of twinning, as G. E. M. Anscombe explains: "Neither of the two humans that eventually develop can be identified as the same human as the zygote, because they can't *both* be so, as they are different humans from one another."[14] It is logically impossible for one organism to be identical to two organisms. And, of course, anything that is logically impossible is biologically impossible. In twinning, two (or more) twins come from a

---

[11] I discussed this point at some length in *Persons and Bodies*, chapter 5.

[12] Norman M. Ford, *The Prenatal Person* (Malden, MA: Blackwell Publishing, 2002), p. 55. Moreover, everything in the natural world comes into existence gradually: solar systems, cherry blossoms, jellyfish, tractors, and other artifacts. Thus, every natural entity has vague temporal boundaries, and hence is subject to vague existence. But it does not follow that there is any vague identity. If a = b and a is vague, then b is vague in exactly the same respects. See chapter 6.

[13] G. E. M. Anscombe, "Were You a Zygote?" in A. Phillips Griffiths, ed., *Philosophy and Practice* (Cambridge: Cambridge University Press, 1985), p. 111.

[14] Ibid., p. 112.

single fertilized egg. But neither of the twins is identical to that fertilized egg, on pain of contradiction.

To see this, suppose that a zygote (a cell cluster) divides and twins result. Call the zygote "A," and one of the twins "B" and the other twin "C." If A were identical to both B and C, then – by the transitivity of identity – B and C would be identical to each other. But B is clearly not identical to C. Therefore, A (the zygote) cannot be identical to B and C. A human organism cannot come into existence until there is no further possibility of "twinning" – about two weeks after fertilization. A frozen embryo that is still capable of twinning is demonstrably *not* a human organism.[15]

Interestingly, the Roman Catholic teaching is not otherwise. The Catholic Church is officially agnostic on the ontological question of whether an embryo is a human organism, but takes the moral stand that, regardless, a fertilized egg must be respected and treated as a person. According to the Second Vatican Council, "Life once conceived must be protected with the utmost care; abortion and infanticide are abominable crimes."[16] This teaching is explicitly independent of the question of the time of the "infusion" of the spiritual soul or of animation.[17] That is, the teaching deems it irrelevant whether or not there is a human organism at stake. The teaching simply is a prohibition: "You shall not kill by abortion the fruit of the womb"[18] – regardless of whether "the fruit of the womb" is a human organism or not. To quote again from the "Instruction on Respect for Human Life in its Origin and on the Dignity of Procreation," "The Magisterium has not expressly committed itself to an affirmation of a philosophical nature [about the time that a person or a human organism comes into existence], but it constantly reaffirms the moral condemnation of any kind of procured abortion. This teaching has not been changed and is unchangeable."

---

[15] This point has an obvious implication for embryonic stem-cell research. There may be reasons to be cautious about stem-cell research, but fear of destroying a human organism is not one of them. A zygote that is still capable of twinning is not yet a human organism.

[16] "Instruction on Respect for Human Life in its Origin and on the Dignity of Procreation; Replies to Certain Questions of the Day," given in Rome, at the Sacred Congregation for the Doctrine of the Faith, February 22, 1987, under the auspices of its Prefect, Joseph Cardinal Ratzinger. I am grateful to John Finnis for alerting me to this work and to the next one.

[17] E.g., "[T]he various opinions on the infusion of the spiritual soul did not introduce any doubt about the illicitness of abortion." "Declaration on Procured Abortion," given in Rome at the Sacred Congregation for the Doctrine of the Faith on November 18, 1974, under the auspices of its Prefect, Franciscus Cardinal Seper.

[18] "Declaration on Procured Abortion."

You may ask: If, as I have argued, a fertilized egg is not a human organism, then – even assuming that our lives are gifts from God – why should a fertilized egg be protected (especially at the expense of the life of a woman, who certifiably is a person with a human life)? The answer that I found is that the fertilized ovum "would never be made human if it were not human already."[19] Notice that the claim that the fertilized ovum is "human already" makes no commitment about whether the fertilized ovum is a human organism; a human cell (from the inside of your cheek, say, that is about to be cloned) is human already. But that is hardly reason for us to treat the cell from your cheek with any special dignity. The Roman Catholic teaching about abortion stands on its own, without any ontological backing. It is simply irrelevant to the Catholic teaching whether an embryo before implantation is a human organism. So, the argument that I gave that such an embryo is not a human organism does not touch Catholic teaching, which is pure decree that does not rest on any "affirmation of a philosophical nature."

In any case, there is no new human organism until after the end of the process of implantation of a blastocyst (a ball of a few hundred cells) in the wall of the womb (about fourteen days after fertilization).[20] Even at implantation, an organism does not come into existence instantaneously. There is no sharp line demarcating the coming into existence of a new human individual organism. There is only a gradual process. But we can say this much: Soon after implantation (the primitive streak stage), the embryo is an individual, as opposed to a mass of cells.[21] At this point, there

---

[19] Ibid.

[20] In making a case for cloning embryos for the purpose of biomedical research, Michael Gazzaniga, a neuroscientist who served on President Bush's bioethics council, points out, "After natural sexual intercourse, an estimated 60 to 80 percent of all embryos generated through the union of egg and sperm spontaneously abort – many without our knowledge. So [he continues] if we use IVF [in vitro fertilization] to create embryos and then implant only a select few, aren't we doing what nature does?" Michael S. Gazzaniga, "The Thoughtful Distinction Between Embryo and Human," *The Chronicle of Higher Education*, April 8, 2005, pp. B10–B12. The quotation is from p. B12. The fact that 60–80 percent of embryos produced by sexual intercourse spontaneously abort with no one's knowing of their existence gives reason to doubt that every fertilized egg is as precious as a person in the eyes of God.

[21] This is a point that has been made by Roman Catholic writers. E.g., see Norman M. Ford, *When Did I Begin? Conception of the Human Individual in History, Philosophy and Science* (Cambridge: Cambridge University Press, 1988), pp. 174–178. See also Anscombe, "Were You a Zygote?"

is an individual human organism that persists through fetal development, birth, maturation, adulthood, until death.

This answers the biological question about human embryos: Before implantation, there is no human organism, just a cluster of human cells. (And, as we have seen, Catholic teaching does not say otherwise; it simply prohibits abortion whether there is a human organism or not.) The main point, however, is that even where there is a human organism, it does not follow that there is a human person.

There remains the ontological question – a further question that is not automatically answered by biology: Granting that a human embryo after implantation is an individual human organism, what is the relation between a human embryo and a human person? On my view, the relation is constitution: A human person is wholly constituted by a human organism, without being identical to the constituting organism. So the coming into existence of a human organism is not ipso facto the coming into existence of a human person. As we shall see, on my view – the Constitution View – a human person is not temporally coextensive with a human organism, but is nevertheless a material being, ultimately constituted by subatomic particles. Human persons have no immaterial parts.[22]

Human persons   A person, as I have said, essentially has a first-person perspective. But as I have described a first-person perspective, then it would seem that an infant, who does not yet think of herself from the "inside," is not a person. Since I do regard infants as persons, I see this consequence as a difficulty that I want to address. My strategy is to say that what I have just described is a *robust* first-person perspective. Now I shall distinguish a robust first-person perspective from a rudimentary first-person perspective, and then apply this distinction to the question of when a person comes into being.[23]

Since our stereotypes of persons are of human persons, my notion of a first-person perspective is tailored to fit specifically human persons. If there are nonhuman persons, they, too, will have robust first-person

---

[22] Again: constitution is not a relation between parts and wholes. If x constitutes y at t, the difference between x and y is that x and y have different properties essentially and different persistence conditions. It is not a matter of y's having a part that x lacks, or vice versa.

[23] I was motivated to distinguish between a robust and a rudimentary first-person perspective by my many critics, including Marc Slors, Anthonie Meijers, Monica Meijsing, Herman de Regt, and Ton Derksen.

perspectives, but they may not have acquired them as a development of rudimentary first-person perspectives. But human persons begin by having rudimentary first-person perspectives:

(Rudimentary FPP) A being has a rudimentary first-person perspective iff (i) it is conscious, a sentient being, and (ii) it has a capacity to imitate; (iii) its behavior is explainable only by attribution of beliefs, desires, and intentions.

The requirement of consciousness or sentience for a rudimentary first-person perspective rules out security cameras as having rudimentary first-person perspectives, even though they may be said to have a perspective on, say, a parking lot. The capacity to imitate involves differentiation of self and other. The capacity to imitate has been linked by developmental psychologists to "some form of self-recognition" that does not require a self-concept.[24] Finally, a being whose behavior is not explainable except by attribution of beliefs and desires has a perspective and can respond appropriately to changing situations. For one's behavior to be explainable only by attribution of beliefs, desires, and intentions is to be a (minimal) intentional agent. So, a being with a rudimentary first-person perspective is a sentient being, an imitator, and an intentional agent.[25]

Human infants have rudimentary first-person perspectives.[26] There is empirical evidence that human infants have the three properties required for a rudimentary first-person perspective. Human infants are clearly sentient. There is abundant research to show that they are imitators from birth. For example, two well-known psychologists, Alison Gopnik and Andrew Meltzoff tested 40 newborns as young as 42 minutes old (the average age was 32 hours) in 1983. They wrote of the newborns' gestures of mouth opening and tongue protrusion: "These data directly demonstrate that a primitive capacity to imitate is part of the normal child's

---

[24] Michael Lewis, "Myself and Me," in Sue Taylor Parker, Robert W. Mitchell, and Maria L. Boccia, eds., *Self-Awareness in Animals and Humans* (Cambridge: Cambridge University Press, 1994), p. 22.

[25] Rudimentary first-person perspectives have what Robert A. Wilson calls "action-traction." See his "Persons, Social Agency, and Constitution," *Social Philosophy and Policy* 22 (2005): 49–69.

[26] An anencephalic infant with only brain-stem functions, or perhaps a severely autistic child, fails to satisfy the conditions for a rudimentary first-person perspective. Because such a being is of a kind (human animal) that at its stage of development normally does satisfy these conditions, we should treat it as if it had a rudimentary first-person perspective.

biological endowment."[27] Imitation is grounded in bodies: newborn imitators must connect the internal feeling of his own body (kinesthesia) with the external things that he sees (and later hears).[28] (Aristotle went so far in his *Poetics* as to say that imitation was a distinguishing mark of human beings.) And finally, according to Ulric Neisser, "Babies are intentional agents almost from birth."[29] So human infants meet the conditions for having rudimentary first-person perspectives. Indeed, developmental psychologists agree that from birth, a first-person perspective is underway.[30]

Higher nonhuman mammals seem to meet the conditions for having rudimentary first-person perspectives as well. Observation of household pets like dogs and cats suggests that they have rudimentary first-person perspectives. They are sentient – they feel pain, for example. (Their brains, as well as their behavior when injured, are similar enough to ours for this to be a secure judgment.) They are imitators; even ducks, who imprint on their mothers, engage in imitative behavior. Although there is some controversy regarding the research on animal intentionality,[31] higher nonhuman mammals appear to be intentional agents. We have apparently successful intentional explanations of animal behavior – e.g., "Fido is digging over there because he saw you bury the bone there and he wants it" – and there are no adequate nonintentional accounts of Fido's behavior. Chimpanzees that pass Gordon Gallup's famous mirror tests even more obviously have rudimentary first-person perspectives.[32]

The conclusion that I draw from the work of developmental psychologists is that human infants and higher nonhuman mammals have

[27] Alison Gopnik and Andrew N. Meltzoff, "Minds, Bodies and Persons: Young Children's Understanding of the Self and Others as Reflected in Imitation and Theory-of-Mind Research," in Parker, Mitchell, and Boccia, eds., *Self-Awareness in Animals and Humans*, p. 171.

[28] Alison Gopnik, Andrew Meltzoff, and Patricia Kuhl, eds., *How Babies Think: The Science of Childhood* (London: Weidenfeld &Nicolson, 1999), p. 30.

[29] See Ulric Neisser, "Criteria for an Ecological Self," in Philippe Rochat, ed., *The Self in Infancy: Theory and Research* (Amsterdam: North-Holland, Elsevier, 1995), p. 23.

[30] See, for example, Jerome Kagan, *Unstable Ideas* (Cambridge, MA: Harvard University Press, 1989).

[31] See, for example, Cecilia Heyes and Anthony Dickinson, "The Intentionality of Animal Action," in Martin Davies and Glyn W. Humphreys, eds., *Consciousness: Psychological and Philosophical Essays* (Oxford: Blackwell, 1993), pp. 105–120.

[32] See Gallup, Jr., "Self-Recognition in Primates." Discussion of the mirror tests has become so widespread that the phenomenom of recognizing oneself in a mirror is routinely referred to simply by the initials MSR ("mirror self-recognition") in psychological literature.

rudimentary first-person perspectives.[33] Moreover, rudimentary first-person perspectives exhaust the first-personal resources of human infants and higher nonhuman mammals; human infants and higher nonhuman mammals exhibit no more sophisticated first-personal phenomena than what rudimentary first-person perspectives account for. Although infants differentiate themselves from others from birth, they do not pass the mirror test until they are about 18 months old. (And chimpanzees and orangutans "show every bit as compelling evidence of self-recognition as 18- to 24-month-old human infants."[34]) According to Jerome Kagan, it is "not at all certain that [human] 12-month-olds, who experience sensations, possess any concepts about their person, and it is dubious that they are consciously aware of their intentions, feelings, appearance or actions."[35] Daniel J. Povinelli and Christopher G. Prince report that "there is little evidence that chimpanzees understand anything at all about mental states."[36] Although more evidence is needed about the cognitive development of chimpanzees, there is no clear evidence that chimpanzees have the capacity to construct higher-order representations that would allow conceptions of themselves as having pasts and futures.[37]

Another similarity between human infants and higher nonhuman mammals is that they are social creatures. There seems to be general agreement among psychologists that developmentally there is a symmetry of self and other, that humans (as well as other higher nonhuman mammals) are social creatures. Ulric Neisser puts the "interpersonal self" in which the "individual engaged in social interaction with another person" at eight weeks.[38] Philippe Rochat flatly asserts that the developmental origins of self-awareness are primarily social.[39] The idea of a first-person perspective is not Cartesian or Leibnizian: we are not monads that unfold according to an internal plan unaffected by our surroundings.

---

[33] I do not expect the developmental psychologists to share my metaphysical view of constitution; I look to their work only to show at what stages during development certain features appear.

[34] Daniel J. Povinelli, "The Unduplicated Self," in Rochat, ed., *The Self in Infancy*, p. 185.

[35] Jerome Kagan, "Is There a Self in Infancy?" in Michel Ferrari and Robert J. Sternberg, eds., *Self-Awareness: Its Nature and Development* (New York: Guilford Press, 1998), p. 138.

[36] Daniel J. Povinelli and Christopher G. Prince, "When Self Met Other," in Ferrari and Sternberg, eds., *Self-Awareness*, p. 88.

[37] Povinelli, "The Unduplicated Self," p. 186. So it looks as if the scope of the self-concept that Gallup postulated to explain mirror behavior is really quite limited, contrary to Gallup's speculation.

[38] Neisser, "Criteria for an Ecological Self," p. 18.

[39] Philippe Rochat, "Early Objectification of the Self," in Rochat, ed., *The Self in Infancy*, p. 54.

So, human infants and higher nonhuman mammals all have rudimentary first-person perspectives, but I hold that human infants are persons and higher nonhuman mammals are not persons (or probably not). If having a first-person perspective is what distinguishes a person from everything else, and if a human infant and a chimpanzee both have rudimentary first-person perspectives, how can a human infant be a person if a chimpanzee fails to be a person? What distinguishes the human infant from the chimpanzee is that the human infant's rudimentary first-person perspective is developmentally *preliminary* to having a robust first-person perspective, but a chimpanzee's rudimentary first-person perspective is not preliminary to anything further.

By saying that a rudimentary first-person perspective is "a preliminary to a robust first-person perspective," I mean to pick out those rudimentary first-person perspectives that developmentally ground or underpin robust first-person perspectives. Unlike chimpanzees, human animals are of a kind that normally develops robust first-person perspectives. This is what makes human animals special: Their rudimentary first-person perspectives are a developmental preliminary to robust first-person perspectives. A being with a rudimentary first-person perspective is a person *only if it is of a kind that normally develops robust first-person perspectives*. This is not to say that a human person will develop a robust first-person perspective: perhaps severely autistic individuals, or severely retarded individuals, have only rudimentary first-person perspectives. However, they are still persons, albeit very impaired, because they have rudimentary first-person perspectives and are of a kind – human animal – that develops a robust first-person perspective. We can capture this idea by the following thesis:

(HP) x constitutes a human person at t if and only if x is a human organism (nonderivatively) and x has a rudimentary or robust first-person perspective at t.[40]

(HP) gives only a necessary and sufficient condition for there being constitution of a *human* person. There may be other kinds of persons: silicon-persons (constituted by aggregates of silicon items) and God (not constituted by anything). (HP) is silent about other kinds of persons.[41]

---

[40] To say that x is a human organism (nonderivatively) is to say that x is of the primary kind *human organism*.

[41] In *Persons and Bodies*, I said that a person comes into being when a human organism develops a robust first-person perspective *or the structural capacity for one*. The effect of (HP) is to mark the onset of personhood to human animals with rudimentary first-person perspectives and not to consider an animal's structural capacity.

In the face of (HP), someone might mount a "slippery slope" argument like the following:[42] "Once we introduce the notion of a preliminary, we have no reason to stop with rudimentary first-person perspectives. Once we consider a being with a preliminary to a robust first-person perspective to be a person, why not consider a being with a preliminary to that preliminary also to be a person? Why stop with a rudimentary first-person perspective? Why not consider a being at some prior stage that is preliminary to a rudimentary first-person perspective to be a person, and so on?" Suppose that, in place of (HP), someone proposed instead (HP*):

(HP*) x constitutes a human person at t if and only if x is a human organism (nonderivatively) and either x has a robust first-person perspective or capacities that, in the normal course of development, produce a being with a robust first-person perspective.[43]

I reject (HP*), and with it the regress argument, for the following reasons. In the first place, note that a robust first-person perspective is itself a capacity – but a capacity of a special sort. A first-person perspective (robust or rudimentary) awaits nothing for its exercise other than a subject's thinking a certain kind of thought. It is an in-hand capacity that can be exercised at will. Let us distinguish between an in-hand capacity and a remote capacity. A hammer has an in-hand capacity at t for driving nails whether or not it is actually driving nails; you have an in-hand capacity at t for digesting food whether or not you are actually digesting food. Unassembled hammer parts (a wooden handle and a metal head) have only a remote capacity at t for driving nails; an embryo has only a remote capacity at t for digesting food.[44] A remote capacity may be thought of as a second-order capacity: a capacity to have or develop a capacity. An in-hand capacity is a first-order capacity.

According to the Constitution View of persons (as revised to include (HP)), a first-person perspective – rudimentary as well as robust – is an in-hand capacity, not a capacity to develop a capacity. According to (HP*), a being with no in-hand capacities at all, but only with a capacity to develop a capacity, is a person. Remote capacities do not suffice for making *anything* the kind of thing that it is. (HP) makes being a person depend on the

[42] Gareth Matthews suggested this argument.   [43] Robert A. Wilson suggested (HP*).

[44] I borrowed the example of the hammer from Robert Pasnau's excellent discussion of "has a capacity." See Robert Pasnau, *Thomas Aquinas on Human Nature: A Philosophical Study of Summa Theologiae 1a 75–89* (Cambridge: Cambridge University Press, 2002), p. 115.

more constrained notion of an in-hand capacity of a (rudimentary or robust) first-person perspective.

The second reason that I reject (HP*) is this: The properties in terms of which rudimentary first-person perspectives are specified are ones we recognize as personal: sentience, capacity to imitate, intentionality. Insofar as we think of nonhuman animals as person-like, it is precisely because they have these properties. The properties that an early- or mid-term human fetus has – say, having a heart – are not particularly associated with persons, or even with human animals. Even invertebrates have hearts. So, not just every property that is a developmental preliminary to a robust first-person perspective in humans specifically contributes to being a person. There is a difference between those properties in virtue of which beings are person-like (the properties of rudimentary first-person perspectives) and the broader class of biological properties shared by members of many taxa. The properties in virtue of which something is a person are themselves specifically personal properties.

Given (HP), then, human infants are persons: when a human organism develops a rudimentary first-person perspective, a new thing comes into existence – a human person. Acquisition of the properties that comprise a rudimentary first-person perspective has different ontological significance for human organisms than for nonhuman primates. Acquisition of those properties by a human organism marks the beginning of a new person. Acquisition of those properties by a nonhuman organism, however, does not mark the beginning of a new person: The rudimentary first-person perspectives of higher nonhuman mammals are not developmentally preliminary to anything further. (If nonhuman primates did develop robust first-person perspectives, then they, too, would come to constitute persons.)

According to the modern synthesis in biology, we are biological beings, continuous with the rest of the animal kingdom. The Constitution View recognizes that we have animal natures. The Constitution View shows how to put together Darwinian biology with a traditional concern of philosophers – our inwardness, our ability to see ourselves and each other as subjects, our ability to have rich inner lives. This first-personal aspect of us – the essential aspect, in my opinion – is of no interest to biologists. The first-person perspective may well have evolved by natural selection, but it does not stand out, biologically speaking.

On the Constitution View, as we have seen, a human person comes into existence when a human organism acquires a rudimentary first-person perspective. There is not an exact moment when this happens – just as there is not an exact moment when a human organism comes into existence. But nothing that we know of in the natural world comes into existence instantaneously.[45] When a human organism acquires a rudimentary first-person perspective, it comes to constitute a new entity: a human person. On this view, a human person comes into existence near birth: what is born is a person constituted by an organism.[46]

LIFE AND DEATH

The usual philosophical approach to life (or death) is to ask what life is (or what death is), and then to ask what things have life. I do not think that this is a good approach. The word "life" by itself is incomplete until we know what kind of thing that we are talking about. The life of x comprises all the events that x is a part of, and what kinds of events x can be a part of depends on what kind of entity x is. So, instead of asking what life in general is, I want to consider what a particular life (say, your life) is. What you are most fundamentally is a person. Your life is the career of a person, you. Your life includes what you do and what happens to you during the time that you exist: you fall off your bicycle, you acquire an allergy to oysters, you get a job, and so on.

Philosophers have often thought of life in terms of biological life, where biological life is understood in terms of the integrated functioning of organs.[47] But my use of the word "life" for a *personal* life like yours or mine is not

---

[45] There is (ontological) indeterminacy at the beginning of everything that comes into existence by means of a process. See chapter 6.

[46] For consequences of this view for thinking about abortion, see my "When Does a Person Begin?". The main consequence is that any argument that relies on a premise that all fetuses are persons is unsound.

[47] Some philosophers have entertained a conception of life that is not an organic or biological one at all. For example, in their influential article, "Eternity" (*Journal of Philosophy* 78 [1981]: 429–458), Eleonore Stump and Norman Kretzmann say, that "anything that is eternal has life" (p. 431). And some materialists at least countenance the possibility of conscious life without biological properties. Richard Boyd says that "there seems to be no barrier to the functionalist materialist's asserting that any particular actual world mental event, state, or process could be – in some other possible world – nonphysically realized." Moreover, Boyd suggests the "possibility that certain kinds of actual world token mental events, states or processes might be realized in some other possible world even if the body of the subject no longer exists." Richard Boyd, "Materialism Without Reductionism: What Physicalism Does Not Entail," in Ned Block, ed., *Readings in the Philosophy of Psychology, Volume I* (Cambridge, MA: Harvard University Press, 1980), p. 101.

just stipulative or metaphorical. Although the word "life" does have a bio-logical use, as evidenced by debates about whether viruses are alive, it also has a nonbiological use, as evidenced by our talk of a person's life as a diplomat. To see that "life" should not be equated with "biological life," consider that when people speak of a living God, they do not mean a living organism.[48] We'd be taken aback in a bookstore to find a new life of Napoleon and discover that it focused on the functioning of his organs. So, it is clear that the word "life" is used both with and without biological implications.[49]

When we speak of human life, we cannot just assume that we are speaking of *both* personal life and organismic life. Since a human organism exists before it constitutes a person, the life of an organism is not identical to the life of any person. Despite our use of the word "life" for both personal and biological aspects of lives, a person constituted by a human organism does not have two lives.[50] Rather, a human person has a single life, a personal life, with many salient biological aspects. A purely bio-logical life is the career of an organism. If the organism constitutes a person, then what would have been a biological life on its own becomes incorpor-ated into a personal life – a life that includes not only health and illness, but also successes and failures, joys and regrets.

So, a person constituted by a body does not have two different lives, but one integrated personal life that has biological as well as nonbiological aspects.[51] The connection between an injury to one's organs and one's resulting dread of a long recovery is a causal connection *within* a personal life. Before a fetus comes to constitute a person, there is biological life; but there is no personal life. Biological life is what is continuous throughout the animal kingdom. But if I am right, biological life is only one aspect of personal life.[52]

---

[48] In John 10:10, Jesus is quoted as saying, "I've come to bring life, and to bring it more abundantly." I am confident that he was not talking about biological functioning.
[49] These two uses of "life" are left undistinguished in phrases like "the sanctity of life" or "the culture of life." It is particularly egregious to use the phrase "the sanctity of life" to suggest that what is sacred is an abstraction called "life"; people may be sacred, but life as an abstraction is not, and real people with real lives should not be made to suffer for the sake of an unanchored abstraction.
[50] I could use the more technical vocabulary of *Persons and Bodies* and say that the person has a personal life nonderivatively and a biological life derivatively and that the organism has a biological life nonderivatively and a personal life derivatively.
[51] Nonhuman persons, if there are any, may have personal lives with no biological aspect at all.
[52] Since organisms constitute persons, and not vice versa, persons are of a higher primary kind than organisms. Hence, it is not the case that a personal life is an aspect of biological life, except perhaps derivatively.

"Life" and "death" are correlative terms. If an entity is alive, the beginning of its life is the beginning of its existence, and the end of its life is death. (For my purposes here, I'll consider life and death to be relative to earthly existence, and not consider the possibility of life after death.) If a person's life consists of everything that one does and everything that happens to one during the time that she exists on Earth, it is natural to consider one's death as the end of one's life and the end of one's existence.[53] When you die, any hopes that you had of seeing the Great Wall of China in the future will remain forever unfulfilled; any amends that you had not made will remain forever unmade. Your death will involve a permanent and irreversible loss. When someone dies, its life (in the here and now, anyway) is over. The book is closed.

Different kinds of entities die under different circumstances. In particular, the death of an organism and the death of a person may coincide, but they need not. The death of an *organism* occurs with the permanent cessation of biological functioning – like respiration, metabolism, circulation of the blood. The death of a *person* occurs with the permanent loss of her first-person perspective, her ability to conceive of herself as herself. Even if she is unconscious, as long as it is physically possible for her to recover enough to entertain a thought like, "Am I dying?" she – the person – still lives. When she permanently loses that ability, the entity that was a person is no longer there. One way that a person may suffer irreversible loss of just her first-person perspective is permanent cessation of her higher brain functioning; another and more common way that a person may suffer irreversible loss of her first-person perspective is permanent cessation of general biological functioning. But in either case, a person leaves this world (so to speak) when she suffers irreversible loss of her first-person perspective.

Hence, a person dies with the irreversible loss of a first-person perspective, and an organism dies with irreversible organ failure. Not surprisingly, there are different criteria for death. The criterion for the death of a human animal (an organism) is now whole-brain death,[54] which occurs when a

---

[53] There are differing views about whether the human organism ends at death, but in no case does the human organism persist through the disintegration of the human body. Many philosophers identify human organisms with human bodies. For example, Fred Feldman holds that human persons are (identical to) human organisms, and that human organisms persist after death as corpses. See Feldman's *Confrontations with the Reaper* (New York: Oxford University Press, 1992), pp. 104–105. Although I do not identify persons and organisms, I do identify organisms and human bodies.

[54] For a defense, see James Bernat, "A Defense of the Whole Brain Concept of Death," *Hastings Center Report* 28 (1998): 18–19. (Thanks to David Hershenov for this reference.)

patient is in an irreversible coma and has no brainstem response, no sign of brain activity on an electroencephalograph recording, and no ability to breathe independently.[55] When the whole brain, including the brainstem that regulates heartbeat and respiration, shuts down, the organism is dead – even if machines continue to support various organs.

Being brain dead must be distinguished from being in a persistent vegetative state. In brain death, the entire brain ceases to function; in a persistent vegetative state, the cerebral cortex, which controls higher, cognitive functions, shuts down. An organism may be capable of unaided respiration and circulation without being capable of any kind of cognitive functioning. Such an organism in a vegetative state still has biological life. But is there still a person there?

According to the Constitution View, it depends. It depends on whether the vegetative state is permanent, on whether it is physically possible for the patient to recover her ability to think "I." If it is not, then, although the organism that used to constitute the person is still alive, there is no person there. This, I believe, was the case with Terry Schiavo: the brain continued to regulate breathing, but the autopsy showed that the brain had so deteriorated that there was no physical possibility of any higher brain function. I believe that Terry Schiavo, the person, had ceased to be there long before she was declared dead.

So, medically speaking, there are criteria that distinguish between the death of a person and the death of an organism that constitutes a person – namely, permanent cessation of higher brain function and cessation of all brain function. Typically, persons and organisms cease living at the same time, but in very difficult and heart-rending cases, the organism may continue to carry on organic-life-sustaining functions when there is no longer a person, no longer an entity with a first-person perspective.[56]

QUASI-NATURALISM AND THE ONTOLOGICAL UNIQUENESS OF PERSONS

A metaphysical account of human persons should accommodate well-known established facts. First, there are the facts of biology that situate

[55] Gazzaniga, "The Thoughtful Distinction Between Embryo and Human," B10.

[56] For a contrasting understanding of life and death that also uses the Constitution View of persons, see David Hershenov's "The Death of a Person," forthcoming in *the Journal of Medicine and Philosophy*.

human persons in the animal world. Darwinism offers a great unifying thesis that "there is one grand pattern of similarity linking all life."[57] Human and nonhuman organisms both find their place in this one grand pattern. Second, there are the facts of self-consciousness that distinguish human persons from other parts of the natural world. People often know what they are thinking, feeling, deciding, etc. They can think about the future, wonder how they are going to die, hope for an afterlife. They can reflect on their own motivations – from Augustine in the *Confessions* to former army generals in their memoirs. Such descriptions all presuppose self-consciousness: they presuppose beings with the ability to be conscious of themselves from a first-personal point of view. And, as far as we know, what they describe is unique to human persons.

I believe that the Constitution View fully honors both these kinds of fact – the biological facts that pertain to human beings as part of the animal kingdom and, for want of a better word, the "personal" facts that pertain to human beings uniquely. On the one hand, human persons are material objects, subject to all the natural laws that apply to other kinds of material objects.[58] Human persons are wholly part of nature, the product of natural processes that started eons before the existence of our solar system, and that account for the existence of everything in the natural world – from atoms and molecules to solar systems and galaxies. On the other hand, human persons have evolved to have the capacity to think of themselves in the first-person. A first-person perspective is the defining property of persons and makes possible their characteristic forms of life and experience.

Not only are human persons a unique part of nature, but also they are an *ontologically* unique part of nature. By saying that persons are ontologically unique, I imply that an inventory of what exists leaving out persons would be incomplete. The addition of a person to the world is the addition of a new entity. Being a person is not just a property of some essentially nonpersonal kind of thing. (Fs are essentially nonpersonal if and only if being a person makes no difference to whether or not an F exists.) I realize that many philosophers do not take ontological uniqueness of persons to be a *desideratum* for an account of persons. Such philosophers are often motivated by doubt about the compatibility of persons' being

---

[57] Niles Eldredge, *The Triumph of Evolution* (New York: W. H. Freeman, 2000), p. 31.

[58] The view that human persons are wholly part of the natural order, I believe, rules out the possibility that human persons have free will as libertarians conceive of it. They do, however, have free will as compatibilists conceive of it. See my "Moral Responsibility Without Libertarianism," *Noûs* 42 (2006): 307–330.

ontologically unique and their being natural products of natural selection. Part of my aim here is to dispel that doubt. I know of no view of human persons other than the Constitution View that satisfies both these *deside-rata*: Human persons are wholly natural, yet ontologically distinctive. In short, a view of human persons should take account of these facts:

(1) Human persons are wholly part of the natural world, produced and governed by natural processes;
(2) Human persons are ontologically unique.

Let me explain further what I mean by these *desiderata*. First, to say that human persons are wholly part of the natural world is to endorse a kind of *quasi-naturalism*. Quasi-naturalism is naturalistic in taking the established results of scientific inquiry seriously: Science is the source of important knowledge of the natural world that is not subject to reinterpretation by philosophers.[59] The natural world is a spatiotemporal order that has its own integrity and autonomy, and that exhibits regularities that can be understood without regard to any immaterial objects or supernatural beings. The sciences are sovereign in their domains (and they are silent about matters outside their domains). Regularities and processes in the natural world have naturalistic explanations – that is, explanations that make no appeal to any supernatural beings.

However, quasi-naturalism falls short of full-blown naturalism in two respects – one epistemological, the other metaphysical: First, quasi-naturalism does not claim that the sciences are the only source of knowledge; rather, it allows there are kinds of knowledge – e.g., personal experience, humanistic studies of history and the arts – that do not belong to the sciences, as standardly understood. A second way that quasi-naturalism falls short of full-blown naturalism is that quasi-naturalism is not a metaphysical thesis at all: it does not claim that the natural world is all there is to reality; quasi-naturalism remains neutral with respect to the existence of anything that transcends the natural world. Another way to put it is that quasi-naturalism is not metaphysical naturalism, according to which science is the final arbiter of all knowable reality. Rather, quasi-naturalism implies only that scientific explanations are genuine explanations, and that most, perhaps all, events have scientific explanations.

---

[59] In reporting the results of science, scientists sometimes give interpretations that depend on philosophical assumptions that philosophers rightly criticize. Although I doubt that there's a sharp line here, I want to rule out philosophers' giving interpretations of scientific results that the scientific community largely rejects.

As the sciences have developed, all scientific explanations are naturalistic: they do not ever advert to immaterial beings. Perhaps the sciences could have developed differently. It seems that some contemporary naturalists like Quine would countenance immaterial objects if there were an explanatory need for them. "If I saw indirect explanatory benefit in positing sensibilia, possibilia, spirits, a Creator," Quine said, "I would joyfully accord them scientific status too, on a par with such avowedly scientific posits as quarks and black holes."[60] This passage manifests Quine's scientific pragmatism; Quine is willing to accord scientific status to all and only those posits that have "explanatory benefit." His position combines methodological naturalism with metaphysical naturalism in a way that I would reject as begging an important question: it precludes there being genuine explanations that do not fall into the domain of any science.

Methodological naturalism, I believe, has come to be a presupposition of science. It is not an ad hoc assumption, or a bias in science: that scientific explanations make no reference to anything supernatural is partly constitutive of science today and partly responsible for its success. The sciences are in the business of discovering natural causes and only natural causes. They do not and cannot appeal to immaterial entities or to supernatural agents.[61]

The issue of the nature of human persons is philosophical. The sciences can tell us about the biology and biochemistry of human persons, but whether the nature of human persons is exhausted by biology and biochemistry is not itself a scientific question. On the one hand, the sciences do not need a foundation in prior philosophy; on the other hand, philosophy is not just "continuous" with science (here I differ from full-blown naturalism). Paradigmatic philosophical questions – What is the nature of necessity and possibility? How should vagueness be understood? Is reality ultimately mind-independent? – are questions that do not arise in the sciences. Although not an extension of the sciences, philosophy, according to quasi-naturalism, should cohere with the results of the sciences.[62]

---

[60] W. V. O. Quine, "Naturalism; or, Living Within One's Means," *Dialectica* 49 (1995): 252. Quoted in Michael Rea, *World Without Design: Ontological Consequences of Naturalism* (Oxford: Clarendon Press, 2002), p. 42. I am grateful to Rea for bringing this passage to my attention.

[61] For this reason, it is wrongheaded to hope to find support for theism in science. The theory of Intelligent Design, advocated by certain Creationists, is a nonstarter as a modern scientific theory.

[62] See my "Philosophy *in Mediis Rebus*," *Metaphilosophy* 32 (2001): 378–394.

Quasi-naturalism is a *desideratum* of an account of persons because the successes of the sciences in the past 400 years command respect. (The absence of any reason to believe that theists make better scientists than atheists or agnostics is evidence that we can discover the nature of things without assuming the existence of God.) Moreover, quasi-naturalism offers protection against metaphysical fantasy. Quasi-naturalism, which requires coherence with science, does not allow wholesale reinterpretation of the sciences or of common sense to conform to an a priori metaphysics. For example, it is ludicrous to try to trump evolutionary explanations of fossils, by saying that God just planted them in order to mislead secular scientists. (Descartes was surely correct to suppose that God is not a systematic deceiver.) Even if there is more to knowable reality than what the sciences can uncover, the success of the sciences – in shaping and reshaping our social and physical environment and the framework for thinking about it – still gives them authority in their domains. Philosophers are in no position to reinterpret, in any large-scale or systematic manner, what scientists say in ways that the scientists themselves do not recognize.

So, I hold views of human persons to be accountable to quasi-naturalism. Specifically, a view of human persons satisfies the *desideratum* of quasi-naturalism only if it is consistent with the following description, which has been bequeathed to us by the sciences: Human persons are part of a natural world that has evolved by means of natural causes over eons. As inhabitants of the natural world, human persons are natural entities that live under the same necessity as the rest of nature (whatever that may be).

The second *desideratum* is that human persons are ontologically unique. To say that persons are ontologically unique is to say that the properties in virtue of which things, in the first instance, are persons are the properties in virtue of which they exist at all.[63] The claim that human persons are ontologically unique is common to the great monotheistic traditions: Judaism, Christianity, and Islam.[64] But I do not rely on this fact to justify ontological uniqueness of human persons as a *desideratum*; rather, a look at the natural world – in ways that I itemized when discussing the

---

[63] I am speaking of nonderivative Fs here. See *Persons and Bodies*, chapter 2. For a discussion of ontologically significant properties, see chapter 11 and my "The Ontological Status of Persons," *Philosophy and Phenomenological Research* 65 (2002): 370–388.

[64] The ontological uniqueness of persons may be explained in more than one way. Some explain it in terms of an immaterial soul; I explain it in terms of the first-person perspective.

Constitution View – gives ample evidence of the uniqueness of human persons.

That human persons are in some respects unique is indisputable; everything is unique in some respects. What is controversial is whether persons are *ontologically* unique – whether, as I hold, the coming-into-being of a new person in the world is the coming into being of a new entity, or whether it is merely the acquisition of a property by an already-existing entity. I submit that our being persons is the deepest fact about us: the properties peculiar to persons are sufficiently different from the properties of nonpersons to warrant the conclusion that persons – with their inner lives that spawn memoirs, confessions, autobiographies, etc. – are a unique kind of being. No other kind of being has values that lead to the great cultural achievements of science, technology, government, the arts, religion, morality, and the production of wealth. The variety and sophistication of the products of human endeavor are good evidence for the ontological uniqueness of persons.[65]

THREE APPROACHES CONTRASTED

Now consider how the three approaches to the nature of human persons each fares with respect to the two *desiderata* – quasi-naturalism and ontological uniqueness.

Animalism   According to Animalism, human persons are fundamentally animals.[66] Animalism does not contravene quasi-naturalism, but some of its proponents do. For example, Animalists consider animals to be what biologists tell us they are. Some Animalists believe that, whereas animals literally exist, their organs (hearts, livers, kidneys, and so on) do not.[67] Anyone who denies the existence of items that are (putatively) in the domain of biology contravenes quasi-naturalism.

---

[65] For more detailed arguments, see my "The Ontological Status of Persons," and "The Difference that Self-Consciousness Makes," in Klaus Petrus, ed., *On Human Persons* (Frankfurt: Ontos Verlag, 2003), pp. 23–39.

[66] Prominent Animalists include Eric T. Olson (*The Human Animal* [New York: Oxford University Press, 1997]) and Paul F. Snowdon, "Persons, Animals and Ourselves," in Christopher Gill, ed., *The Person and the Human Mind* (Oxford: Clarendon Press, 1990), pp. 83–107.

[67] See Peter van Inwagen, *Material Beings* (Ithaca, NY: Cornell University Press, 1990), and Trenton Merricks, *Objects and Persons* (Oxford: Clarendon Press, 2001).

All Animalists deny that human persons are ontologically unique. The basic metaphysical line, as they see it, is between organisms and nonliving things like artifacts. Let me remark in passing that recent work in biotechnology suggests that that line is not metaphysically basic. (Consider the so-called digital organisms, robo-rats, bacterial batteries, genetically engineered viral search-and-destroy missiles mentioned in chapter 3.) But even if there were a sharp organism/nonorganism demarcation, it would not secure the ontological uniqueness of persons, as opposed to organisms generally.

According to Animalists, *person* is a phase sortal. Being a person, like being a student, is a contingent property that some animals have some of the time. A person's persistence conditions are not determined by her being a person. On the Animalist view, being a person is not a deep fact about persons. Ontologically speaking, the world would be no poorer without persons: if an Evil Genius took away all first-person perspectives, but left lower biological functions like metabolism intact, there would be no loss in what exists. If Animalism is correct, then there could be a complete inventory of the objects that exist that neither mentioned persons nor entailed that persons exist. Therefore, according to Animalists, persons are not ontologically unique.

Substance dualism   According to Substance Dualism, human persons have immaterial parts (souls or minds).[68] Substance Dualism – mind-body dualism or soul-body dualism – in contrast to Animalism, does allow for the ontological uniqueness of persons; but Substance Dualism takes human animals to have natures in part outside the purview of biology. Some Substance Dualists take human animals to be radically unlike nonhuman animals in ways that biologists cannot detect.[69] (Hasker takes nonhuman animals, as well as human animals, to have souls.[70]) If part of being a human animal is to have an immaterial soul, and biologists have no truck with immaterial souls, then biologists are not

---

[68] Prominent Substance Dualists include Richard Swinburne, *The Evolution of the Soul*, rev. ed. (Oxford: Clarendon Press, 1997); John Foster, *The Immaterial Self: A Defence of the Cartesian Dualist Conception of the Mind* (London: Routledge, 1991); Charles Talliaferro, *Consciousness and the Mind of God* (Cambridge: Cambridge University Press, 1994); and William Hasker, *The Emergent Self* (Ithaca, NY: Cornell University Press, 1999).

[69] I take Thomism to be a form of Substance Dualism.

[70] According to Hasker, "Animals have souls, just as we do; their souls are less complex and sophisticated than ours, because generated by less complex nervous systems" (*The Emergent Self*, p. 193).

authoritative about the nature of human animals. So, if Substance Dualism is correct, biologists are not authoritative about *biology*.[71] Hence, Substance Dualism violates quasi-naturalism.

The Constitution View It should come as no surprise that the Constitution View, and the Constitution View alone, satisfies both *desiderata*. First, it is quasi-naturalistic: Human animals are exactly as biologists tell us they are. Biologists are authoritative over the animal kingdom, and they agree that the animal kingdom is a seamless whole that includes human animals; there are no significant biological differences between human and higher nonhuman animals. The Constitution View does not have to put a special gloss on biology to accommodate the ontological uniqueness of human persons.

Second, the Constitution View recognizes – nay, insists on – the ontological uniqueness of persons. Although biologists have animals in their domain, we look beyond biology (to the humanities and social studies) for a full understanding of persons that animals constitute. Analogously, although chemists have paint in their domain, we look beyond chemistry (to art history and connoisseurship) for a full understanding of the paintings that the paint constitutes.

According to the Constitution View, each primary kind – persons, paintings, what have you – is a unique kind of reality in some respect or other. But the respect in which human persons are unique is itself unique. With their first-person perspectives, their inwardness, human persons are unique in a special way: uniquely unique, we may say. What saves this from mere hand-waving is that the advent of human persons brings into the world a new kind of reality: first-personal reality.[72]

In sum, the Constitution View makes sense of both the biological claim that we are animals, continuous with nonhuman animals, and the philosophical claim that we are ontologically and morally unique. The Constitution View accommodates both these claims by holding that we are animals in that we are wholly constituted by animals, and yet we are ontologically unique in virtue of having first-person perspectives.

---

[71] Although I agree with Substance Dualists that our person-making properties are not those that biologists care about, on my view, biologists do have the last word on human animals: again, human animals constitute us without being identical to us.

[72] For further discussion of this point, see my "The Ontological Status of Persons" and "The Difference that Self-Consciousness Makes."

CONCLUSION

The Constitution View allows human persons to be part of the material world – as material as statues and traffic signs. It shows both how we are similar to other material things (ultimately constituted by aggregates of atoms), and how we are distinctive (we nonderivatively have first-person perspectives). It allows that we can persist through change of body. We already have artificial hearts and hips; can artificial brainstems be far behind? The *Scientific American* recently had an article on self-replicating machines, in which the authors said, "In a sense, researchers are seeing a continuum between nonliving and living structures."[73] So, it seems to me a good thing to understand persons in terms that are not strictly biological.

---

[73] Moshe Sipper and James A. Reggia, "Go Forth and Replicate," *Scientific American*, August 2001: 43.

PART II

The everyday world

5

Commonsense causation

Commonsense causation is ubiquitous. The everyday world is teeming with ordinary objects that have effects in virtue of having certain properties: the car's backfiring caused the horse to bolt; the door's blowing open caused the alarm to go off; the cook's adding peanuts to the sauce caused the guest's allergic reaction – these are all examples of commonsense causation.[1]

There are countless causal verbs and phrases in ordinary language – "attract," "excite," "tear apart," "open," "remove", "enlarge", and so on – verbs whose use entails causal transactions. G. E. M. Anscombe presented a small sample of causal concepts: "*scrape, push, wet, carry, eat, burn, knock over, keep off, squash, make* (e.g., noises, paper boats), *hurt.*"[2] Each of these verbs expresses a kind of commonsense causation. The root idea of commonsense causation is *making something happen*. To cause is to bring about, to produce, to give rise to something.

Commonsense causation is nonHumean in several ways. First, our experience is not just of successive events, but of causation: we *see* the knife slice the bread, and we *hear* the glass shatter, where slicing and shattering are themselves causal phenomena.[3] Second, singular causal transactions (such as that x's having F has an effect) are local: they do not depend on regularities that extend throughout space and time, but rather only on the instantiation of

---

[1] Objects have effects in virtue of having properties (or by having properties exemplified in certain ways). I take causation by properties to be event-causation, where events are not themselves concrete particulars, but are complexes, as, e.g., an object's having a property at a time. An agent or other thing has an effect in virtue of some event. Properties in the commonsense world are abundant, not sparse.

[2] G. E. M. Anscombe, "Causality and Determination," in *Metaphysics and the Philosophy of Mind, Collected Philosophical Papers, Volume II* (Minneapolis: University of Minnesota Press, 1981), p. 137. I am making no presuppositions here about whether, underlying all the events denoted by this sample, there is a unique relation in nature.

[3] Someone might object that we see the knife slice the bread only by seeing a succession of events, and that all that we directly see are the events. I reject this view for the same reason that I reject sense-data theory. The directly/nondirectly distinction on which it rests cannot be made out nonarbrarily.

the properties by ordinary objects in certain circumstances.[4] Whether or not your car caused the skid marks depends your car and its properties. There need be no universal law that your car and the skid marks instantiate when your car causes the skid marks.[5]

According to Alexander's Dictum, to be real is to have causal powers. For my purposes here, we need only consider the converse of Alexander's Dictum: To have causal powers is to be real. The converse also allows for the possibility of epiphenomena. Many philosophers use the expression "causal powers" as a technical term. I do not: An object x (or a property instance)[6] has causal powers if and only if x has a property F in virtue of which x has effects. Given this informal construal of causal powers, all ordinary objects have causal powers. At the least, any ordinary object affects the direction of local air currents. But more important, ordinary objects have effects in virtue of their having properties that only ordinary objects can have – the shoes' being polished caused them to shine, or the shape of the table caused controversy at the Paris Peace talks.

Nevertheless, many philosophers are dubious about the causal efficacy of ordinary things, and consequently have doubts about the reality of ordinary things. I shall counter such philosophers by giving an account of properties of ordinary things that have two features: they are irreducible to lower-level properties and they are causally efficacious.[7] I am not here offering either a general metaphysical account of causation, or an analysis of the concept *causation*.[8] What I aim to do in this chapter is to vindicate the reality of commonsense causation as I have described it above.

---

[4] Of course, almost all aspects of causation are controversial. For one nonHumean account, however, see Michael Tooley, "The Nature of Causation: A Singularist Account," *Canadian Journal of Philosophy*, Supplementary Volume 16, ed. David Copp (1990): 271–322.

[5] This claim about anomalous causation is distinct from the claim that causal relations are intrinsic to their relata. Armstrong, e.g., rejects anomalous causation, but holds that causal relations are intrinsic to their relata since causation involves universals, and universals are wholly present wherever they are instantiated. See David M. Armstrong, *A World of States of Affairs* (Cambridge: Cambridge University Press, 1997), especially chs. 14 and 15. Conversely, David Lewis sometimes seems to allow anomalous causation, but on his (Humean) view, causal relations are grounded in the whole spatiotemporal world.

[6] Kim speaks of instances of properties as having causal powers. See his "Multiple Realization and the Metaphysics of Reduction," in *Supervenience and Mind: Selected Philosophical Essays* (Cambridge: Cambridge University Press, 1993), p. 326.

[7] For an ontological account of levels of reality, see chapter 11.

[8] For an illuminating survey of views on the metaphysics of causation, see Jonathan Schaffer, "The Metaphysics of Causation," in Edward N. Zalta, ed., *The Stanford Encyclopedia of Philosophy* (Spring 2003 Edition), at: http://plato.stanford.edu/archives/spr2003/entries/causation-metaphysics/.

The view here is one of nonreductive materialism: It is materialistic in that it holds that every concrete particular is made up entirely of microphysical items. It is nonreductive in that it holds that not all objects and not all properties are reducible to physical particles or simples, and their properties.[9] Nevertheless, ordinary things and their commonsense properties contribute to what happens: they are not epiphenomenal. If an ordinary object has some effect in virtue of instantiating having a commonsense property, then the object has causal powers, and the property is causally efficacious.

It is obvious that commonsense properties – in particular, mental properties like your wanting to complete the overdue book review – seem to be causally efficacious. (Your wanting to complete the overdue book review caused you to decline the invitation to the picnic.) Moreover, we cannot help believing in the causal efficacy of such properties. However, there is a powerful argument against nonreductive mental causation, mounted by Jaegwon Kim. I want to meet Kim's challenge and to formulate a property-constitution view that shows how commonsense properties are causally efficacious.

Here is my plan: First, I shall critically examine Jaegwon Kim's strongest argument against nonreductive mental causation, and then show that his argument generalizes to a huge class of nonmental intentional properties that we use successfully in causal explanations and predictions. If Kim is correct, I shall argue, we have the unhappy conclusion that there is no nonmental intentional causation whatever – e.g., that advertising never has caused increased sales, that receiving a bonus never has raised your morale. Since this conclusion is apparently false, we have reason to think that Kim is not correct. Next, I shall formulate a nonreductive version of intentional causation – a version compatible with global supervenience – and show how it vindicates mental causation without reduction.

JAEGWON KIM'S ARGUMENTS AGAINST NONREDUCTIVE MENTAL CAUSATION

Kim's writings support a sustained attack on nonreductive materialism. Unless mental properties are reducible to physical properties, he argues, they are causally inert or else there is massive (and, he thinks, implausible) overdetermination. I shall focus on two of his arguments: briefly, on the

---

[9] See Derk Pereboom and Hilary Kornblith, "The Metaphysics of Irreducibility," *Philosophical Studies* 63 (1991): 125–145.

Overdetermination Argument, and in greater detail, what I call Kim's "Key Argument."[10] Each of the arguments against nonreductive mental causation relies on one or more of the following metaphysical assumptions:

1. The Physical Realization Thesis: A mental property is instantiated only if it is realized by a physical property. If P realizes M, then P is nomologically sufficient for M, and M supervenes on P.[11]
2. The Nomological-Sufficiency Conception of Causation: A causes B only if A is nomologically sufficient for B.[12]
3. The Causal-Realization Principle: If an instance of S occurs by being realized by an instance of Q, then any cause of this instance of S must be a cause of this instance of Q (and of course any cause of this instance of Q is a cause of this instance of S).[13]
4. The Causal-Inheritance Principle: If mental property M is realized in a system at t in virtue of physical realization base P, the causal powers of this instance of M are identical with the causal powers of P.[14]
5. The Causal-Closure Principle: Any physical event that has a cause at t has a complete physical cause at t.[15]
6. The Principle of Causal/Explanatory Exclusion: There is no more than one complete and independent cause (or causal explanation) of any event.[16]

The Overdetermination Argument   Assume that mental events are realized by physical events (in the sense of the Physical Realization Thesis), and hence that mental events supervene on physical events. If one mental event, M, caused another M★, then there would be a physical event P★ that realized M★, and M★ would supervene on P★. Given the Causal-Closure Principle, P★ has a complete physical cause. And given the Principle of Causal/ Explanatory Exclusion, P★ has no more than one complete and independent

---

[10] Jaegwon Kim, *Mind in a Physical World* (Cambridge, MA: MIT Press).

[11] Jaegwon Kim, "The Nonreductivist's Troubles with Mental Causation," in John Heil and Alfred Mele, eds., *Mental Causation* (Oxford: Clarendon Press), p. 200.

[12] Ibid., p. 204. To say that A is nomologically sufficient for B is to say that in every possible world with the same natural laws as our world, if A occurs, then B occurs.

[13] Ibid., pp. 205–206; cf. Jaegwon Kim, "Making Sense of Downward Causation," in Peter Bogh Andersen, Claus Emmeche, Niels Ole Finnemann, and Peder Voetmann Christiansen, eds., *Downward Causation* (Aarhus, Denmark: Aarhus University Press, 2000), p. 310.

[14] Kim, "Multiple Realization and the Metaphysics of Reduction," p. 326.

[15] Kim, "The Myth of Nonreductive Materialism," p. 43.

[16] Jaegwon Kim, "Mechanism, Purpose, and Explanatory Exclusion," in James E. Tomberlin, ed., *Philosophy of Mind and Action Theory* (Philosophical Perspectives 3) (Atascadero, CA: Ridgeview Publishing, 1989), p. 89.

cause. Since M* supervenes on P*, the complete physical cause of P* is also a cause of M*. In that case, M* is overdetermined – by M and by the complete physical cause of P*. So, if mental properties are not identical with physical properties, and mental events have physical effects, then these physical effects are overdetermined: All mentally caused events have complete physical causes as well as mental causes. But it is implausible, claims Kim, that every event with a mental cause is causally overdetermined.

To bolster his case, Kim bids us consider an example of overdetermination. Suppose that there are two assassins acting independently who shoot a politician at the same time. As Kim says, it is not plausible that all events with mental causes are overdetermined in that way. However, as Barry Loewer points out, in contrast to the case of the two assassins, a mental event and a physical realizer of it are not independent; they are metaphysically connected.[17] Indeed, it would suffice to defeat the analogy if they were merely nomologically connected (as dualists hold) or even if they were merely accidentally connected throughout actuality. So, the analogy misfires.

A number of philosophers reply to the Overdetermination Argument by arguing that if there is any overdetermination of mentally caused physical effects, it is harmless.[18] The mental and physical causes are not in competition since mental properties supervene on, and depend on, the physical properties. Such philosophers concede that nonidentity of mental and physical properties leads to overdetermination, but also maintain that the overdetermination involved is quite plausible.

Moreover, there is another line of thought that should lead us not to shun the possibility of overdetermination, but to welcome it. For all we know, there is no fundamental microphysical level.[19] If it turns out that there is no fundamental microphysical level, then we cannot deny overdetermination, lest all the causal powers drain away. Whether there is a "bottom" level is not to be decided by metaphysical argument. So, we may have to countenance overdetermination in any case.

---

[17] Barry Loewer, "Review of J. Kim, *Mind in a Physical World*," *Journal of Philosophy* 98 (2001): 315–324; and Barry Loewer, "Comments on Jaegwon Kim's *Mind in a Physical World*," *Philosophy and Phenomenological Research* 65 (2002): 655–662.

[18] E.g., Amie Thomasson, "A Nonreductivist Solution to Mental Causation," *Philosophical Studies* 89 (1998): 181–195; Derk Pereboom, "Robust Nonreductive Materialism," *Journal of Philosophy* 99 (2002): 499–531; Barry Loewer, "Comments on Jaegwon Kim's *Mind in a Physical World*"; and Thomas Crisp and Ted Warfield, "Kim's Master Argument," *Noûs* 35 (2001): 304–316.

[19] For a discussion of whether there is a fundamental level, see Jonathan Schaffer, "Is There a Fundamental Level?" *Noûs* 37 (2003): 498–517.

In addition, if there is no fundamental level, then the Principle of Explanatory/Causal Exclusion, as it is usually understood, is false. The Exclusion Principle is usually understood to assume that there is a fundamental level – the level at which there is one and only one complete and independent cause (or causal explanation) of an event. If there is no "bottom" level, then each candidate explanation/cause for the title "the single complete and independent explanation/cause" of a particular event will be superseded by a candidate at a lower level. In that case, we must deny the Principle of Explanatory/Causal Exclusion. (Alternatively, we could reinterpret "complete and independent" in such a way that there is not even one complete and independent cause [or causal explanation] of any given event; such reinterpretation would render the Causal-Closure Principle false.) So, not only would the absence of a fundamental level lead to over-determination, it would falsify the Principle of Explanatory/Causal Exclusion or the Causal-Closure Principle. Indeed, if the Principle of Explanatory/Causal Exclusion is assumed to be a necessary truth, then the Principle is refuted by the mere *possibility* of there being no bottom level in a world that still possesses causal activities.

It looks as if we must accept the possibility of overdetermination in a world of causal activity. Moreover, the possibility of overdetermination *supports* nonreductionism. Overdetermination resulting from the absence of a "bottom" level would threaten reductionism but not nonreductive materialism. And we may never know whether there is a fundamental level or not. So, we have good reason to prefer nonreductive materialism to the elimination of overdetermination.

The Key Argument   There is a single argument that can be reconstructed from Kim's writings that, I believe, is his most forceful and sweeping assault on nonreductive materialism. After stating the overall argument (as I–IV below), I'll defend each of its premises by a subargument. (In the process, I'll recast the argument as a reductio ad absurdum.)

Say that a mental property is irreducible if and only if there is no physical property, such that instances of the mental property are identical to instances of the physical property.[20] Then Kim's Key Argument against nonreductive materialism is this:

---

[20] This is an awkward way to put it, but Kim construes identity of instances of a mental property, M, with instances of a physical property, P, to require "either property identity M = P or some form of reductive relationship between them." Jaegwon Kim, *Physicalism, or Something Near Enough* (Princeton: Princeton University Press, 2005), p. 42, n. 9.

   I. If mental properties are both irreducible and causally efficacious, then there is downward causation by irreducible mental properties.
   II. If there is downward causation by irreducible higher-level properties, then there are two distinct nomologically sufficient conditions of a single event.
   III. There are not two distinct nomologically sufficient conditions of a single event.[21]
∴.IV. Mental properties are not both irreducible and causally efficacious.

Now turn to the arguments for the Premises I–III. If mental states are causally efficacious, then one irreducible and causally efficacious mental state may cause another mental state. Suppose that M and M$\star$ are mental states realized by physical states, P and P$\star$, respectively, and that M $\neq$ P and M$\star$ $\neq$ P$\star$.

  Argument for Premise I:

   1. M causes M$\star$. (supposition for reductio)
   2. If M causes M$\star$, then M causes P$\star$. (Causal Realization Principle)
∴.3. M causes P$\star$. (1,2 MP)

Argument for Premise II:

   4. If M causes P$\star$, then M is nomologically sufficient for P$\star$. (Kim's Nomological-Sufficiency Conception of Causation)
   5. M is nomologically sufficient for P$\star$. (3,4 MP)
   6. P is nomologically sufficient for P$\star$. (Causal-Closure Principle + Kim's Nomological-Sufficiency Conception of Causation)
∴.7. M and P are distinct nomologically sufficient conditions for P$\star$. (5,6 conjunction + assumption that M is irreducible.)

Argument for Premise III:

   8. P is nomologically sufficient for M. (Physical Realization Thesis)
   9. If 7 & 8, then P is the only genuine cause of P$\star$. (Causal-Closure Principle + Principle of Causal/Explanatory Exclusion)[22]
∴.10. P is the only genuine cause of P$\star$.
   11. If P is the only genuine cause of P$\star$ and M is not reducible to P, then M does not cause P$\star$. (conceptual truth)
   12. If M does not cause P$\star$, then M does not cause M$\star$. (Causal-Realization Principle)
∴.13. M does not cause M$\star$. (10–12 MP twice)

---

[21] Since Kim takes causation to be nomological sufficiency, his ban on causal overdetermination is a ban on nomological overdetermination.
[22] Although I have already shown that the Principle of Causal/Explanatory Exclusion is false (due to the possibility of there being no fundamental level), I am here presenting what I believe is Kim's most detailed argument against irreducible mental causation.

Hence, given Kim's principles, the supposition that one irreducible mental state causes another leads to a contradiction (1 and 13). The only causally efficacious properties are microphysical (or micro-based macrophysical properties that are mereological aggregates of subatomic properties – see next section). Therefore, it appears that if nonreductive materialism is correct, mental states are causally inert, and epiphenomenalism carries the day. I shall respond to the Key Argument by proposing a different model of nonreductive causation, which, if correct, shows that the Key Argument is unsound. (In particular, lines (2), (8), and (9) are false.) Before proposing my own model, however, I want to revisit an old controversy about the scope of Kim's conclusion.

DOES KIM'S KEY ARGUMENT GENERALIZE TO ALL MACROCAUSATION?

The Key Argument has an extremely strong conclusion. It seems to apply not just to mental properties, but to any putatively irreducible macrophysical property. The grounds for the principles supporting his argument against nonreductive mental causation equally support an argument against all causation by irreducible higher-level properties. Roughly, Kim takes the idea of a higher-level property to be this: P_2 is a higher-level property than P_1 iff the entities where P_2 makes its "first appearance" have "an exhaustive decomposition, without remainder, into entities belonging to the lower levels."[23]

If Kim's argument against nonreductive mental causation is sound, then there may be no higher-level (e.g., macrophysical) properties that are both irreducible and causally efficacious.[24] Kim has replied to the charge that his arguments against mental causation generalize to threaten all macrocausation. I shall respond that although Kim's arguments against mental causation do not threaten *all* macrocausation, they do threaten enough macrocausation to render them untenable.

---

[23] Kim, *Mind in a Physical World*, p. 15.

[24] See Tyler Burge, "Mind–body Causation and Explanatory Practice," in Heil and Mele, eds., *Mental Causation*, pp. 97–120; Lynne Rudder Baker, "Metaphysics and Mental Causation," in Heil and Mele, eds., *Mental Causation*, pp. 75–96; and Robert van Gulick, "Who's in Charge Here?" in Heil and Mele, eds., *Mental Causation*, pp. 233–258 for arguments that Kim's claims against mental causation generalize to all macroscopic properties.

Kim made a two-pronged reply to the charge that his arguments threaten all macrocausation:[25]

(i) Kim's first prong: Macroproperties that are micro-based are reducible (and hence, causally efficacious). Micro-based macroproperties are properties of macro-objects that can be characterized in terms of microstructure: "P is a micro-based property just in case P is the property of being completely decomposable into nonoverlapping proper parts, a1, a2,..., an, such that P1(a1), P2(a2),... Pn(an), and R(a1,... an)."[26] For example, being a water molecule is a micro-based property: it is the property of having two hydrogen atoms and one oxygen atom in a certain bonding relationship among them. Micro-based properties, Kim argues, are both macroproperties and causally efficacious.[27] For example, my table's having a mass of 10 kg is a micro-based property: it is the property of being completely decomposable into 10 nonoverlapping parts each weighing 1 kg. Having a mass of 10 kg is a property of the table that is causally efficacious (it makes the pointer on the scale read "10 kg") and is not a property of the table's proper parts. Hence, says Kim, we were mistaken to suppose that all macrophysical properties fall to the argument against nonreductive mental causation. Micro-based macroproperties are causally efficacious.

(ii) Kim's second prong: All properties of a single bearer are at a single level. Hence, mental properties and their realizers are on the same level. For example, my property of intending to lock the door is at the same level as my property of having microparts with such-and-such microproperties and related in a certain way. So, the competition between mental and physical properties is intralevel. Belief properties and the neural properties that realize them are at same level; I have both. Hence, there is (or may be) mental causation, but it is reductive: mental properties and their physical realizers are on the same level.

Levels must be distinguished from orders. Belief is a second-order functional property: Belief is the property of having a first-order property that plays a certain causal role. The distinction between first- and second-order properties should be distinguished from a micro-macro hierarchy of levels: "the realization relation does not track the micro-macro relation."[28] Neural properties are the first-order properties – the realizers – that play the causal role. Since mental properties and the neural properties that

---

[25] Kim, *Mind in a Physical World*, pp. 77–87.   [26] Ibid., p. 84.
[27] Note that micro-based properties are not irreducible, however.
[28] Kim, *Mind in a Physical World*, p. 82.

realize them are on the same level, they can be identified. And since neural properties are micro-based, they are causally efficacious. In general, macro-properties that are reducible to their realizers are causally efficacious.

On Kim's view, a property can have a realizer only if it can be "functionalized" – that is, only if it can be construed "as a property defined by its causal/nomic relations to other properties, specifically properties in the reduction base."[29] Kim ties realization to supervenience: If P realizes M, then M supervenes on P.[30] The functional property and its realizers – the supervening property and its base – are on the same level. In short, says Kim, the problem of mental causation does not generalize to cross-level causation because mental and neural properties are at the same level, and neural properties are micro-based and hence are causally efficacious. So, neural properties, and other micro-based macroproperties generally, are not susceptible to an analogue of the problem of mental causation raised for irreducible mental properties.

RESPONSE TO KIM'S KEY ARGUMENT

Let me respond to Kim's argument. Despite his argument for reducibility of mental properties, there remains a huge class of important non-micro-based *nonmental* properties that Kim's view cannot accommodate. Kim thinks that mental properties can avoid epiphenomenality by being reduced (perhaps in a species-specific way). But macroproperties that do not fit Kim's schema for reduction – properties that will be rendered epiphenomenal by Kim's view[31] – are properties mentioned in causal explanations of psychology, economics, and political science, as well as in everyday life. They are properties without which we cannot begin to make sense of the everyday world.

Recall the huge class of properties that are "intention-dependent" or, for short, ID properties. ID properties are properties that cannot be instantiated in a world without beings with propositional attitudes – e.g., being in debt, being a driver's license, being a delegate. Nobody can be in debt and

---

[29] Jaegwon Kim, "Making Sense of Emergence," *Philosophical Studies* 95 (1999): 10.

[30] Kim, "The Nonreductivist's Troubles with Mental Causation," pp. 196–197.

[31] Kim accepts Alexander's Dictum, according to which "to be real is to possess causal powers" (Jaegwon Kim, "Downward Causation' in Emergentism and Nonreductive Physicalism," in Ansgar Beckermann, Hans Flohr, and Jaegwon Kim, eds., *Emergence or Reduction?* [Berlin: de Gruyter, 1992], p. 134). So, his view will render the properties appealed to by psychology and the social sciences nonexistent.

nothing can be a driver's license in a world without beings with propositional attitudes. Call any property that either is a propositional-attitude property (like believing, desiring, or intending) or is one whose instances presuppose that there are beings with beliefs, desires, and/or intentions an "intention-dependent" property – or ID property. These are properties, nonmental as well as mental, whose instances depend on there being creatures with intentionality. ID properties that we are familiar with include being a wedding, being a carrot scraper, being a treaty, and so on. Other communities may be familiar with other kinds of ID properties; but all communities recognize many kinds of ID properties – as well as other ID objects like pianos and paychecks, and ID phenomena like conventions and obligations. All artifacts and artworks, and most human activities (getting a job, going out to dinner, etc.), are ID phenomena: They could not exist or occur in a world without beliefs, desires, and intentions. ID properties are not plausibly construed as micro-based properties. Kim says that "we can microstructurally explain why a micro-based property has a certain set of causal powers."[32] Since ID properties are multiply realizable in indefinitely many ways, they (the properties, not the property-instances) are not decomposable into lower-level physical properties and relations, whose causal powers determine the causal powers of the original ID properties.

However, there is overwhelming empirical evidence that ID properties are causally efficacious properties. We could not begin to make sense of the world without supposing that ID properties – like being employed, being an elected representative – have effects. Without ID properties, we could explain almost nothing that happens in the everyday world – a president's ordering an invasion, a dean's cutting the departmental budget, a business's going bankrupt. If so, then ID properties provide an enormous set of counterexamples to Kim's view.

It is highly unlikely that on Kim's account, ID properties turn out to be causally efficacious. An ID property is causally efficacious on Kim's view only if it is reducible, and it is reducible only if it meets three conditions: First, it must be "functionalized." That is, it must have a functional definition in terms of having some property that plays a particular causal role. Second, there must be a physical realizer in a physical reduction base that *plays* the causal role. Indeed, the causal efficacy of a higher-level property resides in its physical (micro-based) realizer. Third, there must be a theory that shows *how* the physical realizer plays the causal role.

---

[32] Kim, *Mind in a Physical World*, p. 116.

I doubt that ID properties satisfy any of these conditions, but I'll focus only on the second condition – the condition that says that there must be a physical realizer that plays the causal role that defines the property: Consider the property of being the payment of a debt. It is difficult even to think of a *candidate* to be a physical realizer in a physical reduction base of being payment of a debt. Here's why:

Kim ties realization to supervenience: If P realizes M, then M supervenes on P. So, an instance of the property of being payment of a debt supervenes on the instances of its nonintentional realizer. Thus, given a nonintentional realizer of an instance of the property of being a payment of a debt, necessarily, the property of being a payment of a debt is instantiated. But the nonintentional properties on which any instance of being a payment of a debt supervenes are not locally instantiated. In order for it to be possible for an event to be a payment of a debt, the practices of owning and borrowing must *already* be in place. So, the properties involved in those practices of owning and borrowing must be instantiated before a payment of a debt is even possible. Moreover, owning and borrowing are also ID properties. We have no idea what are the base physical properties on which being a payment of a debt can supervene. Yet, if Kim is right, the causal efficacy of the payment of the debt resides in the physical realizer (whatever that is). So, when your payment of the debt causes an end to harassing phone calls from your creditor, the causation involved is all going on at the micro-level. Kim's view would have us transform a causal connection that we all understand, and that we can predict – the causal connection between your paying your debt and putting an end to harassing phone calls from your creditor – into a causal connection between totally unknown physical properties.[33]

Moreover, even if Kim's conditions for functionalization were met, ID properties (though obviously causal) would still violate his Causal Realization Principle. The Causal Realization Principle, you recall, is this: If an instance of S occurs by being realized by an instance of Q, then any cause of this

---

[33] This latter objection may smack of being "merely epistemological." The fact that we do not know how to carry out a reduction, as we are often reminded, does not imply that there is no reduction to be carried out. (See Louise Antony and Joseph Levine, "Reduction With Autonomy," in James E. Tomberlin, ed., *Mind, Causation and World [Philosophical Perspectives 11]* [Malden, MA: Blackwell, 1997]: 83–106.) I tendentiously reply that if we have no clue about how to find a reduction, we are in no position to claim that it can be carried out in principle. Without the "merely epistemological," one has little grounds for confidence in the loftily metaphysical. In any case, I also give nonepistemological reasons to hold that Kim's view cannot accommodate causally efficacious ID properties.

instance of S must be a cause of this instance of Q (and of course any cause of this instance of Q is a cause of this instance of S). So, on Kim's view, if, say, Jones's payment of his debt is to have the effect of putting an end to harassing phone calls from his creditor, the payment of the debt must bring about the *physical realizer* of the property of putting an end to harassing phone calls. But the physical realizer of the property of putting an end to harassing phone calls must include the physical properties on which already-existing practices supervene. So, there is nothing that Jones (or anyone else) can do today that is nomologically sufficient for putting an end to harassing phone calls. Since similar arguments apply to other ID properties, I conclude that no ID properties satisfy Kim's Causal Realization Principle.

The reason that Kim cannot recognize nonmental intentional properties of the social sciences and everyday life as causally efficacious is that, on his view, a macroproperty is causally efficacious only if it is micro-based, and a property is micro-based only if it is supervenient on *locally* instantiated microproperties. That is, the same object that instantiates the causally efficacious macroproperty must have parts that instantiate its supervenience base.[34] But if nonmental intentional properties – like paying a debt – supervene on anything, they do not supervene on locally instantiated properties. Your paying a debt does not supervene on physical properties of parts of your body.

So, if Kim were correct, I doubt that there would be any nonmental intentional causation whatever. What is at stake is all causation by objects' having properties whose instances depend on there being things with propositional attitudes – e.g., being written in German, being married, being an ambassador. If we are realists about causal explanation (as Kim and I both are), then without ID properties, we would have no causal explanations of, say, the success of a political candidate's election campaign – or of any other historical, political, economic, social, or legal phenomenon. So, Kim may be right that the problem of mental causation does not generalize to all macroproperties; but it does generalize to a great class of macroproperties that realists about causal explanation cannot do without.[35]

Although your paying a debt does not satisfy Kim's requirements for reduction, paying a debt obviously has consequences: Your payment of a

---

[34] This follows from the definition of "micro-based" property. Micro-based macroproperties supervene on micro-properties of parts of the object that instantiates the micro-based macroproperty. Kim, *Mind in a Physical World*, p. 84.

[35] Of course, someone may contend that ID causal explanations are just higher-level descriptions of microphysical transactions. But I just argued that ID properties are not

debt has the effect of clearing your name, and putting an end to harassing phone calls from your creditor. So, payment of a debt is causally efficacious. Hence, instances of paying one's debt – along with instances of other ID properties – show that Kim's account of causation is inadequate.

Indeed, if Kim is correct, then there is no genuine downward causation either. In that case, what are we to say about suggestive empirical evidence that various kinds of experience cause changes in the brain? Here are some examples of what seems like downward causation: (1) When people learn to juggle, the motor and visual areas of the brain get larger; and when they stop practicing, the areas retract. A senior lecturer in medical imaging said that "what we do in everyday life might have an impact not just on how our brains function but on the structure at a macroscopic level."[36] (2) A study of taxi drivers in London showed that the more time taxi drivers spent on the job, the larger the hippocampus grew. The leader of the research team said, "The hippocampus has changed its structure to accommodate their huge amount of navigating experience."[37] (3) *Scientific American* reported on a study by the National Academy of Sciences that found a link between psychological stress and telemere shortening. (Telemeres are chromosomal caps that promote genetic stability; they naturally shorten with age.) The team leader said, "The new findings suggest a cellular mechanism for how chronic stress may cause premature onset of disease. Chronic stress appears to have the potential to shorten the life of cells, at least immune cells."[38] These are just a few of recent results that strongly suggest the causal efficacy of ID properties.[39]

In sum, the overwhelming empirical evidence for the causal efficacy of ID properties generally gives us good reason to reject any theory that deems them epiphenomenal, or nonexistent.

---

micro-based, and hence not reducible. So, at this point, the claim that ID causal explanations are just higher-level descriptions of microphysical transactions amounts to the claim that ID properties are epiphenomenal. The latter claim is empirically falsified every day.

[36] BBC News. http://newsvote.bbc.co.uk/mpapps/pagetools/print/news.bbc.co.uk/1/hi/health/3417045.stm. Accessed June 3, 2006.

[37] BBC News, March 14, 2000. http://news.bbc.co.uk/1/hi/sic/tech/677048.stm. Accessed February 23, 2005.

[38] Scientific American.com. http://www.sciam.com/print_version.cfm?articleID=0005525A-9A84-1AB-9A8483414B. Accessed December 7, 2004.

[39] To deny that these examples are examples of downward causation by giving a reductive interpretation seems like a "work-around," especially in light of the fact that no one has an inkling of what a reduction of, say, learning your way around London might be or of how to go about finding it.

AN ACCOUNT OF NONREDUCTIVE CAUSATION

I take it to be a condition of adequacy on any account of materialism that it allow that ID properties generally are causally efficacious.[40] I want to propose a new version of nonreductive materialism – I'll call it the "PC View", "PC" for "property-constitution"[41] – and to suggest that it refutes Kim's arguments against nonreductive mental causation. Moreover, it recognizes the causal efficacy of ID properties, of which propositional attitudes are a special case.

Let me set out my view in contrast to Kim's in three ways. First, according to the PC View, there are a multiplicity of ontological levels – levels in reality. On Kim's view, levels must be understood as levels of description or levels of explanation, not as levels of reality.[42] Kim defines levels mereologically: objects that have properties at one level of description are parts of objects that have properties at higher levels of description.

---

[40] Even some versions of *nonreductive* materialism do not recognize the causal efficacy of ID properties generally. Versions of nonreductive materialism that hold that instances of mental properties confer (or are) causal powers and are *intrinsic* to their bearers will not generalize to account for other ID properties like the property of being written in Dutch or the property of being a delegate – putative properties whose realizations may have nothing in common. If predicates like "having a credit card" or "being a felon" do not designate properties, then we have no idea of any causal explanations of ordinary phenomena like being able to buy things without cash or of losing certain rights. Many ordinary phenomena are ID phenomena whose causal explanations appeal to (nonintrinsic) ID properties. Examples of such versions of nonreductive materialism that do not accommodate nonmental (noninstrinsic) ID properties include Pereboom, "Robust Nonreductive Physicalism"; Lenny Clapp, "Disjunctive Properties: Multiple Realization," *Journal of Philosophy* 98 (2001): 111–136; Sydney Shoemaker, "Causality and Properties," in *Identity, Cause and Mind*, 2nd ed. (Oxford: Clarendon Press, (2003), pp. 206–234. All these philosophers use the term "constitution," but my view differs significantly from each of theirs.

[41] I say "property-constitution" for convenience. What is constituted are property instances, not properties themselves. Property-constitution is analogous to the idea that I developed in *Persons and Bodies: A Constitution View* (Cambridge: Cambridge University Press, 2000) for understanding material objects in terms of what I simply called "constitution."

[42] Kim takes the difference between levels to be the difference between wholes and their parts, and – on Kim's view – a whole is identical to the sum of its parts. Entities "at any level higher than the lowest level must have a full decomposition into parts all of which belong to the lower levels" (Jaegwon Kim, "The Layered Model: Metaphysical Considerations," *Philosophical Explorations* 5 [2002], p. 15). Levels turn out just to be a matter of *description* in terms of wholes or of sums of parts. They have no ontological significance for Kim. Likewise, Kim construes higher-level properties as "properties of wholes [that] are fixed by the properties and relations that characterize their parts." So, higher-level properties are had by entities that have "an exhaustive decomposition, without remainder, into entities belonging to the lower levels" (Kim, *Mind in a Physical World* [1998], pp. 18, 15).

On Kim's view, all that exists are fundamental physical entities and their properties and relations, and sums of fundamental physical entities and their properties and relations. (That's what makes him a reductive physicalist [leaving aside epiphenomenal qualia].) Because of this mereological conception of levels and higher-level properties, ontologically speaking, Kim's levels all collapse into one, a microphysical level. So, in the end, the differences among Kim's levels are descriptive or conceptual.[43]

On my view, by contrast, reality is characterized by distinct ontological levels. Different kinds of material objects are on different ontological levels.[44] For example, mountains are on a lower level than ID objects like credit cards or passports, and atoms are on a lower level still.[45] Concrete material objects come in kinds: Every object is of some *primary kind* or other.[46] An object's primary-kind property determines the object's level and confers on the object causal powers that cannot be manifested at lower levels. But the object also has other causal powers at lower levels, as well as at the level of its primary-kind property. For example, a bronze statue has some causal powers in virtue of being a statue and some causal powers at a lower level in virtue of being made of bronze. An ordinary woman has causal powers at a personal level (she can make her friends feel good), as well as at a subpersonal level (she can rearrange air molecules when she dives into the swimming pool).[47] Making one's friends feel good is not a micro-based property. An individual can have properties at many levels, whether the properties are micro-based or not. So, the first way in which I differ from Kim concerns the notion of levels.

The second way the PC View differs from Kim's concerns my notion of property-constitution, in place of Kim's notion of realization. Kim's Realization Principles, as we have seen, are very strong – so strong that they doom nonmental intentional causation. I reject his conception

---

[43] In chapter 11, I give a nonKimean and nonmereological account of levels that allows for ontological (not just descriptive) distinctness among levels.

[44] Although I agree with Kim that atoms and sums of atoms are on the same ontological level, I do not believe that material objects can be understood as sums of atoms.

[45] In chapter 11, I give a sufficient ontological condition for "Q is a higher-level property than P." There is only a partial ordering of levels.

[46] See chapter 9, and *Persons and Bodies*, chapter 2. Again, concrete material objects are constituted objects, where constitution is *not* a mereological relation.

[47] *Pace* Kim, *Mind in a Physical World*. I take an object to be the bearer of all properties at the different levels. (This is a result of my rejecting Kim's mereological conception of levels, according to which all properties with a single bearer are on the same level.) To put the point in terms of *Persons and Bodies*, an object's properties include all those that the object has nonderivatively or derivatively.

of realization and replace it with the much weaker notion of property-constitution. The heart of my view – the PC View – is the idea of property-constitution: Property instances are constituted by other property instances at a lower level. A property's constituter on a given occasion may be a proper part of a supervenience base for the property, but the relation of property-constitution is not the relation of supervenience: A constituting instance does not by itself suffice for the property-instance that it constitutes. For example, being an extension of an arm out of a car window does not by itself suffice for there being a left-turn signal. Property-constitution is a much weaker notion than supervenience or nomological sufficiency: Whether or not one property-instance constitutes another depends on circumstances. For example, nothing is constituted by instances of being a sodium atom and instances of being a chlorine atom unless the atoms are in circumstances of bonding.

I call the circumstances in which an instance of F can constitute an instance of G "G-favorable circumstances."[48] G-favorable circumstances are the milieu in which something can have the property of being a G. The addition of an appropriate F to G-favorable circumstances gurantees that there is an instance of G.[49] A siren in certain circumstances constitutes an all-clear signal. A hand motion in certain circumstances constitutes a salute. Here, then, is a schema for property-constitution:[50]

(P-C) x's having F at t constitutes x's having G at t $=_{df}$

  (a) G is a higher-level property than F; &
  (b) x has F at t and x has G at t; &
  (c) x is in G-favorable circumstances at t; &

---

[48] The schema for constitution of properties differs from the one for constitution of particulars given in *Persons and Bodies* and elsewhere. In the schema for constitution of particulars, F and G are x's and y's primary-kind properties, respectively; and x and y are guaranteed to be nonidentical. In the schema for constitution of property-instances, F and G are any properties; and although F and G are guaranteed to be nonidentical, there may be a single bearer of the properties F and G.

[49] I individuate property-instances in such a way that the same property-instance could have occurred in different circumstances. Any G-instance must be in G-favorable circumstances, but if a G-instance is constituted by an F-instance, the F-instance (which in fact is in G-favorable circumstances) could have occurred in non-G-favorable circumstances.

[50] The objectual quantifier "x" ranges over constituted objects (e.g., chairs) that have some properties nonderivatively (e.g., being comfortable) and some properties derivatively (e.g., weighing 5 kg). The relation of "having a property" in (P-C) should be understood as having a property either derivatively or nonderivatively. For details, see chapter 8. The quantifiers "F" and "G" range over properties (ID and nonID).

    (d) It is necessary that: $\forall z[(z$ has F at t & z is in G-favorable circumstances at
        t$) \rightarrow z$ has G at t]; &
    (e) It is possible that: x has F at t & x lacks G at t.[51]

The potential constituters of an instance of G may have nothing in
common, other than their suitability to constitute an instance of G in various
circumstances.[52] For example, a single instance of the property of voting
may be constituted by an electronic signal, a mark on paper, a hole in paper
or something else.[53] There is no general answer to the question of how
much latitude there is among potential lower-level property-instances that
may constitute a single higher-level property-instance. My only point is that
there is some latitude: a constituted property-instance may have any of a
variety of different kinds of nonintentional constituters, and there may be no
physical similarities among the potential constituters.[54]

Actually, the definition (P-C) is too broad. It allows that, say, an instance
of the property of having mass constitutes an instance of the property of
being a passport. To remedy that, we may define "direct property constitution" as follows:

(DP-C) x's having F at t directly constitutes x's having g at t $=_{df}$

    (a) x's having F at t constitutes x's having G at t, &
    (b) There is no H such that x's having F at t constitutes x's having H at t
        and x's having H at t constitutes x's having G at t.

---

[51] x has F but lacks G at t if the F-instance is not in G-favorable circumstances. X's having the
property of being a salt molecule is constituted by x's having the compound property of
being a sodium atom and being a chlorine atom – but only in salt-favorable circumstances.
If the properties of being a sodium atom and being a chlorine atom were instantiated in
circumstances that prevented bonding, there would be no salt molecule.

[52] This feature distinguishes my idea of property-constitution from ideas of constitution
found in Pereboom's "Robust Nonreductive Materialism" and from Clapp's "Disjunctive
Properties: Multiple Realization."

[53] For a defense of this claim, see Pereboom and Kornblith, "The Metaphysics of Irreducibility."

[54] My view differs from Pereboom's in his "Robust Nonreductive Materialism" in several
important ways. Most significantly, (i) Pereboom sets aside "any fundamentally relational
causal powers." (ii) Pereboom takes the relation between levels to be realization, where a
realizer is nomologically sufficient for the realized property. (iii) Pereboom takes the causal
powers of the realized property to be determined by ("constituted by") those of the
realizer. I differ on all scores: (i′) Assuming that causal powers derive from properties in
virtue of which something has an effect, I take almost all intentional causal powers to be
relational. (ii′) I take the relation between levels to be constitution, where a constituter is
not nomologically sufficient for the constituted property, and (iii′) I take the causal efficacy
of ID properties *not* to be determined by their constituters.

Although an instance of having mass at t may constitute an instance of being an instance of being a passport at t, there are intermediate constituters (e.g., being an aggregate of pieces of paper, plastic, and ink). So, the instance of having mass at t does not directly constitute the instance of being a passport at t. When needed, the notion of direct property constitution is available.

The third way in which my view differs from Kim's is that I reject his Causal Inheritance Principle and replace it with a principle of Independent Causal Efficacy. The causal powers of higher-level property-instances cannot be reduced to the causal powers of their constituters. Constituted property-instances confer causal powers that are "over and above" the causal powers of their constituters. The effect of a vote exceeds the effect of the constituting hand motion alone.

Some nonreductionists hold that a property-instance has independent causal efficacy if and only if it would have had its effect even if its constituter had been different.[55] I would add that the causal powers of the constituted properties are not determined by those of the constituter alone. So,

(IC) A property-instance that has an effect e has *independent causal efficacy* if and only if (i) it would have had its effect e even if its constituting property-instance had been different, and (ii) it confers causal powers that could not have been conferred by its constituting property-instance alone.

Any property whose instances have independent causal efficacy is a genuine causal property. My thesis, then, is this: ID properties generally (with mental properties as a special case) are causal properties because their instances have independent causal efficacy. Consider an example.

Let: V be Jones's voting against Smith at t.
    P be Jones's hand's going up at t
    V★ be Smith's getting angry at Jones at t′
    P★ be Smith's neural state at t′.
    C be circumstances that obtain at t in which a vote is taken by raising hands ("vote-favorable circumstances").

Suppose that V is constituted by P and that V★ is constituted by P★. By (IC), the causal powers conferred by the constituted property-instance (Jones's voting against Smith) are independent of the causal powers conferred by the constituter (Jones's hand's going up). The causal powers

---

[55] Pereboom in "Robust Nonreductive Materialism" and Pereboom and Kornblith in "The Metaphysics of Irreducibility" explain this point fully and persuasively.

conferred by Jones's hand's going up include the power to block someone's view. The causal powers conferred by Jones's voting against Smith
include the power to anger Smith – no matter how the vote was cast.

If Jones's hand had gone up in circumstances in which its going up did
not constitute a vote against Smith, its going up would not have had the
effect of angering Jones. And conversely, if the vote had been taken some
other way than by raising hands, Jones's vote still would have angered
Smith regardless of there not being a hand's going up. The contribution of
Jones's hand's going up to Smith's anger was exhausted by the fact that the
hand's going up constituted a vote against Smith. Jones's voting against
Smith would have angered Smith – no matter how the vote was cast. In
short, the causal efficacy of constituted property-instances – of mental
property-instances and of instances of ID properties generally – is independent of the causal efficacy of their constitutors. The PC View thus
shows how mental properties make a causal contribution to what happens.

The PC View also shows how constituted objects differ in their nonderivative causal powers from their constituters.[56] As we have just seen,
Jones's voting for Smith is constituted by Jones's hand's going up. Jones has
the property of voting for Smith nonderivatively; Jones has the property of
his hand's going up derivatively, in virtue of being constituted by a certain
body that has the property of its hand's going up nonderivatively. So, Jones
has different nonderivative causal powers (e.g., voting for Smith) from
Jones's body, which can only derivatively vote for Smith in virtue of
constituting something that nonderivatively votes for Smith.

SAVING NONREDUCTIVE MATERIALISM

Now I shall apply this new version of nonreductive materialism to the
metaphysical principles underlying Kim's arguments against nonreductive
mental causation. *Any* nonreductive materialist, I believe, will have to reject
three of Kim's Principles, as he intends them:[57] (a) The Physical-Realization

---

[56] I mentioned the idea of having properties (non)derivatively in chapter 2, and I shall spell
out the idea in detail in chapter 8.

[57] As I said, the term "realizer" is used in many ways by different philosophers. What is under
consideration here is Kim's use, according to which if P realizes M, then M supervenes on
P (Kim, "The Nonreductivist's Troubles with Mental Causation," pp. 196–197). Some
nonreductivists may construe "realizer" in a way that would allow them to accept (a) and
(b), suitably interpreted. I do not believe that anyone who accepts (c) should be counted as
a nonreductivist.

Thesis, which guarantees that a putatively higher-level property can be instantiated only if it is realized by lower-level properties, where realization is tantamount to reduction – since realizing properties are micro-based and hence reducible.[58] (b) The Causal-Realization Principle, which requires that the cause of any higher-level property must bring about its realizer (again, on Kim's view, its supervenience base), and thus guarantees that no irreducible higher-level property can be causally efficacious; and (c) The Causal-Inheritance Principle, which guarantees that no higher-level property-instance confers on its bearer any new causal powers.

Since each of these principles precludes irreducible, higher-level, causally efficacious properties, each should be disavowed by any nonreductionist. Indeed, the PC View provides the resources to justify rejection of each: if the PC View is correct, then the relevant relation for understanding causation is property(-instance) constitution, not physical realization; if the PC View is correct, then the Causal-Realization Principle and the Causal-Inheritance Principle are both false. Hence, if the PC View is correct, each of the principles (a)–(c) is false.

The Physical-Realization Thesis and the Causal-Realization Principle were both needed for Kim's Key Argument; the Causal-Inheritance Principle insures that higher-level properties have no independent causal efficacy. Hence, the PC View, if correct, renders Kim's argument unsound. (Conversely, of course, if Kim's argument is sound, then the three principles are true, and the PC View is incorrect.) My aim, however, is only to show that there is a coherent version of nonreductive materialism that vindicates intentional causation and that justifies discarding these three principles. No nonreductionist of any stripe can accept the three principles, and the availability of the PC View provides the grounds for rejecting them.

Finally, consider the Causal-Closure Principle. The Causal-Closure Principle says, roughly, that any physical event that has a cause at t has a complete physical cause at t.[59] On my view, all property-instances are physical in this respect: any property-instance is either identical to or ultimately *constituted by* microphysical property-instances.[60] ID properties

---

[58] Kim, *Mind in a Physical World*, p. 80. See also Kim's "Making Sense of Emergence," p. 10.

[59] Kim, "The Myth of Nonreductive Materialism," p. 280. This principle is important, says Kim, because to deny it "is to accept the Cartesian idea that some physical events have only nonphysical causes."

[60] If there is no fundamental level, then property-instances have no *ultimate* constituters at all. In that case, as I argued earlier, either the Causal-Closure Principle or the Explanatory

thus are physical properties. So, the causal efficacy of ID properties does not violate the Causal-Closure Principle.

Someone may object that ID properties as I have construed them are not really physical properties: the only physical properties are microphysical or "micro-based properties" that are just aggregates of microphysical properties.[61] Even so, the PC View would not violate the Causal-Closure Principle. Consider a case of basic action: Suppose that Jane is going through the security gate at a US airport, and she is instructed by a Federal agent to raise her arms, so that the agent can "wand" her. Jane wills[62] to raise her arms (M) and she raises them (M★). Suppose that her willing to raise her arms causes her to raise them. Let MP be the microphysical constituter of Jane's willing to raise her arms and let MP★ be the microphysical constituter of Jane's raising her arms. (Note that the relations between MP and M, on the one hand, and MP★ and M★, on the other hand, are not instances of Kim's realization relation but of my constitution relation.)

On the PC view, the microphysical *constituter* of Jane's willing to raise her arms (MP) is not a complete cause of the microphysical constituter of Jane's raising her arms (MP★). (To see that (MP) is not nomologically sufficient for (MP★), consider a world with the same laws as ours in which Jane's brain is in a vat in the same microphysical state that it's in in the example. In that world, (MP) would not cause (MP★), because in that world Jane doesn't have arms to raise. Hence, (MP) is not nomologically sufficient for (MP★). But the fact that (MP) is not a complete cause of (MP★) is no problem for causal closure. The Causal-Closure Principle requires only that MP★ *have* a complete microphysical cause, not that MP *be* that complete cause of MP★. MP is only a proper part of a larger aggregate of microproperties that is nomologically sufficient for MP★.

On the PC view, the relation between P and MP is not supervenience, but constitution. MP is only a proper part of a larger collection of microproperties that is nomologically sufficient for MP★.[63] There is no difficulty for the property-constitution view in saying: (i) Jane's willing to raise her

Exclusion Principle will have to be rejected. Here I am assuming that we will still count a microphysical cause as a *complete* cause, even if, in the absence of a fundamental level, there is no *ultimate* cause.

61 Kim, *Mind in a Physical World*, p. 114.

62 I am using "will" as an all-purpose term that covers choosing, deciding, forming an intention for the immediate future. "Will" carries no metaphysical weight here.

63 Compare Paul Noordhof, "Causation by Content?" *Mind & Language* 14 (1999): 291–320; Gabriel Segal and Elliott Sober, "The Causal Efficacy of Content," *Philosophical Studies* 63 (1991): 1–30; and E. J. Lowe, "The Causal Autonomy of the Mental," *Mind* 102 (1993):

arms is constituted by MP; (ii) Jane's raising her arms is constituted by MP★; (iii) Jane's willing to raise her arms causes her to raise her arms; but (iv) MP does not cause MP★.[64] If the microphysical state of one sizable spatiotemporal region that ends at the time of Jane's willing caused the microphysical state of a slightly later sizable region that begins at the time of Jane's raising her arms, then the Causal-Closure Principle is honored.[65] So, although the PC View does not require MP to be causally sufficient for MP★, the PC View nevertheless does not violate the Causal-Closure Principle.[66]

One last question about the PC View: What is the relation between constitution and supervenience? Although constitution is not itself a supervenience relation, constitution is compatible with global, or near-global, supervenience. Although a constituted property-instance does not supervene on its constituting property-instances, it may supervene ultimately on its subatomic constituters *together with* the microphysical supervenience base of all the circumstances in which the instance of the constitution relation obtains.[67] The supervenience base will be very broad – too broad to be specified or to be useful in explanation – but it may be metaphysically sufficient for the constituted property-instance. So, there is no logical conflict between global supervenience and the PC View.[68]

CONCLUSION

In this chapter, I have done four things: (1) I set out in detail Kim's Key Argument against nonreductive mental causation and showed that it is

---

629–644. I discovered these articles after I had written the paragraph to which this note is appended.

[64] Of course, on Kim's view MP does cause, and cause completely MP★, but I am trying to show that one can deny that the micro-constituter of a willing to raise her arms (MP) completely causes the micro-constituter of her raising her arms (MP★) without violating the Causal Closure Principle.

[65] There is much more to be said about the Causal-Closure Principle. Kim holds that physicalism "need not be, and should not be, identified with micro-physicalism." In that case, if we disentangle the Causal-Closure Principle from the thesis of mereological supervenience, my own nonreductive view satisfies the Causal-Closure Principle. See Kim, *Mind in a Physical World*, p. 117.

[66] We may still have a harmless kind of overdetermination. But note that the overdetermination is generated by the whole supervenience base, not by the constituter.

[67] Constitution is contingent and highly context-dependent; supervenience is necessary and independent of context.

[68] Even if near-global supervenience is correct, I suspect that we will never come close to specifying even one supervenience base for any ID property. And hence, we will never come close to specifying a complete microphysical cause for any ID event.

valid. (2) I showed that, if Kim's Key Argument were sound, it would make nonmental intentional properties epiphenomenal; and this is good reason to think that the Key Argument is unsound. We have no idea how to do without nonmental intentional properties in causal explanation. (3) I presented a nonreductive model of causation – the PC View – that vindicates irreducible intentional causation with mental causation as a special case. The PC View justifies rejection of Kim's Key Argument. (4) I have shown where my view is and is not consistent with Kim's metaphysical principles.

The property-constitution version of nonreductive materialism vindicates commonsense causation. It shows how ordinary things can be causally efficacious in virtue of their everyday properties. It also provides a principled reason to reject reductive views that exclude commonsense causation. Nonreductive materialism in general is the most promising metaphysical view for understanding the everyday world – the world filled with ordinary things like people and artifacts and artworks. Only nonreductive materialism offers a metaphysics that takes ordinary things and their interactions with them at face value and makes them intelligible.[69]

[69] I am grateful to Jonathan Schaffer, Gareth B. Matthews, and Hilary Kornblith for reading drafts of this chapter and making helpful suggestions.

6

Metaphysical vagueness

Vagueness has become a central topic in analytic philosophy. It is obvious that much of our language is vague. Words like "fat," "wealthy," "friendly," "tall," "happy" are unquestionably vague: each is subject to borderline cases where the predicate in question neither clearly applies nor clearly fails to apply. Every concept that applies to the everyday world – every empirical concept – is subject to borderline cases, and hence is vague.[1] One might think that the vagueness of our empirical concepts is to be explained by vagueness in the world; however, many philosophers begin with the pre-supposition that the reality to which our concepts apply is not vague: The standard view today is that reality itself is precise. Given the fact that all of our empirical evidence suggests that the world, as well as our language, is vague, one may wonder why philosophers are so intent on denying what seems obvious. Well, there is a reason.

Typically, interest in vagueness stems from interest in logic and semantics: Philosophers are looking for logic and semantics to handle vague language. Concern about logic and semantics leads one to treat vagueness in a way that preserves, for example, the law of excluded middle, according to which "p v ∼p" is a logical truth. And vagueness in the world would seem to threaten the law of excluded middle. If there were vagueness in the world and Sam, say, was borderline bald, then there would be cases where "Sam is bald or Sam is not bald" would not be true, and the law of excluded middle would be violated. The concern to understand vague language in a way that saves the classical logical truths has led philosophers to suppose that reality, considered apart from language-users, is perfectly precise; vagueness is a matter of language and thought.

---

[1] Bertrand Russell thought so, anyway. See his "Vagueness," *Australasian Journal of Philosophy and Psychology* 1 (1923): 84–92.

Let me sketch two influential approaches that explain vague language in ways that preserve the law of excluded middle – epistemicism and supervaluation. Epistemicism is the view that borderline cases are only a matter of language, of the crudeness of our discriminatory powers. There really is some number n such that a person with n hairs or fewer is bald, but a person with n + 1 hairs is not bald. There are cut-off points in nature. Vagueness is wholly a matter of our language and is a result of our ignorance of the cut-off points in reality. So, no matter how many hairs Sam has, "Sam is bald" is definitely true or definitely false; we just do not know which. So, if epistemicism is correct, there is no threat to classical logic.

The other common strategy for explaining vague language without assuming vagueness in the world is supervaluation. Consider a vague word like "young". Some people are definitely young (e.g., 10-year-olds); some people are definitely not young (e.g., 85-year-olds); and some are neither definitely young nor definitely not young (e.g., 32-year-olds and 54-year-olds). The supervaluation strategy is to sharpen or to "precisify" the predicate "young" by considering all the different ages, within the area of "neither definitely young nor definitely not young" – an area where lines may be drawn to distinguish between "young" and "not young." Each line marks an age, at which or younger than which a person counts as young; and older than which a person counts as not young. Given such a line – a "precisification" – the borderline cases are eliminated, and each sentence is either true or false relative to it.

If Sam is borderline young – neither definitely young nor definitely not young – the vague sentence "Sam is young" will be true on some precisifications (places to draw a line between "young" and "not young") and false on others. On each such precisification, "Sam is young" will be true or false relative to that precisification. For a sentence to be true (or false) *simpliciter*, however, is for it to be true (or false) on *all* admissible precisifications. Such sentences are called "supertrue" (or "superfalse"). Any sentence that is neither supertrue nor superfalse lacks truth value. Since "Sam is young" is true on some admissible precisifications and false on others, "Sam is young" has no truth value. By contrast, "Sam is young or Sam is not young," and all the other truths of classical logic, are true on all admissible precisifications and hence are supertrue. In this way, supervaluationists hold, the word "young" is vague, but reality need not be vague: in the world, there are just people at various ages, on which the word "young" may be sharpened. We need not attribute any vagueness to the world. On supervaluationism, every sentence is either supertrue or superfalse or it lacks truth value altogether (and is vague).[2] All the logical truths (e.g., "Sam is young or Sam is not young") hold; they are true on all admissible precisifications, and thus are supertrue. And this is so even if "Sam is young" remains vague. The effect of supervaluation is to acknowledge vague language but to render it irrelevant to logic.

It is to protect classical logic and formal semantics, I believe, that many philosophers locate vagueness wholly in language and thought. (There is a vast technical literature that reflects this interest.)[3] Although I share some of that interest, I do not take formal semantics to be an end in itself, and I do not take the law of excluded middle as an a priori constraint on reality. It is less than self-evident that reality must conform to the law of excluded middle – in light of the facts that all the empirical evidence suggests the contrary and that there are alternative systems of formal logic.[4] As I argued in chapter 1, metaphysics should be rooted in reflection on matters for which we have empirical evidence. Methodologically, formal semantics should follow metaphysics, and not the other way around.

In order to motivate my views about metaphysical vagueness – vagueness in the world – let me give two simple direct arguments for the conclusion that not all vagueness is linguistic. Then, I shall locate vagueness in constituted objects (specifically, in their spatial and temporal boundaries) and in the constitution relation itself. Finally, I shall turn to the sorites arguments that hold centerstage in standard discussions of vagueness.

ARGUMENTS FOR METAPHYSICAL VAGUENESS

The view that vagueness is not in the world, but in our language, was forcefully expressed by David Lewis:

---

[2] In "Vague, So Untrue" (*Noûs*, 41 (2007): 133–156), David Braun and Theodore Sider argue that no sentence that contains a vague term (not even "a person with zero hairs is bald") is true; hence almost no English sentence is true. But they argue that this claim does not have dire consequences since vagueness should be (and typically is) ignored.

[3] For an excellent overview of the positions on vagueness, see Timothy Williamson, *Vagueness* (London: Routledge, 1994). See papers in Delia Graff and Timothy Williamson, eds., *Vagueness* (Burlington, VT: Ashgate Publishing Co., 2002); Rosanna Keefe and Peter Smith, eds., *Vagueness: A Reader* (Cambridge, MA: MIT/Bradford, 1996). For an argument that all vagueness is either metaphysical or epistemic – and that there is no third variety of vagueness that is linguistic – see Trenton Merricks, "Varieties of Vagueness," *Philosophy and Phenomenological Research* 62 (2001): 145–157.

[4] J. C. Beall and Greg Restall, "Logical Pluralism," *Australasian Journal of Philosophy* 78 (2000): 475–493.

The only intelligible account of vagueness locates it in our thought and language. The reason it's vague where the outback begins is not that there's this thing, the outback, with imprecise borders; rather there are many things, with different borders, and nobody has been fool enough to try to enforce a choice of one of them as the official referent of the word "outback." Vagueness is semantic indecision.[5]

Lewis may be right about the outback, but I do not believe that we can account for vagueness generally as semantic indecision. I have two very simple one-step arguments against those who deny that there's vagueness in reality, and locate all vagueness in our language or concepts.

Argument from semantic indecision

1. All vagueness is a matter of semantic indecision only if, for every instance of vagueness, it is within our ability to eliminate it by making some semantic decision.
2. Much vagueness is ineliminable: it is not within our ability to eliminate it by making some semantic decision.
∴3. Not all vagueness is a matter of semantic indecision.

Premise 1: Some – but admittedly not all – who argue that all vagueness is linguistic, in fact do argue that vagueness could be eliminated.[6] They say, e.g., that we could be precise about what is baldness – e.g., having fewer than n hairs on one's head – but we do not bother, because such specificity is not useful. The point of holding that all vagueness is a matter of semantic indecision (however the thesis is expressed) is that vagueness is held to be "up to us"; it is not in "the world as it is in itself." If vagueness is up to us, it would seem that we could eliminate it if we wanted to.[7]

Premise 2: But we could not eliminate vagueness – even if we wanted to.[8] If we could, then for any predicate "F" that is vague, we could we

---

[5] David Lewis, *On the Plurality of Worlds* (Oxford: Blackwell, 1986), pp. 212–213.

[6] Some philosophers who take vagueness to be semantic indeterminacy may reject Premise 1 of Argument 1; but Argument 2 applies to them. Also, epistemicists about vagueness do not hold that all vagueness is a matter of semantic indecision, but rather that vagueness is our ignorance of what our words mean. So this first argument may not apply to epistemicists; but I believe that the second argument does apply to epistemicists. For a discussion of the various approaches to vagueness (such as supervaluationism, epistemicism, many-valued logics, etc.), see Williamson, *Vagueness*.

[7] Supervaluationists who reject Premise 1 owe us an explanation of the fact (that they acknowledge) that we cannot eliminate vagueness from language. The most plausible explanation seems to me to be that vagueness in language often reflects vagueness in the world.

[8] The fact that vagueness is ineliminable explains why good judgment is such an important virtue, and why good judgment cannot be replaced by algorithms.

draw a line as the example of "bald" (misleadingly) suggests. But any line (like having fewer than so many hairs on one's head) reveals new vague predicates – in this case, "is a hair." (Is a broken follicle a hair?) Vagueness may be pushed around, but not eliminated, by our decisions. (Interestingly, Bertrand Russell would have agreed: all natural language, he argued, is infected with vagueness, and hence [he thought] unsuitable for logic.[9])

A word may be vague in one of two ways: the items in the extension of the word may each be precise, but it may be indeterminate which of a range of individually precise items is in the extension of the word. If hairs were precisely individuated, for example, then "bald" would be vague in this first way: we could just draw a line at such-and-such number of hairs, and declare anyone with fewer than that number of hairs to be bald.[10] There is another way that a word can be vague, however: The items in the extension of the word may themselves be vague.[11] Not only do politically charged expressions (like "sexual harassment") have extensions that are vague in this second sense,[12] but so do less charged words like "gossip," and uncharged words like "paying attention" or the word "vague" itself.[13] The extensions of such words are vague, not because we have failed (or declined) to draw a line, but rather because there is no line to be drawn. To try to "sharpen" such words would be to lose them altogether. Therefore, not all vagueness is a matter of semantic indecision. As we shall see, the vagueness in language cannot be isolated from vagueness in the world.

---

[9] For a critical discussion, see Williamson's *Vagueness*, pp. 52ff.

[10] Even this would be inaccurate since baldness also depends on the location and distribution of hairs.

[11] Consider the concept of "killing." The concept of killing seems clear enough: a kills b if and only if a causes b's death. Killing does not even require an intention: lightning can kill. Here is a partly fictional case: A middle-aged professional woman (call her "Jane") has an affair with a vain and famous doctor (call him "Bill"), who is about to abandon Jane for a younger woman. Jane loves Bill and in her desperation, she takes a small revolver and goes to Bill's house – intending, as she says later, to kill herself in front of him. Bill grabs the gun; in the scuffle with both Bill's and Jane's hands on the gun, the gun goes off at close range. Bill is fatally shot. Did Jean kill the doctor? (This story is loosely based on my recollection of the killing of the celebrated "diet doctor," Dr. Tarnower by Jean Harris. Harris was convicted by a jury of murder.)

[12] Wittgenstein on rule-following comes to mind here. There are too many ways of harassing that no one has yet thought of that may or may not end up in the extension of the concept.

[13] J. L. Austin pointed out, " 'Vague' is itself vague." *Sense and Sensibilia* (Oxford: Oxford University Press, 1962), p. 125.

Argument from natural processes

1. If, independently of our concepts, there is anything that exists or occurs in the world that does not have a precise beginning, then there is vagueness in objects that is not simply a product of how we decide to use our words.
2. Independently of our concepts, natural processes occur in the world and do not have precise beginnings.
∴ 3. There is vagueness in objects that is not simply a product of how we decide to use our words.

Premise 1: Premise 1, on a straightforward reading, is just a matter of definition.[14] If, independently of our concepts, something comes into existence, and there is no precise instant before which it definitely failed to exist, and after which it definitely existed, then, by definition, it has a vague beginning independently of our concepts. If something has a vague beginning independently of our concepts, then our concepts are irrelevant to its vagueness. If our concepts are irrelevant to the vagueness of something, then then there is vagueness in objects that is not simply a product of how we decide to use our words.

Premise 2: Premise 2 is a matter of taking special sciences – like astronomy and biology – at face value. Astronomers and biologists understand their domain to be natural processes that occur in nature, independently of our concepts – processes that would transpire in the absence of any of our concepts. The evolution of our solar system is an example of a natural process. Astronomers give us good reason to believe that our solar system evolved, and that its evolution was a natural process. If the best astronomy today is correct, then our solar system did not begin at a precise instant. For example, there are times at which the sun definitely does not exist, and times at which the sun definitely exists, and countless times in between when the sun neither definitely exists nor definitely fails to exist.

Everything that comes into being by a process (natural or artifactual) has a vague beginning. The sun, for example, would have had a vague beginning even if we (with our words and concepts) had never existed. If astronomers are correct in saying that our solar system evolved over eons, then that's the way the world is, regardless of our language. If the

---

[14] I mention a straightforward reading of Premise 1, because supervaluationists may interpret Premise 1 as a metalinguistic statement about the truth-values of various sentences.

sun has a vague temporal boundary that does not depend on our concepts, then there is metaphysical vagueness.[15]

We may cast the point as a dilemma: Either there are sharp cut-off points in reality or there are not. If there are no sharp cut-off points in reality, then there is metaphysical vagueness. If there are sharp cut-off points in reality, then no science that conceptualizes objects as lacking sharp boundaries (e.g., astronomy and biology), can be correct.[16] Not only would such a claim be prima facie implausible, but also it should be unattractive to realists of any naturalistic stripe. So, there is metaphysical vagueness.

WHERE IN THE WORLD IS VAGUENESS?

What, then, in the world is vague? What sorts of things are vague? I shall argue that there are several kinds of vagueness in the world:

(1) There are vague objects, in that there are objects with indeterminate spatial and temporal boundaries.[17]
(2) The constitution relation itself is vague, in two ways:
   (a) There are cases in which it is indeterminate whether a (putative) constituter constitutes anything at some time t; and
   (b) Even where there definitely is a constituted object, there are cases in which it is indeterminate what microphysical constituter constitutes it at t.[18]

---

[15] My claim that there is vagueness in the world is consistent with Lewis's and Sider's claim that composition is never vague. Constitution is a distinct relation from mereological composition. See chapters 9 and 10.

[16] Granted that scientists still find Newtonian physics useful even if incorrect. But the case of objects' lacking sharp boundaries is not analogous to the case of Newtonian physics. Newtonian physics was superseded by relativity theory, but there is no prospect of current sciences being superseded by sciences that conceptualize objects as having sharp boundaries. I doubt that scientists would see any need to replace their theories for such metaphysical reasons.

[17] For a sample of other discussions of vague objects (construed in various ways), see Michael Tye, "Vague Objects," *Mind* 99 (1990): 535–557; Peter van Inwagen, "How to Reason About Vague Objects," *Philosophical Topics* 16 (1988): 255–284; Michael Morreau, "What Vague Objects are Like," *Journal of Philosophy* 99 (2002): 333–361; Eddy M. Zemach, "Vague Objects," *Noûs* 25 (1991): 323–340; Brian Garrett, "Vague Identity and Vague Objects," *Noûs* 25 (1991): 341–351; Harold W. Noonan, "Are There Vague Objects?" *Analysis* 64 (2004): 131–134.

[18] The indeterminacy is not a matter of ignorance of which aggregate is the constituter at t. As we saw in chapter 1, we have no conceptual access to particular microphysical aggregates. We have no way to identify particular microphysical aggregates that may constitute an ordinary object at a time, except by reference to the ordinary object.

All these kinds of vagueness in the world may be grouped together as vagueness of states of affairs. Following Williamson, we may take states of affairs to be ontological correlates of sentences.[19] If x is an object, P is a property and t is a time, there is the state of affairs that x has P at t. That state of affairs obtains if and only if x has P at t. Then a state of affairs, s, is borderline if and only if it is vague whether s obtains – that is to say if and only if s neither definitely obtains nor definitely fails to obtain. If any state of affairs is borderline, then there is vagueness in the world.[20]

When I say that ordinary objects are vague objects, I am speaking of objects that exist *simpliciter* (i.e., are in the ontology; see chapter 11), but have certain properties vaguely – properties like existing at t, having a certain part at t.[21] So, my talk of vague objects is talk of borderline states of affairs. Although I eschew vague identities, talk of vague identities can also be construed as talk of borderline states of affairs, the state of affairs of x's being identical with y. In the next two sections, I shall consider the various kinds of vagueness in the world – the various kinds of states of affairs that are subject to borderline cases.

SPATIAL AND TEMPORAL BOUNDARIES

Everyday objects are liable to particular types of vagueness: indeterminacy of spatial boundaries and indeterminacy of temporal boundaries. Although there are spatial points and temporal points at which it is indeterminate whether x exists *there* or *then*, the indeterminacy of x at those spatial and temporal points is parasitic on the *determinacy* of x's existence elsewhere. For example, it is never the case that it is indeterminate whether an object exists at t unless there is some other time at which it determinately exists. So the indeterminacy of temporal boundaries of an object presupposes that the object exists at some time or other. The vagueness of an object with indeterminate temporal boundaries may be understood as the vagueness of

---

[19] Timothy Williamson, "Vagueness in Reality," in Michael J. Loux and Dean Zimmerman, eds., *The Oxford Handbook of Metaphysics* (Oxford: Oxford University Press, 2003), pp. 699–701.

[20] So, I am not taking metaphysical vagueness to imply that there is any vagueness in matters of identity, or that there is indeterminate identity. See Gareth Evans, "Can There Be Vague Objects?" *Analysis* 38 (1978): 208.

[21] Others use the term "vague objects" differently. E.g., Williamson, "Vagueness in Reality," pp. 701–704.

a state of affairs – the object's existing at t.[22] In short, ordinary objects are vague in that they have imprecise spatial and temporal boundaries.

Spatial vagueness

Consider a hair on your dog that is coming out. Does that hair help make up the dog or not? That is, is that hair a constituent of the dog? Many would agree that it is indeterminate whether that hair is a constituent of the dog. The dog's spatial boundaries are vague.[23] The problem generalizes. Consider any ordinary object – your house, say. There are numerous aggregates of particles in the vicinity of your house only minutely different from each other, each of which is an equally good candidate for constituting the house. Hence, your house's spatial boundaries are vague – as are the spatial boundaries of every medium-sized object.

Part of the idea of x's being spatially vague is that at any time that x exists, there is some spatial region that x occupies. In that region, there are some places – e.g., the place where the head joins the torso of the dog – where the dog definitely (but not entirely) exists, and there are some other spatial places – e.g., the place where the loose hair is – where it is indeterminate whether the dog exists there. Any primary kind, F, whose instances are in the everyday world, has instances that exist at t such that there is some spatial place l, that is definitely within the region occupied by the F at t, and there is some other spatial place l', that is neither definitely within the region occupied by the F at t nor definitely outside the region occupied by the F at t. So, it is indeterminate whether the F exists at l' at t or not.

My opponents agree that the spatial boundaries of the dog are vague, but they trace the indeterminacy to indeterminacy in the concept *dog*. On their view, the vagueness is just a matter of reference; we just have not decided whether the expression "dog" should refer to the precise thing that contains the hair or the mostly overlapping precise thing that does not contain the hair. On my view, the vagueness is not exhausted by any

---

[22] The relation between an object's existing at t and existing simpliciter (being in the ontology) is discussed in detail in chapter 11.

[23] I speak of spatial boundaries rather than of parts here because I believe that the role of parts has been vastly (and misleadingly) overemphasized in contemporary metaphysics. But the vagueness of spatial boundaries of ordinary objects may also be thought of as vagueness of parts.

indeterminacy in the concept *dog*. An animal that may have loose hairs is what the concept *dog* is a concept *of*.

On my view, then, the vagueness is metaphysical: the vagueness in our concepts is (at least sometimes) a result of the vagueness in objects. Primary-kind concepts of medium-sized objects (*dog*, *table*, etc.) are concepts of things that lack precise spatial boundaries; anything that falls under such concepts in fact lacks precise spatial boundaries. My point does not concern the determinacy of the extension of *dog*, or whether there are borderline cases of dogs. Rather, my point concerns the things that definitely are dogs. Whether the extension of *dog* is determinate or not, Fido is such that: it is determinate that he is in the extension *dog* and it is indeterminate that he has exactly such-and-such spatial boundaries. Our concept *dog* is not just an imprecise way of picking out something that is precise. Medium-sized objects are typically spatially vague.

Temporal vagueness

Consider a model house that you build. At the time when you acquire the blocks and the inverted v-shaped piece for the roof out of which you plan to build the model house, there definitely is no model house (yet). When you give the completed model house to your daughter as a present, there definitely is a model house. Is there a precise moment in which the model house comes into existence? I believe that the answer is no.

There is no precise instant at which you finish the model house either. Let t be a time after which you have finished building the model house. Let B be the aggregate of the blocks and the inverted v-shaped piece. Since B is in model-house-favorable circumstances at t, according to the Constitution View, there is a model house such that B constitutes it at t.

Now consider a slightly earlier time, t', at which you had put the blocks together but had not yet put the roof on. At t', the constituter B (the aggregate of all the blocks and the inverted v-shaped piece for the roof) definitely existed, but B was not in model-house-favorable circumstances at t' inasmuch as the inverted v-shaped piece was still on the floor then. Let B' be the aggregate of the blocks without the inverted v-shaped piece. Did the model house exist at t'? It is not definitely true that the model house existed at t' since the v-shaped piece for the roof was still on the floor. So, it is either definitely false that the model house existed at t' or it is indeterminate that the model house existed at t'. I take it to be indeterminate that the model house existed at t'. We can give a necessary (but hardly sufficient) condition for the indeterminacy about whether B′ constitutes a model house at t′: It is indeterminate whether a model house exists during t′ only if: there is something (viz., B′) that exists at t′ in some but not all model-house-favorable circumstances, and there is something (viz., B) related to B′ in an appropriate way and some time t (≠t′) such that B constituted a model house at t.

So, on a constitutional approach to temporal vagueness, its being indeterminate whether x exists at t′ requires that there is some other time, t, such that x definitely exists at t. Determinate objects (i.e., objects that determinately exist) may have indeterminate temporal boundaries. (And conversely, any object that has an indeterminate temporal boundary is a determinate object.) Indeterminate existence is thus parasitic on determinate existence. In this way, there is something that definitely exists at some time that we refer to when we say that it is indeterminate whether *it* exists at t′.[24]

There is a perhaps surprising epistemic asymmetry in this view: On the one hand, if, after the model house was completed, you removed the roof, we would know that it is indeterminate that the model house exists then. We would know this, because we know that the model house definitely existed before the roof was removed. But on the other hand, we cannot know at t′, before the house is completed, that it is indeterminate whether B′ constitutes a model house then. We cannot know this, because we do not know at t′ whether there ever definitely exists a model house in the vicinity. If you had got bored at t′ and had stopped building before putting the roof on top, then there would not have been a model house that existed indeterminately at t′. There would have been no model house at all. This is a consequence of the dependence of indeterminate existence on determinate existence.

"Surely," someone may object, "you were building something. What was it if not a model house?" To which I reply: Building something is an intentional activity, subject to the phenomenon of "intentional inexistence." You can be building something that never gets built in the same way that you can hunt for something (like unicorns) that never exist. If there is never definitely a model house in the vicinity, then there is never a time at which an aggregate indeterminately constitutes a model house in the

---

[24] So, there is no vague identity. The house such that it is indeterminate that it exists at t is identical to the house such that it is determinate that it exists at t′. Thus, we do not need indeterminate identity statements that, as Gareth Evans showed, lead to contradiction when coupled with the thesis that there are vague objects. See Evans, "Can There Be Vague Objects?" p. 208.

vicinity. (So, it is not indeterminate how many objects there are simpliciter; what is indeterminate is that at any time t, there are n objects at t.)[25]

Cases of temporal vagueness are not just confined to artifacts. Anything that comes into existence by means of a process is subject to this kind of indeterminacy. Temporal vagueness (as well as spatial vagueness) affects natural objects like animals as well. When does an animal come into existence? Is there an exact moment? No. A mammalian fertilized egg is not an animal. A fertilized egg is capable of twinning and producing two animals. If such a fertilized egg were an animal, then it would follow that one thing could be identical to two things. But it is logically impossible for one animal to be identical to two animals. So, an animal does not come into existence at fertilization. Moreover, fertilization itself is not instantaneous; it too is a process. It takes time for the sperm to enter the egg. There is a temporal interval during which it is indeterminate whether the egg has been fertilized.

Every kind of macroscopic entity encountered in the natural world admits of borderline cases of existence. If F is a macro-primary-kind property (e.g., being a frog, being a table), then individuals that have F as their primary-kind property are temporally vague. By saying that an object is temporally vague, I mean that there are times when it is indeterminate whether or not it exists at those times. When your house is partially built, it is neither true nor false that there is a house there. No objects that we encounter in the world pop into existence or go out of existence instantaneously. Again, I am not talking about our concepts, but rather about what our concepts are concepts *of.* Our concepts are concepts of things that come into existence gradually. For any x, if x comes into existence gradually, then x has an indeterminate temporal boundary.

THE VAGUENESS OF THE CONSTITUTION RELATION

The constitution relation is a vague relation.[26] That is, there are circumstances in which it is indeterminate whether the constitution relation holds

---

[25] For a discussion of existence simpliciter and existence at a time, see chapter 11. For a critical discussion of Sider's assumption that no numerical sentence of the form "There are n concrete objects" can ever be indeterminate, see Kathrin Koslicki's "The Crooked Path from Vagueness to Four-Dimensionalism," *Philosophical Studies* 114 (2003): 107–134.

[26] This is one reason to distinguish constitution from mereological composition. David Lewis: "If composition obeys a vague restriction, then it must sometimes be a vague matter whether composition takes place or not. And that is impossible." *On the Plurality of Worlds,* p. 212.

at t between x and y, or even whether x constitutes anything at t. In chapter 9, I shall argue that, at each moment of its existence, every ordinary object is constituted at some level by some microphysical aggregate or other. (Since I am accepting universalism in mereology, an aggregate is a mereological sum or fusion.) The identity conditions of an aggregate are obvious: Aggregate A = Aggregate B just in case A and B contain exactly the same objects. Since the identity of an aggregate is wholly determined by the objects aggregated, an aggregate – unlike a constituted object – is precise. An aggregate of, say, my dining room chairs is precise, despite the fact that the chairs are themselves vague objects.[27]

The point is twofold: every constituted object is vague and is constituted, perhaps vaguely, by a nonvague microphysical aggregate. The distinction between precise microphysical aggregates and the vague objects they constitute will allow us to explain vagueness of spatial boundaries, of temporal boundaries, and of parts of constituted objects. I'll give three examples of vagueness in the world, none of which leads to indeterminacy of identity:[28]

First, by distinguishing between aggregates and constituted objects, we can acknowledge objects with vague spatial boundaries. Let "Schmeverest" refer to a mountain-shaped object just like the referent of "Everest" except that Schmeverest includes slightly more of the foothills (say an inch in diameter around the bottom) than Everest. Now ask:

(1) Is Everest identical to Schmeverest?

This question has spawned a huge line of literature, because it seems to lead to a puzzle: If the answer to (1) is yes, then since Everest and Shmeverest differ in spatial boundary, Leibniz's Law (the indiscernibility of identicals) is violated. But if the answer to (1) is no, then we are left wondering in virtue of what does "Everest" refer to in the object with the slightly smaller spatial area?

---

[27] For details, as well as a discussion of parthood relations, see chapter 9. Every constituted object at some level is constituted by an aggregate. But, of course, not all constituters are aggregates: a silver dollar is constituted by a piece of silver, which in turn is constituted by an aggregate of Ag atoms.

[28] Again, see Evans, "Can There Be Vague Objects?" (p. 208) for an influential argument that identity cannot be vague. Also, see Nathan P. Salmon, *Reference and Essence* (Oxford: Blackwell, 1982). For an opposing view, see van Inwagen, "How to Reason About Vague Objects."

This puzzle disappears on the Constitution View. There is only one mountain where Everest is. There are not multiple overlapping mountains; we do not have to decide which one is Everest. The vagueness concerns which aggregate constitutes Everest, the one and only mountain that we are talking about. "Everest" determinately refers to a vague spatial region, rather than being indeterminate in reference between a number of precise regions.[29] In ordinary language, "Everest" refers to a mountain – an object with vague boundaries. If the answer to (1) is yes, then "Schmeverest" refers to the very same mountain, with the every same vague boundaries. The questioner who asks (1) seriously must be using "Everest" and "Schmeverest" (non-standardly) to refer to aggregates, not to mountains. In this case, the answer to (1) is straightforwardly no: "Schmeverest" definitely refers to a different aggregate from "Everest."

The vagueness arises, not from what "Everest" refers to, but from the availability of many candidates to be the aggregate that constitutes Everest. What is vague in reality is which of the many candidate aggregates is the constituter of (spatially vague) Everest. So, on the Constitution View, there is no puzzle of identity.[30] The puzzle putatively about identity arises from failure to distinguish the mountain from the aggregate that constitutes it. But reality includes the vague mountain as well as all the precise microphysical aggregates as genuine objects in the ontology. And it is the mountain that is of primary interest in a metaphysics of everyday life.

Second, by distinguishing between aggregates and constituted objects, we can acknowledge objects with vague beginnings. Suppose that construction is underway of a house that you contracted to have built. At time t, it is partially built, but is not definitely a house. Does a house partially exist at t? Not on my view. It is either indeterminate or false that there exists a house at t. If the construction stops, and there is never definitely a house there, then it is (definitely) false that a house exists at t. All that exists at t is an aggregate in some but not all house-favorable circumstances; but there's no house at t. On the other hand, if the construction continues to completion at t', and at t' there is definitely a house there, then it is indeterminate that a house exists at t. The house that exists at t' had a vague beginning, and the house is such that it indeterminately existed at t

---

[29] This is a paraphrase of Williamson, where he is arguing that this sort of treatment is not inconsistent with the Evans–Salmon argument. *Vagueness*, p. 256.

[30] However, in "Vague Identity and Quantum Indeterminacy," *Analysis* 54 (1994): 110–114, E. J. Lowe has argued that there are quantum-mechanical cases in which there is no fact of the matter about whether an electron x is identical to electron y.

and determinately exists at t′. As we have seen, vagueness of beginning existence is parasitic on determinate existence. And in the next case, we shall see that determinate existence is compatible with vagueness of (spatial) parts of ordinary objects.

Third, by distinguishing between aggregates and constituted objects, we can acknowledge objects with vague parts. Consider Jane's cat, Felix, who is shedding, and one of his loose hairs, x, is on the verge of falling out at t. Is x a part of Felix at t? The answer does not depend on the identity of Felix; as before, it depends on which aggregate constitutes Felix at t. (Jane has only one cat, and she takes good care of that one cat.) It is indeterminate which aggregate constitutes Felix at t. We know that Felix exists at t and that he has various hairs in various states of falling out at t. (So, we also know that Felix is not identical to any aggregate since aggregates are precise.) The object that Jane loves is Felix, the cat. Of course, there is a fact of the matter about which cat he is. (He is essentially a cat.) There is no fact of the matter about which aggregate of particles constitutes Felix.

Although I believe that there is vagueness in the world, my view is consistent with holding that there is no vagueness in the number of things that exist in a world of finite things.[31] On my view, it may be indeterminate which properties an object has (such as when it came into existence). But in order for there to be such an indeterminacy the object must definitely exist at some time. Objects may be (and usually are) vague in that they have vague spatial and temporal boundaries without there being any indeterminacy in identity. As Stalnaker pointed out: "[I]f we insist that, say, Mt. Rainier is a vague individual, and that the name 'Mt. Rainier' refers determinately to this individual, we do not thereby commit ourselves to vague identities."[32]

SORITES ARGUMENTS

The mention of vagueness brings to philosophers' minds the sorites argument. The sorites is a logical paradox – a problem in logic, not in metaphysics. Nevertheless, one may wonder, if, as I have argued, there is vagueness in

---

[31] Although, for any time, there may be indeterminacy about the number of objects that exist then, there is no indeterminacy in the number of objects that ever exist, or exist simpliciter. For discussion, see Peter van Inwagen, "The Number of Things," *Philosophical Issues 12, Realism and Relativism* (2002): 176–196.

[32] Robert Stalnaker, "Vague Identity," in David Austin, ed., *Philosophical Analysis* (Dordrecht, Holland: Kluwer Academic Publishers, 1988), p. 359.

the world, how should an advocate of metaphysical vagueness respond to the sorites? Here's an example of a sorites that follows from the Argument from Natural Processes given earlier. Recall that even if existence simpliciter is not a property, existing at time t is. So, where x exists simpliciter, x's existing at t is a state of affairs:

Let t_1 be 1 year after the Big Bang (measured by oscillations of cesium atoms).
Let t_n be midnight (Greenwich Mean Time) 1/1/2007 CE.
Let $t_i = t_{i-1} + 1$ minute. (So, $t_{i-1} = t_i - 1$ minute.)

Now consider this argument:[33]

At t_1, the Earth did not exist.
If at t_1 the Earth did not exist, then at t_2 ($= t_1 + 1$ minute) the Earth did not exist.
If at t_2 the Earth did not exist, then at t_3 ($= t_2 + 1$ minute) the Earth did not exist.
.
.
.
If at $t_n - 1$ minute, the Earth did not exist, then at t_n the Earth did not exist.
∴ At t_n the Earth did not exist.

Since t_n is midnight GMT 1/1/2007 CE, the conclusion is this:

At midnight GMT 1/1/2007 CE, the Earth did not exist.

The argument is valid: in all models in which all the premises are true, the conclusion is true.[34] The first premises are true. Since there does not seem to be an exact cut-off point at which the Earth began to exist, each of the intermediate premises seems true. But the conclusion is patently false: The Earth definitely existed at midnight GMT 1/1/2007 CE. A logical conundrum! Although there is a huge literature on the sorites paradox, no one, I think, has a satisfactory solution.[35] Among the solutions are ones that take vagueness to be handled by truth-value gaps, and proponents of

---

[33] Time is dense: Between any two instants, there is another instant. So, after t, there is no next instant. But to state the temporal sorites, we must appeal to next times (minutes, nanoseconds, etc.) – times that are intervals not instants. Hence, in stating the temporal sorites, we are already abstracting from reality.

[34] Or at least: In no models in which all the premises are true is the conclusion false. The sorites looks valid on either construal of validity.

[35] The leading theories – supervaluation, epistemicism, multi-valued logic, and fuzzy semantics – all have counterintuitive consequences. According to supervaluationism, "p v ~p" is supertrue even though neither "p" nor "~p" is supertrue; moreover, "∃xFx" may be true, yet there may fail to be any object a such that "Fa" is true. According to fuzzy semantics, the degree of truth of a conjunction is not a function of the degrees of truth of its conjuncts. (See Williamson, *Vagueness*, pp. 135–138.) According to epistemicism, there is a number n, such that someone with n dollars or more is rich, but

metaphysical vagueness can avail themselves of such solutions. Although a technical discussion of logics with truth-value gaps is beyond the scope of this book, I can describe the situation that I take the advocate of metaphysical vagueness to be in:

1. The doctrine of metaphysical vagueness implies that there was a time at which the Earth definitely did not exist, a time at which the Earth definitely did exist, and a time in between at which it was vague or indeterminate whether the Earth existed or not. These are facts about the Earth, not facts about language.
2. From this, it will be the case that there are times t such that "The Earth exists at t" is false, times t such that "The Earth exists at t" is true, and times t such that "The Earth exists at t" is vague or indeterminate. These facts about language will be true on theories that admit truth-value gaps.
3. A solution to the sorites consists in finding a logic that shows how to evaluate an argument in a language containing indeterminate sentences. Proponents of the doctrine of metaphysical vagueness can use solutions that recognize indeterminacy in a language – whether or not their proponents take all vagueness to be linguistic.

The upshot is that the proponent of metaphysical vagueness is in no worse position than one who takes reality to be precise and all vagueness to be linguistic. Hence, the sorites leaves open the way to the conclusion that is obvious both to commonsense and to many of the sciences. In the course of nature, things' coming into existence and going out of existence unfold over time: Natural processes have no sharp cut-off points.[36] Ordinary objects have vague temporal and spatial boundaries.[37] Indeed, the thesis that there is vagueness in reality provides a straightforward explanation of the unsoundness of the sorites: The reason that many of its premises are neither true nor false is simply that they depict states of affairs that neither obtain nor fail to obtain.

---

someone with only n–1 dollars is not rich. According to supervaluationism, vague words do not have unique extensions. According to epistemicism, vague words do have unique extensions, but we do not know what they are.

[36] Events that seem instantaneous (e.g., explosions) are not really instantaneous; they have slightly earlier and later parts. Truly instantaneous events, if there are any, are rare.

[37] Recall that only things that definitely exist simpliciter can have indeterminate boundaries. So the vagueness of ordinary objects is vagueness of boundaries, not vague existence simpliciter.

If the thesis of metaphysical vagueness is correct, not only is there vagueness about whether a given state of affairs obtains, but there is also higher-order vagueness. Higher-order vagueness appears when we try to determine the point at which the first-order vagueness starts and ends. So, in addition to there being no precise moment exactly at which the Earth comes into existence, there is no precise moment at which the state of affairs of the Earth's existing at t begins to be vague. There is vagueness about vagueness. The same truth-value-gap treatment (whatever it turns out to be) that handles first-order vagueness can be applied over again to higher-order vagueness. After all, I am not trying to eliminate vagueness from the world.[38]

Let me conclude this brief discussion by showing that sorites arguments are not just logical puzzles, but that they also have practical importance.[39] Many of the phenomena that we encounter everyday are subject to sorites: One day without rain is not a drought; a sorites leads to the (false) conclusion that 1000 days without rain is not a drought. One death from flu is not an epidemic; a sorites leads to the conclusion that 1,000,000 deaths from flu is not an epidemic. One locust is not a plague; a sorites leads to the conclusion that 100,000 locusts is not a plague. Eating one potato chip does not break a diet; a sorites leads to the conclusion that eating 500 potato chips does not break a diet. Catching one fish a day from the bay is not overfishing; a sorites leads to the conclusion that catching 1000 fish a day from the bay is not overfishing. One millimeter of running water on a city street is not a flood; a sorites leads to the conclusion that 10,000 millimeters of running water on a city street is not a flood. And so on.

Many sorites are of moral and legal importance as well. For example, on March 3, 1991, after a high-speed car-chase on a California highway, the California Highway Patrol stopped the car driven by Rodney King. Local police officers and a police helicopter were on the scene. Rodney King, who was drunk and uncooperative, was pulled from the car and beaten severely. From a nearby apartment, George Holliday captured the beating on videotape. Several officers hit and kicked King; one stomped on King's shoulder, causing King's head to hit the pavement hard. The videotape, recording some 56 baton blows and kicks, was shown on TV. According to polls,

---

[38] I am grateful to Ed Gettier for many helpful discussions about the sorites paradox. Of course, he is not responsible for any errors or obscurities that may remain.

[39] In "Why it is Impossible to be Moral," *American Philosophical Quarterly* 36, (1999): 351–359, Stephen P. Schwartz also takes vagueness and sorites problems to be relevant to morality.

92 percent of the people who saw the tape believed that the police had used excessive force.[40] Several policemen were indicted and tried.

To the surprise of many, the videotape was successfully used by the defense to produce acquittal of the officers. The defense lawyers argued that only reasonable force was used against King. In a frame-by-frame analysis, they asked of each blow, whether *it* was the blow that tipped the scales to excessive force? Suppose that the lawyers had framed the series like this: "The first blow was not use of excessive force. If the first blow was not the use of excessive force, was the second blow? And if the second blow was not use of excessive force, was the third blow?. . . and If the 55th blow was not use of excessive force, was the 56th blow?" The lawyers wanted the jury to presume that all the questions should be answered no, and that, therefore, no excessive force was used. They argued that since there was no cut-off point at which reasonable force became excessive force, there was no excessive force used.[41] The jury did acquit the officers.

This historical case illustrates a sorites argument. In effect, the defense lawyers convinced the jury to believe each of the premises below. If each of the premises is true and if the blow 56 was the last blow, then it follows validly that no excessive force was used:

1 blow is not use of excessive force.
If 1 blow is not use of excessive force, then 2 blows is not use of excessive force.
If 2 blows is not use of excessive force, then 3 blows is not use of excessive force.
.

.
If 55 blows is not use of excessive force, then 56 blows is not use of excessive force.
∴ 56 blows – the 56th was the last blow – is not use of excessive force.

In order to make the moral import of the sorites clear, let us disregard the conclusion so far and continue the premises beyond the actual case of the King beating.

---

[40] www.law.umkc.edu/faculty/projects/ftrials/lapd/lapd.html. Accessed June 14, 2006.

[41] If the lawyers asked, "Was *this* blow, considered in isolation, use of excessive force?" they would have committed the fallacy of composition; that is, they would have fallaciously argued that since each blow *by itself* was acceptable use of force, *the sum* of the blows was acceptable use of force. I do not have a transcript of the trial, and the phrasing of the lawyers' series of questions may have been ambiguous between a fallacy of composition and a genuine sorites. I only want to point out that a genuine sorites is a reasonable interpretation of the line of argument. (Indeed, since a sorites argument is valid [though unsound], and an argument containing the fallacy of composition is invalid, it is more reasonable to interpret the lawyers' argument as a sorites than as a fallacy of composition. I suspect [hope?] that astute jurors would have spotted a fallacy of composition.)

If 56 blows is not use of excessive force, then 57 blows is not use of excessive force.

.

.
.

If 999 blows is not use of excessive force, then neither is 1000 blows use of excessive force.

∴ 1000 blows is not use of excessive force.

If all the premises are true, and if blow 1000 was the last blow, then it follows that no excessive force is used – no matter what condition the prisoner was in. Since the argument is valid and the conclusion is false, at least one of the premises is not true, and the theories under discussion all yield that result. On epistemicism, the argument is unsound: it has a false premise; we just do not know which one is false. On supervaluationism, the argument is unsound: it has many premises that are neither supertrue nor superfalse. So, we have logical and semantic accounts for the unsoundness of the argument.

That the argument is unsound is a morally as well as a logically desirable result. If the argument were sound, we could run an analogous valid argument with the conclusion "n blows are morally permissible," for any number n, no matter how large. Logic would compel us to conclude that if a single blow is morally permissible, any number of blows – a million, say – are morally permissible. Although all the theories under discussion avoid this morally disastrous outcome, I think that the view that there is vagueness in reality best comports with the unsoundness of the moral sorites. If there is no vagueness in reality and epistemicists are correct, then there are facts of the matter about what is morally permissible that we can never know. In that case, we should be skeptics about moral permissibility. If there is no vagueness in reality and supervaluationists are correct, then the moral permissibility of a state of affairs is just a matter of how we choose to use the words "morally permissible." On some supervaluationist theories, no sentences containing vague words like "morally permissible" are true, and hence there are no truths about what is and is not morally permissible.[42] However, if there is metaphysical vagueness, the unsoundness of the sorites arguments is explained by the fact that many of their premises depict states of affairs that neither obtain nor fail to obtain.

The view that reality itself is vague at least allows us to understand the moral uncertainties felt by every morally perceptive person as being

---

[42] If Braun and Sider are right in "Vague, So Untrue," no sentence in which any vague word appears is true. So, not even "a person with 0 hairs on his head is bald" is true.

appropriate (and inevitable) responses to reality. Sometimes, the difficulty of deciding what is the right thing to do is neither a matter of our ignorance nor of our use of language, but of vagueness in reality. So, reflection on moral sorites, and on moral experience in general, gives further credence to the view that there is vagueness in reality.[43]

---

[43] For examples of moral sorites in literature, see Franz Kafka's short story, "In the Penal Colony," and Arthur Miller's play, *The Crucible*.

7

Time

The everyday world is a temporal world: the signing of the Declaration of Independence was later than the Lisbon earthquake; the Cold War is in the past; your death is in the future. There is no getting away from time.

The ontology of time is currently dominated by two theories: Presentism, according to which "only currently existing objects are real,"[1] and Eternalism, according to which "past and future objects and times are just as real as currently existing ones."[2] In my opinion, neither Presentism nor Eternalism yields a satisfactory ontology of time. Presentism seems both implausible on its face and seems in conflict with the Special Theory of Relativity, and Eternalism gives us no handle on time as universally experienced in terms of an ongoing now. (There is a third theory, the Growing Block Universe, according to which the past is real but the future is not; but it also conflicts with the Special Theory of Relativity.[3]) So, I shall by-pass these theories for now and return to them later.

This chapter aims to develop a way to understand time that is adequate both to physics and to human experience. It begins with McTaggart's framework of the A-series and the B-series – the framework that underlies both Presentism and Eternalism.[4] I shall set out a theory (that I call "the BA theory") that shows how the A- and B-series are related without reducing

[1] Theodore Sider, *Four-Dimensionalism: An Ontology of Persistence and Time* (Oxford: Clarendon Press, 2001), p. 11.

[2] Ibid. See also Thomas Crisp, who characterizes Eternalism as "the view that our most inclusive domain of quantification includes past, present and future entities" (in Dean Zimmerman, ed., "Defining Presentism," *Oxford Studies in Metaphysics* Vol 1 [Oxford: Clarendon Press, 2004], pp. 15–20; quote is on p. 19); and Ned Markosian, "In Defense of Presentism," in Zimmerman, ed., *Oxford Studies in Metaphysics*, pp. 47–82.

[3] Michael Tooley, *Time, Tense and Causation* (Oxford: Clarendon Press, 1997), ch. 11, suggests modifying the Special Theory of Relativity in a way that entails absolute simultaneity while maintaining consistency with experimental results. See also C. D. Broad, *Scientific Thought* (London: Routledge & Kegan Paul, 1923).

[4] Michael Rea notes that we cannot equate the A-theory and Presentism, nor the B-theory and Eternalism. See Michael C. Rea, "Four-Dimensionalism," in Michael J. Loux and Dean

either to the other. Then, I shall draw out some metaphysical implications of the view and try to move beyond Eternalism and Presentism.

THE A-SERIES AND THE B-SERIES

There are two distinct ways in which we conceive of time: in a "tensed" way, in terms of past, present, and future ("You will be dead in 60 years," "It's now 4:00," "The Earth is millions of years old," "The play has just started") and in a "tenseless" way, in terms of clock times ("The play starts at 8 p.m.") and relations of succession and and simultanety ("The sinking of the *Titanic* is earlier than the beginning of WWI"). McTaggart named these two ways of temporally ordering events the "A-series" and the "B-series," respectively.[5] He said:

> I shall give the name of the A-series to that series of positions which runs from the far past through the near past to the present, and then from the present through the near future to the far future, or conversely. The series of positions which runs from earlier to later, or conversely, I shall call the the B-series.[6]

Events change with respect to their A-properties (pastness, presentness, futurity). For example, the death of Queen Anne was once in the future, then it was present, then past. So, there are really many different A-series, not just one. By contrast, events do not change with respect to their B-relations (earlier than, simultaneous with, later than). For example, if the signing of the Declaration of Independence is later than the Lisbon earthquake, then the signing of the Declaration of Independence is always later than the Lisbon earthquake. The term "tenseless" refers to the fact that, given an inertial frame, B-relations between events do not change over time: once "earlier than," always "earlier than."

Although the expressions "past," "present," and "future" are characteristic of the A-series, those expressions may be used to designate B-series relations. For example, "in the past" is an A-series term only if it's used with a shifting reference – as in "The McCarthy era is in the past," where

W. Zimmerman, eds., *The Oxford Handbook of Metaphysics* (Oxford: Oxford University Press, 2003), pp. 246–280. Nevertheless, Eternalism is *a* B-theory, and Presentism is *an* A-theory, albeit a truncated one that singles out only the present as real.

[5] J. M. E. McTaggart, "Time," from *The Nature of Existence*, Vol. 2 (Cambridge: Cambridge University Press, 1927, Book V, ch. 33, in *The Philosophy of Time* Richard Gale, ed., (London: Macmillan, 1968), pp. 86–97. I take "earlier than" and "later than" to denote temporal relations; hence, there is no question that the B-series is a temporal series.

[6] McTaggart, "Time."

"in the past" is relative to now. If "past" is used relationally – as in "The McCarthy era is in the past in 2005," "past" has nothing to do with the A-series. "The past at t" is a B-series term equivalent to "earlier than t," a paradigmatically B-series expression. Similarly, for "in the future." For example, "in the future" is an A-series expression in "In the future, call me before 9 o'clock," where "in the future" means in the future relative to now. But "in the future" is a B-series expression in "In August 1939, the beginning of WWII was in the future" where "in the future" means "later than 1939." "In the future in 1939" is a B-series expression that applies to the same times (any time later than 1939) no matter when it is used. Parallel remarks apply to "now at t" (B-series) and to "now" (as in "I'm ready to adjourn the meeting now" – A-series). So, the expressions typical of the A-series actually presuppose the A-series only if they are used in ways that have different referents on different occasions of their use. The definitive difference between the A- and B-series is this: A-properties are transient, and B-relations are not.

Verb tenses, as well as terms like "past," "present," and "future," are associated with the A-series. We report facts ordered by the A-series by use of tensed verbs and copulas: "He will not be going home," "That happened 6 weeks ago," "They're off!" yelled by the announcer at a horse race. A-sentences (as I'll call them) are true on some occasions of their utterance, but not others. By contrast, B-sentences – e.g., "In 2006, Tony Blair (tenselessly) is Prime Minister of England" – is true (if true at all) on all occasions of its utterance. Unlike the tensed "is" of the A-series that contrasts with "was" and "will be," the "is" in B-sentences should be understood tenselessly.

Let me pause for a comment on Eternalism: Eternalism is often characterized, as I noted at the beginning, as the view that past, present, and future times and objects are equally real.[7] That characterization is highly misleading for a B-theory. The B-series, which is the basis for Eternalism, makes no appeal to past, present, or future at all: "Past," "present," and "future" are A-series terms. (As I just pointed out, all that can be countenanced by the B-series is "past at t," "present at t," and "future at t"; but these designations are eliminable in favor of B-series terms "earlier than t,"

---

[7] The term "Eternalism" seems to me to be a misnomer for *any* theory of time: According to a B-theory of time, temporal objects exist tenselessly. Something that exists eternally – e.g., God or the square root of 2 or the set of possible worlds – exists "outside" of time altogether. (E.g., to say that God exists eternally is to *deny* that God is in time; the term "semipeternal" is used to mean that God exists at all times.)

"simultaneous at t," and "later than t.") Past, present, and future – along with the ongoing now – are irrelevant to the B-series. From the perspective of the B-series, nothing is really past, present, or future – just past at t, present at t, or future at t. Inasmuch as Eternalism calls into question the referents of A-series words, using ostensibly A-language to characterize Eternalism leads to confusion.

It is important not to confuse the tenselessness of the B-series with timelessness. The mathematical relation "greater than" is timeless, but "earlier than" is paradigmatically a temporal relation. The name "Eternalism," together with the metaphor of a block universe and the claim that the B-series "spatializes" time, wrongly suggest that time is all laid out *now* or that all time is present. Such suggestions make no sense on the B-series. The B-series (taken alone) is a temporal ordering that accords no metaphysical significance to the past, present, or future. It is also wrong to think that the B-series implies fatalism. As J. J. C. Smart, a four-dimensionalist advocate of the B-series (without the A-series) observed, the B-series "is compatible both with determinism and with indeterminism, i.e., both with the view that earlier time slices of the universe are determinately related by laws of nature to later time slices and with the view that they are not so related."[8]

THE INDISPENSABILITY OF BOTH A- AND B-SERIES

It is tempting to think that we can dispense with either the A-series or the B-series in favor of the other. On the contrary, I am convinced that we require both the A-series and the B-series to understand all the temporal facts. Neither the A- nor the B-series can be eliminated in favor of the other.

Here are three reasons to think that the B-series is not dispensable in favor of the A-series:

(1) Prima facie, the A-series is incomplete as an account of time: we need the relations "earlier than," "later than," and "simultaneous with," in addition to "past," "present," and "future" to describe familiar temporal facts – e.g., causes are typically earlier than their effects. Indeed, the natural way to understand the past is as earlier than now, and the natural way to understand the future is as later than now.

---

[8] J. J. C. Smart, *Philosophy and Scientific Realism* (London: Routledge & Kegan Paul, 1963), p. 142. For a full discussion of the matter of determinism and indeterminism with respect to the A-series, see Adolf Grünbaum, "The Status of Temporal Becoming," in Gale, ed., *The Philosophy of Time*, pp. 28–36.

(2) Although the B-series is required for physics, the A-series is never appealed to in theories of physics. (Time's having a direction depends on physical asymmetries, like the increase of entropy; the directionality of time in no way implicates the A-series with its ongoing now.) If one is at all a realist about physics, then one will take the B-series to be essential for temporal reality.

(3) Although I cannot discuss it here, I believe that attempts to ground the B-series in the A-series have failed.[9] So, I do not believe that the B-series can be eliminated or reduced to the A-series.

Nor is the A-series dispensable in favor of the B-series. Again, there are three reasons:

(1) The B-series without the A-series leaves out the paradigmatic temporal properties of past, present, and future altogether, along with the ongoing nows that order our experience.

(2) There are many temporal facts that the B-series without the A-series cannot recognize – e.g., that this is the twenty-first century or that social services in the US used to be more secure that they are now. The B-series offers no way for the doctor to tell you that you have less than a year to live, or for you to assure the school board that the Earth is millions of years old now. (And your having less than a year to live and the Earth's being millions of years old now are by no means "subjective" or a product of psychological attitudes.)

(3) The A-series is required for the occurrence of many kinds of ordinary phenomena – for making and executing plans, for regret, for making sense of ourselves and the world. A-series facts are explananda that need A-series explanations. Why are you so sad today? Because someone close to you died last night. (Being sad at t because someone died at t–1 is not the same at all as being sad today; being sad today because someone died last night has the sting of grief that the tenseless fact of being sad at t because someone died at t–1 just does not have.)

---

[9] E.g., McTaggart's attempt to define "earlier than" in terms of A-properties is circular. See Richard Gale, *The Language of Time* (New York: Routledge & Kegan Paul, 1968), p. 90. More recently, L. Nathan Oaklander has subjected William Lane Craig's version of A-time – Presentism – to a convincing critique. L. Nathan Oaklander, "Presentism: A Critique," in Hallvard Lillehammer and Gonzalo Rodriguez-Pereya, eds., *Real Metaphysics* (London: Routledge, 2003), pp. 196–211.

So, I conclude that we can neither eliminate the B-series in favor of the A-series, nor eliminate the A-series in favor of the B-series.

Before setting out a theory of temporal reality that integrates the B- and A-series, let me motivate the need for a *metaphysical* theory. What's the point of a metaphysical (as opposed to a merely semantic) approach to the A-series? After all, David Kaplan and others have shown how to treat indexical sentences containing "now," and, it may be thought, no more need be said.[10] There is nothing special about the present: "Now" is just a word that applies to every time t, at that time t.[11]

Indexical theories, in general, leave important questions unanswered. An indexical theory of "now" cannot tell you where you are in time: If you are Rip van Winkle and don't realize what year it is when you wake up, don't expect the B-theory, or a token-reflexive theory of "now," to tell you; every time is "now" at that time and only at that time. An indexical theory of "I" does not distinguish you from anyone else: Complete knowledge of every scientifically established third-person fact will not tell you which person you are; every person is 'I' to herself. An indexical theory of "actual" does not single out our world as special: it will not tell you which world you live in; every world is "actual" to its inhabitants.

Although such indexical theories may be useful in semantics, metaphysicians should not stop with them. There is information that indexical theories cannot account for – e.g., facts about what time it is now and which person is you and which world you live in. It seems a rather significant fact that it is now 4:00 and not midnight, or that I am LB and not George Washington, or that this is the twenty-first century and not the eighteenth. These are temporal facts that one may be right or wrong about. Those who accord no metaphysical import to the A-series will point out that the only propositions involved here (on the standard semantic treatment) are B-series

---

[10] David Kaplan, "Demonstratives," in J. Almog, J. Perry, and H. Wettstein, eds., *Themes from Kaplan*, (New York: Oxford University Press, 1989), pp. 481–614.

[11] Some philosophers speak of the reduction of the tenses by B-language. E.g., Sider, *Four-Dimensionalism*, p. 20. But what is meant by "reduction of the tenses" is that there are tenseless truth conditions for tensed tokens, e.g., "S is now F" uttered at t is true just in case S is F at t. For example, after Kennedy was assassinated, a doctor said, "It is too late to help him; he has died." We can supply tenseless truth conditions for an utterance of "It is too late to help him" at time t concerning an event (the death of Kennedy) that tenselessly takes place earlier than t. However, those tenseless truth conditions cannot convey to listeners the tensed information that it was already too late to help him. As I interpret the important papers of John Perry and others, the existence of tenseless truth conditions does not signal that indexicals and tensed language can be dispensed with. See John Perry, "The Problem of the Essential Indexical," *Noûs* 13 (1979): 3–21.

propositions. I reply: The propositions expressed by "This is the twenty-first century" and "I am LB" and "It is now 4:00," according to the standard treatment, are tautologies: "The twenty-first century is the twenty-first century" and "LB is LB" and "4:00 is 4:00." Tautologies are trivial. But it is far from trivial that this is the twenty-first century or that I am LB.[12] I can only conclude that nonindexical propositions as such do not yield a complete account of reality.

Moreover, indexical theories of the language of the A-series are mute in the face of the transiency of experience, the ineluctable ordering of our lives in terms of an ongoing now. Note the dissimilarity between "here" and "now": The reference of "now" shifts inexorably. Your next utterance of "now" will refer to a different time from your preceding utterance of "now." But your next utterance of "here" will not refer to a different place from your preceding utterance of "here" unless you have moved, and you may move in any direction. There is no spatial analogue of temporal becoming – the property by which, no matter what we do, events recede away from us into the past.

The A-series is required in order to know what one's temporal location is, and one's A-series temporal location is crucial for understanding ordinary events: Consider a politically engaged high-school student whose eighteenth birthday is a day too late to vote in some national election. She says, "I wish that I were a day older than I am." (Since an obstetrician could have induced labor in her mother a day earlier, our high school student might have been a day older.) Without the A-series, I see no possibility of understanding the thought that she expressed; the A-series is needed for understanding both *her* thinking of herself as *then* being a certain age, and *our* attributing to her that A-series understanding of her temporal location. Consider a real life example: Laurence Summers, former President of Harvard University, was quoted as saying, "If I could turn back the clock, I would have said and done things very differently."[13] There is no way to understand this thought without the A-series.

To take a less prosaic example, recall Andrew Marvell's famous words, "But at my back, I always hear/Time's wingéd chariot hurrying near."[14]

---

[12] I discussed these matters at length in "Underprivileged Access," *Noûs* 16 (1982): 227–241.
[13] The *New York Times*, http:www.nytimes.com ("Harvard Professors Confront Its President"), February 16, 2005.
[14] Andrew Marvell, "To His Coy Mistress."

Again, the thought that Marvell expresses would make no sense apart from the A-series. Our understanding of experience in terms of an ongoing now – an understanding that is universal – is not fully captured by non-indexical language and a metaphysical theory is in order.

Thus, the standard semantic treatment of A-series phenomena needs supplementing. The trivial rendering of "now" as applicable at t to each t, does not fully capture temporal reality. I have no quarrel with indexical theories, as far as they go. They just do not go far enough to answer all the questions about time: The present moment has privileged status in our experience; we order our lives according to an ongoing present.

In sum, the world that we encounter and interact with is a world ordered both by the B-series and by the A-series. Neither is a dispensable part of temporal reality. What can be gleaned from physics is only that time is ordered by the B-series (and that relative to inertial frame). But the B-series ordering does not exhaust temporal reality. Much temporal information, important temporal information – like "It's now 4:00," "You have less than a year to live," or "The Earth is now millions of years old" – is simply invisible within the framework of the B-series. And almost all of the temporality of "lived experience" is inexplicable from the framework of the B-series. So, time cannot be fully understood without the A-series as well as the B-series. Indeed, it is an important fact about time (not just about us) that it is ordered in terms of past, present, and future. Now let's turn to my sketch of a theory of temporal reality that draws on both the A-series and the B-series.

A THEORY OF TIME

As I mentioned, I'll call my proposed view "the BA theory of time." My aim is to take the B-series as basic, but to jack up the A-series so that it too reveals an aspect of the nature of time. According to the BA theory, time has two irreducible aspects: one that depends on there being self-conscious entities (the aspect of the A-series, the ongoing now) and one that does not depend on self-conscious entities (the aspect of the B-series, simultaneity and succession). The BA theory will show how these two aspects are related.

According to the BA theory, it is part of the nature of time to be ordered by "earlier than," etc. (the B-series); but it is also part of the nature of time that it is experienced by self-conscious beings as ordered by past, present, and future (the multiple A-series). Everything that a self-conscious being is aware of—what someone else is saying, natural events, one's own thoughts, one's rememberings, what have you—is always experienced as being present. In the absence of self-conscious beings, we might say that the A-series is dormant (or merely potential, or not manifest). So, my BA theory will be a metaphysical account of how the B-series can accommodate an A-series ongoing now. Hence, it is not to the point to respond that, trivially, every time is now (at that time).

(I realize that some philosophers take it to be a metaphysical mistake to claim that any aspect of reality depends on there being self-conscious entities. The claim looks like a mistake only on an assumption that I do not share—namely, the assumption that what depends on us has no ontological significance. I'll return to this point later, but now let's see how the B-series and the A-series fit together.)

In the absence of self-conscious beings, events occur (tenselessly) at various times, and some events are (tenselessly) later than others.[15] But there is no ongoing now. Given that the B-series makes no appeal to what is occurring now, we must ask: In virtue of what does an event occur now, in the present?[16] Modifying the view of Adolf Grünbaum, I say that an event's occurring now depends on someone's being judgmentally aware of it now.[17] (Judgmental awareness is "awareness that": if you are aware that you are feeling something soft, then you are judgmentally aware of feeling something soft.) Consider, for example, a sudden snap of my fingers. The following are sufficient for your hearing the finger snap's occurring now:

(1) You hear the snap.
(2) You are now judgmentally aware of hearing something.
(3) Your judgmental awareness is simultaneous with your hearing the snap.

Because your hearing the snap is (nearly) simultaneous with the snap, the snap also occurs now. The finger snap occurs now in virtue of someone's

---

[15] The locution "at t" is neutral between an absolute and a relational theory of time. Relationalists like Grünbaum freely use "at t." As Grünbaum observed, an event occurs "in a network of relations of earlier and later and thus can be said to occur 'at a certain time t.' Hence to assert tenselessly that an event exists (occurs) is to claim that there is a time or clock reading t with which it coincides." See, Grünbaum, "The Status of Temporal Becoming," p. 24.

[16] The following discussion is from my Ph.D. dissertation, *Linguistic and Ontological Aspects of Temporal Becoming* (Vanderbilt University, 1972). At that time, I joined Grünbaum in denigrating what is "mind-dependent." I have since come to my senses.

[17] Grünbaum, "The Status of Temporal Becoming," p. 17. Also see Grünbaum's *Philosophical Problems of Space and Time* (New York: Alfred A. Knopf, 1963), Part II.

being judgmentally aware (now) of hearing something, together with the simultaneity of the judgmental awareness with hearing the snap. You need know nothing about the clock time of the snap. If the snap is unperceived, then it may still qualify as occurring now if it is simultaneous with some other event that meets the awareness requirements.[18] Occurring now or in the present is a primitive property of all judgmental awareness at the time of the judgmental awareness.

There is no conflict between this view and the Special Theory of Relativity. The appeal to simultaneity is local – indeed, initially, it is between mental events of a single person.[19] A physical event qualifies as occurring now only by being perceived (or by being simultaneous with some other physical event that is perceived). Absence of absolute simultaneity does not deprive reality of simultaneity; it only implies that simultaneity is relative to frame. Physics still appeals to relations of "earlier than" and "simultaneous with" – only now these relations on standard views are taken to be relative to inertial frame.[20] Similarly, metaphysics may still use "past," "present," and "future" – only now these properties should be taken to be relative to self-conscious beings.

The nowness of judgmental awareness is, I believe, primitive. So, this view is not reductive; indeed, it is circular: What I am judgmentally aware of is *now* because my judgmental awareness is (primitively) now. I do not think that this circularity is avoidable; I think that it is a mark of an inextricable link between time and self-consciousness. Again, all of our self-conscious awareness is experienced as being present. Indeed, it is *constitutive* of our conscious lives that they are ordered by the A-series' ongoing nows.

Many events unperceived by me or by anyone else qualify as occurring now, viz., all those unperceived events that are simultaneous with physical events which, by virtue of someone's conceptualized awareness, themselves qualify as being present or occurring now. The A-series is naturally

---

[18] I have defended this view in "Temporal Becoming: The Argument From Physics," *Philosophical Forum* 6 (1974–75): 218–236 and in "On the Mind-Dependence of Temporal Becoming," *Philosophy and Phenomenological Research* 39 (1979): 341–357.

[19] "In the first instance, it is only an experience (i.e., a mental event) which can ever qualify as occurring now." Grünbaum, "The Status of Temporal Becoming," p. 19.

[20] Anja Jauernig pointed out that if I'm standing still and you jump, then we are not in the same inertial frame since you are accelerating. But I still experience your jumping as occurring in the present. So, we should loosen the simultaneity requirement between the judgmental awareness and the physical event that occurs now, and speak of near-simultaneity. (Since judgmental awareness is not instantaneous, no judgemental awareness is simultaneous, strictly speaking, with an instantaneous physical event anyway.)

taken as presupposing the B-series: Past events are those that occur earlier than those occurring now. Since past events include events that occurred during the formation of the solar system, when there was no judgmental awareness, Grünbaum's view has the odd, but tolerable, consequence that there are past events that were never present.

For example, if everyone were in a dreamless sleep at t, things would happen at t (hearts would beat, etc.), but in the absence of judgmental awareness, t would not be present. But when someone woke up and some later t′ was present, then t would be past in virtue of being earlier than t′, which would then be present. (Note that to say that "t′ would then be present" is, like "t is past at t′," B-series talk.) Even though t was never present, events still occurred at t and at all the other times while everyone was asleep. By the time someone awoke and t′ was present, all the events earlier than t had occurred. Again, t is present in virtue of someone's judgmental awareness at t. The A-series of past, present, and future is a product of our self-consciousness, but the A-series is no less part of what time is for all that. We, by means of our self-consciousness, contribute to temporal reality.

The BA theory has the virtue of empirical adequacy: it is adequate both to our experience and to the demands of physics. Anything that we self-consciously experience is perforce ordered by an A-series, but the A-series cannot stand alone. The BA theory takes the B-series to be basic – basic, but not exclusive or exhaustive. On the B-theory, events just occur at different clock times. The B-theory is often thought of as a static view of time. On the BA theory, three-dimensional objects move through time, but their doing so depends on their being self-conscious beings. It is also part of the nature of time that any self-conscious experience has – must have – A-properties.

METAPHYSICAL IMPLICATIONS

Superficially, I may seem to be in league with Grünbaum: Without self-conscious beings, there are no A-series. Without self-conscious beings, events would be related only by succession and simultaneity; there would be no ongoing now, and thus no past, present, or future. But there is a huge metaphysical difference between Grünbaum and me: Grünbaum took his view to show that the A-series has no ontological status, that it is merely "mind-dependent," with emphasis on the "merely."[21] In contrast

---

[21] There is even less similarity between Hugh Mellor and me. According to Hugh Mellor, temporal reality is purely B-series; but we think about it in A-series terms. We need A-series beliefs in order for our actions to be successful. Nevertheless, there are no A-series facts. See

to Grünbaum and many others, I do not take the mind-independent/ mind-dependent distinction as the basis for metaphysics. (See chapter 1.) Metaphysics should concern reality. We self-conscious beings are part of reality. We self-conscious beings contribute to what there is: Much that exists depends – depends ontologically, not just causally – on us: pacemakers, cell phones, particle accelerators. If a piece of plastic physically indistinguishable from your Mastercard spontaneously coalesced in outer space, it would not be a credit card: Nothing would be a credit card in a world without beings with propositional attitudes and their conventions and legal and financial arrangements.

We people contribute not only to material reality, but to temporal reality as well. What we contribute to temporal reality is the A-series: "nowness" is a product of self-consciousness, but no less part of the reality of time for all that.[22] To deny that we add to material reality is to refuse to take the world that we interact with (the world with pacemakers, credit cards, personal computers) as metaphysically significant. The world that we interact with is ordered temporally by both the B-series and the A-series. The Cold War (tenselessly) concludes in 1989; the Cold War is in the past. These are both temporal facts.

I can hear an objection: "Time as it is *in itself* is only the B-series. On the view that you just sketched, the A-series is extrinsic to time, not part of what time is." To such an objection, I reply that it is a very general and widespread mistake to think that what something is is determined wholly by its intrinsic properties. What makes something a portrait, a credit card, or a personal computer (or any other kind of artifact) are relational and intentional properties. Of course, some philosophers think that there are no artifacts; but, then, some philosophers think that there are no material objects at all. As I have said, I am concerned with the world as we encounter it, and we encounter it as full of artifacts, and as temporally ordered by ongoing nows – indeed, as saturated with A-series temporality.

Time is not something extraneous to us, or something nontransient (as the B-series alone would have it) that simply causes us to experience the world as transient. Our relation to time is much more intimate than is

---

Hugh Mellor, "The Time of Our Lives," lecture delivered on 22 October 1999 in London to the Royal Institute of Philosophy. www.dspace.cam.ac.uk/bitstream/1810/753/1/ TimeLives.html.

[22] That now is relative to an inertial frame only means that there is no unique now; there is no unique A-series. But this casts no doubt on there being an ongoing now relative to us – just as the fact that the truth of an utterance of "It's 4:00 now" depends on time zone casts no doubt on its really being 4:00.

effect to cause. Contrast time with heat, say. The phenomenon of heat is nothing but the motion of particles; that motion causes our sensations of heat. We can readily imagine living in a world in which there were no sensations of heat; the motions that cause sensations of heat in our world could cause other kinds of sensations or no sensations at all. But time is not like that: We cannot imagine living in a world without the passage of time. We are not just contingently related to time (as we are to heat) as a cause of certain experiences. We are wrapped up in time (indeed, we are carried away by time's wingéd chariot). Passing time is the medium of our lives: To live is to get older, and to get older is for time to pass. There is something about time, not just about us, that makes our experience transient.

So, to say that the A-series requires self-consciousness does not exclude the A-series from being an aspect of time. It is an important feature of time that it has a disposition toward A-properties, which are manifest only in relation to self-conscious beings. Recall the reasons that the A-series is not dispensable in favor of the B-series: The B-series alone simply renders too many temporal facts invisible. Indeed, the temporal facts that the B-series leaves out are ones of great import – like the A-series fact that you are alive now or that someone you love is now dying. In short, I do not see how to make sense of the world that we encounter without metaphysical appeal to transiency; and the best metaphysical theory of transiency, I believe, is that time's passing depends on our self-conscious experience.

BEYOND PRESENTISM AND ETERNALISM

As I mentioned, the metaphysics of time is currently dominated by two theories: Presentism, according to which "only currently existing objects are real," and Eternalism, according to which "past and future objects and times are just as real as currently existing ones."[23] It is typical of philosophers, when faced with two ways of conceiving of some phenomenon (say, P and Q), to divide over whether to say that P is real and Q is not, or that Q is real and P is not. Presentists take the A-series (but not the B-series) to be real; Eternalists take the B series (but not the A-series) to be real. Neither side seeks to expand the available options.

In my opinion, as I said, neither Presentism nor Eternalism yields a satisfactory ontology of time. If Presentism – which as I mentioned is both

---

[23] Sider, *Four-Dimensionalism*, p. 11.

implausible on its face and in conflict with the Special Theory of Relativity – were correct, it is difficult to see how we could understand the difference between our meaningful talk about Plato and our meaningful talk about Pegasus. Pegasus never existed; Plato existed in the past. We speak meaningfully of Plato and we speak meaningfully of Pegasus; and it seems that our meaningful talk of Plato is grounded in Plato himself, whereas our meaningful talk of Pegasus is grounded in ancient stories. But according to Presentism, neither Plato nor the ancient stories exist since neither is temporally present. So, it is difficult to see how, if Presentism is correct, we can even recognize the difference between what grounds meaningful talk about Plato and what grounds meaningful talk about Pegasus, much less explain the difference. (Actually, Presentists are very clever, and go through all sorts of contortions to make the sentences that we all take to be true to come out true on a Presentist scheme; it is just that the sentences do not mean what we thought that they did. How much smoother and more satisfactory to avoid the contortions and take sentences at face value!)

Eternalism fares a bit better, but is still inadequate. Once we clear away Eternalism from the A-series' appeal to past, present, and future (as opposed to the B-series' appeal to past-at-t, which is equivalent to earlier-than-t), we can see that the B-series provides no way to understand that the Earth is millions of years old, that we are all going to die, and other nonpsychological facts. Eternalism provides no handle on time as universally experienced in terms of an ongoing present.

So, I have bypassed both Presentism and Eternalism and tried to sketch a theory of time that is both physically respectable and adequate to our experience. In chapter 11, I'll connect this account of time to ontology in a way that (*pace* Eternalism) makes room for ontological novelty and that (*pace* Presentism) does not presuppose the A-series.

CONCLUSION

I argued that *both* the B-series (that orders time in terms of unchanging relations like "earlier than") and the A-series (that orders time in terms of changing properties like "being past," "being present," and "being future") are needed for an adequate account of time. Neither series is dispensable, and neither by itself is a sufficient account of time: An A-theory cannot stand alone. On a B-theory alone, things just exist at different clock times: nothing moves through time; there is no passage. On the BA-theory, objects move through time, but their doing so depends on the existence of self-conscious beings. Conversely, our experience as self-conscious beings would be impossible without transiency. Although the B-series is the more fundamental of the two orderings, it is a deep fact about time that it can be experienced only as transient.

Some of my relatives in Tennessee recently attended a funeral during which the old Southern preacher said, "Time ain't as long as it used to be." That seems to me to be an insight into the reality of time. If you agree, then you'll take both the A-series and the B-series to order temporal reality.

PART III

Metaphysical underpinnings

8

Constitution revisited

The Constitution View is a metaphysical view of concrete entities in the natural world. These concrete entities include the familiar objects that we interact with daily, as well as electrons and quarks. To review: everything is of one primary kind or another. An object x's primary kind answers the question: What is x most fundamentally? Trigger most fundamentally was a horse (not an animal TV star); Michaelangelo's *David* most fundamentally is a statue (not a piece of marble). Neither could Trigger cease to be a horse, nor *David* cease to be a statue without going out of existence. Different primary kinds have associated with them different persistence conditions. One of the differences between the primary kinds *horse* and *statue* is that horses have different persistence conditions from statues.

According to the Constitution View, there is constitution "all the way down," whether there's a fundamental level of reality or not. (See chapter 2.) If there is no "bottom" level, then every entity is constituted.[1] Letting "y" range over material objects and "t" range over times, if there is no "bottom" level,

∀y∀t[y exists at t → ∃x(x exists at t & x constitutes y at t)].

If there is a "bottom" level, then entities at the bottom are unconstituted constituters:

∀y∀t{y exists at t → [∃x[(x exists at t & x constitutes y at t) v ~(∃z(z is a part of y at t & z ≠ y)]]}

Many philosophers will have no truck with the idea of constitution-without-identity.[2] By contrast, I find the idea of constitution-without-identity very natural: it obviates the need for contingent identity, relative

---

[1] See Jonathan Schaffer, "Is There a Fundamental Level?" *Noûs* 37 (2003): 498–517.
[2] I tried to respond to qualms in chapter 2 by considering Aristotle's idea of numerical sameness without identity, and by considering metaphysical motivations (repeated above) for an idea of unity-without-identity.

identity, temporal identity, or any other kind of faux identity. Moreover, it provides the best (perhaps the only) way to make ontological sense of the everyday world in terms that we can recognize.

DEFINITION OF "X CONSTITUTES Y AT T"

In *Persons and Bodies*, I set out a series of definitions of the main terms at the core of the view – in particular, "x constitutes y at t," "x has H (non)-derivatively at t," and "x is the same F as y." Some of these definitions and the claims using the defined terms have properly been criticized. I now want to concede some points to my critics and offer some revised definitions, followed by further defense of the Constitution View.

Recall that if F and G are primary kinds, and an F constitutes a G at t, then the F is in G-favorable circumstances. Only in circumstances with certain laws and conventions in force does a piece of plastic constitute a driver's license; only in circumstances including organic environment and perhaps even evolutionary history does a conglomerate of cells constitute a human heart. G-favorable circumstances are the milieu in which something can be a G. The G-favorable circumstances are conditions such that the addition of an appropriate F makes it the case that there is a G, but not so comprehensive that just anything in G-favorable circumstances guarantees that there is a G. Then, when a suitable F is in G-favorable circumstances, it comes to constitute a G. (To be suitable, an F cannot cease to be an F when put in G-favorable circumstances.) G-favorable circumstances may be characterized by open sentences which are satisfied by an appropriate F.

There will never be a general account of K-favorable circumstances for kinds generally. There are too many different kinds of primary kinds, with different kinds of favorable circumstances for instances of each. Indeed, it is impossible to specify all the primary kinds; some have not even been invented yet. (See chapter 11.) However, we can illustrate the idea of K-favorable circumstances with particular cases, and illustration is all that is needed to understand the idea of K-favorable circumstances.

Consider the circumstances in which C, a piece of cloth, constitutes F, the flag made by Betsy Ross. The flag-favorable circumstances can be specified by a list of open sentences true of the piece of cloth when it constitutes a flag. E.g., "x is in a context in which there are conventions of national symbols"; "x is rectangular, flat, and nonrigid"; "x is approximately 3 feet by 5 feet"; "x is in the possession of someone who knows how to

160

sew, has a well-stocked sewing basket, and has intentions to make a national symbol and carries out those intentions." These sentences can be satisfied by things that are not pieces of cloth, and by things that are not flags; but when a piece of cloth does satisfy them all, there is a flag.

One final preliminary point: I am a universalist about mereological sums; hence, any aggregate of things is a mereological sum. (See chapter 9.) In chapter 6, I argued that aggregates (i.e., mereological sums) can constitute ordinary objects that have vague boundaries. In such a case, there will be vagueness in the constitution relation. That is, it will be indeterminate exactly which mereological sum of atoms, say, constitutes a particular vague object. Hence, when we require that the constituter and the constituted object be spatially coincident, we cannot be requiring *absolute* spatial coincidence.[3] We should construe the requirement of spatial coincidence of constituter and constituted object in Clause (2) loosely: Clause (2) requires *near* spatial coincidence of the constituter and constituted object.

Now we can define "constitution."[4] Let "F$\star$x" stand for "x has F as its primary kind property" and likewise for other predicate variables.

(C$\star$) <u>x constitutes y at t</u> = df. There are distinct primary-kind properties F and G and G-favorable circumstances such that:

(1) F$\star$x & G$\star$y &

(2) x and y are spatially coincident at t, and ∀z(z is spatially coincident with x at t and G$\star$z → z = y), &

(3) x is in G-favorable circumstances at t; &

(4) It is necessary that: ∀z[(F$\star$zt & z is in G-favorable circumstances at t)→ ∃w(G$\star$wt & z is spatially coincident with w at t)].

(5) It is possible that: ∃t{(x exists at t & ~∃w[G$\star$wt & w is spatially coincident with x at t])}; &

(6) If x is of one basic kind of stuff, then y is of the same basic kind of stuff.

Let me make some comments on the clauses of the definition.

Clause (2): The (new) second clause of (2) insures that nothing can constitute two distinct things of the same kind at once. It thus blocks

---

[3] Indeed, it is less than clear, in any case, how to understand "absolute spatial coincidence." See my *Persons and Bodies: A Constitution View* (Cambridge: Cambridge University Press, 2000), pp. 208–212.

[4] (C$\star$) replaces (C) in *Persons and Bodies*. The definition was improved with the help of Dean Zimmerman. Clauses (1), (3), (4), (5) are unchanged from (C) in *Persons and Bodies*. The second clause of (2) is new, and (6) is slightly generalized.

Sider's counterexample.[5] Sider's counterexample was this: Suppose that a constitutes b at t, and there's a crazy-matter-thing c such that (i) c is spatially coincident with a at t and (ii) c is of the same kind as b. In that case, a (also) constitutes c at t. So, a body could constitute two persons at t. Bad news! The new second clause of (2) to the rescue: Sider's counterexample has x constituting two things of the same kind at the same time. The new second clause of (2) rules that out.

In addition, the new second clause of (2) fends off counterexamples from philosophers who advise adding a mereological clause to the definition of "constitution."[6] The clause that they advise adding is, roughly, that x and y have all the same parts – e.g., "Every part of y has a part in common with some part of x, and vice versa."[7] I think that sameness of parts should be a consequence of constitution, not a condition of constitution. (See chapter 9.) Constitution is a comprehensive relation that applies to persons and their bodies, as well as to credit cards and pieces of plastic. I want the Constitution View to illuminate all these relations, and what all these kinds of things have in common is obscured by mereological considerations. In any case, I think that the new second clause of (2) avoids the need for a mereological clause.

Clause (3): As before, G-favorable circumstances are such that if there is something of primary kind F in those circumstances, then there is a G. G-favorable circumstances are almost, but not quite, sufficient for there being a G. They would become sufficient for there being a G if something of a suitable primary kind (viz., F) were in them. As the case of Betsy Ross's flag illustrates, G-favorable circumstances may be formulated in terms of open sentences that are satisfied by something of a suitable primary kind.

Clause (4): In cases in which it is not necessary that all things with the primary-kind property G are constituted by things with the primary-kind property F, (4) guarantees that constitution is asymmetric. That is, when things of a single primary kind (e.g., statue) may be constituted by things of several different primary kinds (e.g., pieces of bronze, pieces of marble), (4) guarantees asymmetry of constitution.

---

[5] Theodore Sider, "Review of *Persons and Bodies: A Constitution View*," *Journal of Philosophy* 99 (2002): 45–48.

[6] E.g., Anil Gupta (in conversation), Dean W. Zimmerman, "*Persons and Bodies*: Constitution Without Mereology?" *Philosophy and Phenomenological Research* 64 (2002): 599–606, and Sider's "Review of *Persons and Bodies*."

[7] Zimmerman, "*Persons and Bodies*: Constitution Without Mereology?," p. 604.

One of the most serious challenges to this definition has come from Derk Pereboom, who offered a counterexample to my definition of "constitution" in *Persons and Bodies*.[8] The problem is that it seems that (4) can be falsified, and, worse, what seems to falsify (4) is its role in securing the asymmetry of constitution.[9]

Clause (4) is to insure the asymmetry of constitution: If x (of primary-kind F) constitutes y (of primary-kind G) at t, then it is not the case that y constitutes x at t. For example, by (4) it is necessary that: if a piece of marble is in statue-favorable circumstances, then there is a statue spatially coincident with the piece of marble. But it is not necessary that: if a statue is in piece-of-marble-favorable circumstances, then there is a piece-of-marble spatially coincident with the statue. Piece-of-marble-favorable circumstances would include being within certain ranges of temperature and pressure. If a sum of certain molecules (calcium carbonate) were in those circumstances, there would be a spatially coincident piece of marble. Consider a bronze statue in piece-of-marble-favorable circumstances: If a bronze statue were in those circumstances, there would not be a spatially coincident piece of marble.

Pereboom asks: "If a statue can be a bronze statue even when it is in piece-of-marble favorable circumstances, why can't a lump be a plant-pot even when it is in statue-favorable circumstances?" I answer: "It can." Then, Pereboom goes on: "And if this is possible, then the statue won't be constituted of the lump, by Baker's definition."[10] According to (4), anything whose primary kind is a lump and is in statue-favorable circumstances would constitute a statue – even if in fact that lump already constituted a plant pot.

I should bite the bullet and hold onto (4): necessarily, any lump in statue-favorable circumstances constitutes a statue.[11] Consider a lump that

---

[8] Derk Pereboom, "On Baker's *Persons and Bodies*," *Philosophy and Phenomenological Research* 64 (2002): 618.

[9] I responded to Pereboom by amending my definition. See Lynne Rudder Baker, "Replies," *Philosophy and Phenomenological Research* 64 (2002): 630–635. Since I no longer believe that my response is adequate, I want to retain (4) and take another crack at responding to Pereboom's counterexample.

[10] Pereboom, "On Baker's *Persons and Bodies*," p. 618.

[11] In my reply to Pereboom in *Philosophy and Phenomenological Research*, I added a clause to the effect that "x doesn't have any property of a higher order than F that doesn't entail G." I hereby recant. Tomasz Kakol has convinced me that the clause (more precisely, the conjunction of two clauses that he adds, his (7) and (8)) makes constitution dependent

constitutes a plant pot and then is put in statue-favorable circumstances. There seem to be three possibilities compatible with (4):

(i) The plant pot goes out of existence, and is replaced by a statue (perhaps it is hammered so that there was no longer a plant pot there).

(ii) The plant pot itself can come to constitute a statue; in that case, the lump constitutes a statue in virtue of constituting a plant pot that in turn constitutes a statue.

(iii) There could be branching:[12] The lump constitutes a plant pot, and the lump constitutes a statue. But the plant pot does not constitute a statue.

I think that filling out the story in different ways could make any of these three possibilities plausible, and leave clause (4) undisturbed. The change in my view is that I am now countenancing "branching." An object x may constitute y and z at t, where $y \neq z$, but only if y and z are of different primary kinds (in accordance with clause (2)).[13]

Clause (5): As before, (5) guarantees that constitution is irreflexive and contingent. Even the relation between an aggregate of a sodium atom and a chlorine atom and a salt molecule is contingent: the aggregate of that sodium atom and that chlorine atom would still exist if the two atoms were miles apart, but the salt molecule would not. In cases in which necessarily all things with the primary-kind property G are constituted by things with the primary-kind property F, (5) guarantees that constitution is asymmetric.

Clause (6): Clause (6) is a slightly generalized version of the old (6), according to which no wholly material thing can constitute anything

---

on the time of acquiring properties, and it makes constitution intransitive. See Tomasz Kakol, "The SameP-Relation as a Response to Critics of Baker's Theory of Constitution," *Journal of Philosophical Logic* 34 (2005): 561–579.

[12] Both David B. Hershenov and Robert A. Wilson suggest the permissibility of allowing branching for some cases of constitution. See David B. Hershenov, "Problems with a Constitution Account of Persons," in preparation, and Robert A. Wilson, "Persons, Social Agency, and Constitution," *Social Philosophy and Policy* 22 (2005): 49–69.

[13] Kakol uses a nonbranching lemma to prove transitivity of "sameP." (Kakol also took nonbranching to be required for constitution in light of a response to Pereboom; but I am responding to Pereboom in another way from the one he was assuming.) If branching is a problem, I could use Kakol's lemma of the one-to-oneness of constitution: Define $C^{\star\star}$:

$xC^{\star\star}y = x$ constitutes y or there exist (finitely many) $z1, z2, \ldots, zn$ such that x constitutes $z1, z1$ constitutes $z2, \ldots zn$ constitutes y.

Then, prove: $\forall x, y, z(yC^{\star\star}x \ \& \ yC^{\star\star}z \rightarrow xC^{\star\star}z \lor x = z)$. This rules out the branching case, but the others remain options.

immaterial. By "basic kind of stuff," I mean to include (mythical) ectoplasm or some other immaterial stuff. Basic kinds of matter include particulate matter and "gunk." The aim of (6) is to preclude the constitution of any immaterial thing by a material thing: a body cannot constitute a soul or a body/soul composite.

Constitution is an irreflexive, asymmetric, and transitive relation.[14] Asymmetry is to be secured by clause (4) of the definition of "constitution," with suitable filling out of G-favorable circumstances. Several people (e.g., Derk Pereboom and Michael Rea) have raised doubts about asymmetry.[15] Here I just want to emphasize that asymmetry is not at all in danger, because I can easily get asymmetry on the cheap: First, define a symmetric relation, "constitution(s)," that is just like constitution without the claim of asymmetry. Then define "constitution" as this relation: x constitutes y at t if and only if x constitutes(s) y at t and y does not constitute(s) x at t. So, there is no danger that for technical reasons, I would have to give up asymmetry.[16]

It should be clear that it is a mistake to suppose that constitution is simply co-location. Many philosophers who discuss constitution-without-identity understand constitution to be simple spatial coincidence, or co-location. On my view, that is a mistake. Constitution can not be understood just in terms of co-location. In the first place, constitution is asymmetric and co-location is not. In the second place, philosophers typically construe co-location to be a mereological idea: x and y are co-located at t if and only if x and y share all parts at t. But constitution, as I have been at pains to show, is not itself a mereological idea. In the third place, co-location makes unity a mystery. Whereas constitution, with the allied notion of having properties derivatively, accounts for the unity of a constituted object, co-location does not. Co-location raises a question that constitution can

---

[14] In *Persons and Bodies*, I said that constitution was nontransitive, but that there were chains of constitutionally related entities all the way down to aggregates of particles. Dean Zimmerman showed me a flaw in my argument for nontransitivity. I am happy for constitution to be transitive. But if it is not, we can simply define another relation, C* as follows: C*xy iff x constitutes y or there exist some z1, z2,... zn such that x constitutes z1, z1 constitutes z2,... zn constitutes y. Then, C* is transitive. See Tomasz Kakol, "The SameP-Relation as a Response to Critics of Baker's Theory of Constitution."
So, now I recant: constitution is transitive. That is all right with me. Transitivity is certainly more elegant than the separate instances of constitution that I postulated all the way down to aggregates of particles.

[15] These appeared in the Book Symposium on *Persons and Bodies*, in *Philosophy and Phenomenological Research* 64 (2002): 592–635.

[16] Jaegwon Kim pointed out this strategy to me in (about) 1996.

answer but co-location cannot: Why are statues and pieces of marble co-located, but bulldogs and fireplugs never co-located? (That is, why do statues and pieces of marble sometimes share the same matter and locations, but bulldogs and fireplugs never do?) Co-location is mute in the face of this question, but constitution furnishes at least a beginning of an answer in terms of primary kinds. Bulldogs and fireplugs are of primary kinds unsuited for constitution. Some pairs of primary kinds are related in the way given by the definition of "constitution"; others are not.[17] So, constitution is a much richer notion than co-location.

UNITY WITHOUT IDENTITY

In chapter 2, we saw that constitution is not identity. Now we are in a position to see how, nevertheless, constitution allows for unity. If x constitutes y at t, x and y are not just two things that happen to be at the same place at the same time.[18] Rather, if x constitutes y at t, there is a unified individual whose identity is determined by y's primary kind. If a piece of marble constitutes a statue, the piece of marble does not cease to exist, but (I can only put it metaphorically) its identity is encompassed or subsumed by the statue. The unified individual is the statue-constituted-by-a-piece-of-marble. If you went into a gallery of the Louvre that is lined with works by Antonio Canova and you identified them only as pieces of marble, you would be missing what is there. The constituted thing has ontological priority over its constituter. (This further bolsters the anti-reductive thrust of my view.)

A statue has some of its properties (weight, color, texture) in virtue of being constituted by a piece of marble, say; and the piece of marble has some of its properties (being worth $20 million, being selected for the cover of *ArtNews*) in virtue of constituting the statue. So, as I said in chapter 2, we need to distinguish between *having a property derivatively* and *having a property nonderivatively*. Now I can be more precise. Let the

---

[17] Many philosophers who take constitution just to be co-location consider co-location without identity to be mysterious. But co-location is no more mysterious than the mereological idea of overlap, which many philosophers profess to understand. Overlap is a species of co-location: x overlaps y iff x and y have a part in common, where having a part in common is x's having a part at the same place and time as y. So, any mystery about co-location seems to be equally a mystery about the notion of overlap. Derk Pereboom suggested this to me.

[18] I'll drop the time indices unless they seem needed.

expression "x has constitution relations to y at t" abbreviate "x constitutes y at t or y constitutes x at t." Then, to have a property derivatively is to have it in virtue of constitution-relations to something that has it independently of *its* constitution-relations. A constituted thing inherits many properties from its constituter; and a constituter inherits many properties from what it constitutes. This two-way borrowing further indicates the unity of a constituter and what it constitutes.

Not all properties may be had derivatively. There are four classes of properties that cannot be had derivatively: (1) alethic properties (properties expressed in English by locutions like "essentially," "possibly," "primary-kind" (as in "has F as its primary-kind property"), and their variants; (2) identity/constitution/existence properties (properties expressed in English by "is identical to" or "constitutes" or "exists," or their variants); (3) properties rooted outside the times that they are had (properties whose instantiation entails that the bearer existed at earlier or later times[19] – such as "was in the quarry yesterday"); (4) hybrid properties (conjunctive properties that entail or are entailed by two or more primary-kind properties – such as the property of being a human person). Call properties in any of these four classes "excluded properties."

Let "having a property" be an undefined notion of generic exemplification.[20] Now, as a preliminary to defining "x has H derivatively at t," first define "y has H at t independently of its constitution relations to x":

(I) y has H at t independently of y's constitution relations to x at t = $_{df}$
    (a) H is not an excluded property; and
    (b) y has H at t; and
    (c) Either (1) (i) y constitutes x at t, and
                (ii) y's having H at t (in the given background) does not entail that y constitutes anything at t; or
            (2) (i) x constitutes y at t, and

[19] This idea comes from Roderick Chisholm, *Person and Object* (LaSalle, IL: Open Court Publishing Co., 1976), p. 100.

[20] I am grateful to Dean Zimmerman for showing me how to set out the theory this way. He not only improved my definitions, but also he showed me how to avoid a "reductive" interpretation that defined derivative exemplification in terms of an undefined notion of nonderivative exemplification. See Dean W. Zimmerman, "The Constitution of Persons by Bodies: A Critique of Lynne Rudder Baker's Theory of Material Constitution," *Philosophical Topics: Identity and Individuation* 30 (2002): 295–338.

(ii) y's having H at t (in the given background) does not entail that y is constituted by something that could have had H at t without constituting anything at t.

Now we can define "having properties derivatively" as follows:

(D) x has H at t derivatively = $_{df}$.

   (a) H is not an excluded property;
   (b) There is some y such that:
      (1) y has H at t independently of y's constitution relations to x at t; and
      (2) it is not the case that: x has H at t independently of x's constitution relations to y at t.

Now we can define having a property nonderivatively:

(N) x has H at t nonderivatively = $_{df}$

   (a) x has H at t; and
   (b) Either: (1) H is an excluded property; or
             (2) There is no y such that:
                (i) y has H at t independently of y's constitution relations to x at t; and
                (ii) It is not the case that: x has H at t independently of x's constitution relations to y at t.

(I), (D), and (N) are reductive definitions of derivative and nonderivative exemplification in terms of the undefined notion of generic exemplification and constitution. "Has" in (Ib) and (Na), along with "having" in (Ic1ii) and (Ic2ii), denotes the generic exemplification relation. A substantive axiom concerning the notion of generic exemplification is this:

(G) x has H at t if and only if: either

   (a) x has H at t derivatively, or
   (b) x has H at t nonderivatively.

Let me illustrate the definitions. The piece of marble that constitutes Michelangelo's *David* has the property of being a statue derivatively, and the property of being white nonderivatively. *David*, constituted by that piece of marble, has the property of being a statue nonderivatively, and the property of being white derivatively.

The kind of independence at issue in (I) is not causal, but rather logical or metaphysical. For example, if the winning team hoists the Coach in celebration, the position of the Coach's body is not causally independent of its constituting the Coach – the team would not have hoisted that body if it hadn't been the body of the winning Coach – but the position of the Coach's body is logically independent of its constituting the Coach.[21] The Coach has the property of being, say, five feet off the ground derivatively – in virtue of being constituted by a body that is five feet off the ground independently (in the relevant noncausal way).

As I see it, then, there are two ways to have a property – nonderivatively or derivatively.[22] Although to have a property derivatively is to have it in virtue of constitution-relations to something that has it nonderivatively, to have a property derivatively is still really to have it: Mary's property of having a broken leg is a property that Mary has derivatively – in virtue of being constituted by a body that has a broken leg; but she really has a broken leg. It would be literally false for her to say, "I don't have a broken leg; it's just my body whose leg is broken." If her body has a broken leg, then Mary has a broken leg.

The idea of having properties derivatively does important work in the Constitution View. It explains how it is that when x constitutes y, x and y have so many properties in common without being identical: x and y have properties derivatively from each other. It also explains how it is that, although I am a person and my body is a person and I am not identical to my body, there are not two persons where I am: Since my body has the property of being a person derivatively, its being a person is a matter of its constituting something that has the property of being a person nonderivatively. Hence, my body is not another person in addition to me.

THE SAME F

The reason that the idea of having properties derivatively can serve these purposes is this: The relation of constitution occupies an intermediate position between strict identity, on the one hand, and separate existence, on the other. (The fact that "constitution" can be defined using familiar logical and modal ideas by (C★) indicates that the idea is not incoherent.) What constitution-without-identity shows is that there are two ways for

---

[21] I am assuming that a possible world in which the Coach's team lost is closer, in the given background, than a world in which the team mistakenly thought that someone else was the Coach and hoisted the wrong person. (That's why I thought it safe to say "the team would not have hoisted the body if it hadn't been the body of the winning Coach," without hedging by saying "the team would not have hoisted the body *if they hadn't believed* that it was the body of the winning Coach.")

[22] Since "having a property derivatively" is defined in terms of constitution-relations, the property of having F derivatively is itself an excluded property (an identity/constitution/ existence property), and hence is not subject to being had derivatively.

things to fail to be identical (two ways to be numerically different, if you prefer). By the term "identity," I always mean classical, strict identity. But the idea of *nonidentity* divides into two more fine-grained notions: constitution and separate existence.

We have already seen what constitution is. It remains to spell out the idea of separate existence. With these two notions of constitution and separate existence – and without modifying the classical notion of identity – there are two ways for things to be nonidentical. In order to define the notion of separate existence, we need first to extend John Perry's notion of *being the same F* to accommodate constitution. (Perry's notion is that x and y are the same F if and only if (x = y and Fx).)[23] I'll adopt Perry's notion of "the same F" for excluded properties and introduce a new condition for nonexcluded properties: x and y are the same F at t if and only if: (x = y or x has constitution relations to y at t) and Fxt. Then the fully general definition of "x and y are the same F at t" is this:

(Same-F) x and y are the same F at t = $_{df.}$

> ∀F∀t{Either: (1) (i) F is an excluded property (i.e., F cannot be had derivatively) and
> (ii) (x = y & Fxt);
>
> or (2) (i) F is not an excluded property (i.e., F can be had derivatively) and
> (ii) [(x = y or x has constitution relations to y at t) & Fxt]}

With this definition of "the same F," we can define a second way that things can be nonidentical besides constitution:

(SE) x and y have separate existence at t = $_{df.}$

> (1) x and y exist at t and
> (2) There is no F such that x and y are the same F at t.

So, now we have two ways to be nonidentical at t: constitution at t and separate existence at t. In some respects, constitution is like identity: if x constitutes y at t and Fxt (for nonexcluded Fs), x and y are the same F at t. Cicero and Tully are the same person in virtue of being identical; my body and I are the same person in virtue of being constitutionally related.[24]

---

23 Cf. John Perry, "The Same F," *The Philosophical Review* 79 (1970): 181–200. I'm taking "x has the property personhood" to be equivalent to "x is a person."

24 The phrase "my body and I are the same person but not identical" should not suggest relative identity. (I do not hold that statements of the form "x = y" are incomplete or

In other respects, constitution is like separate existence: if x constitutes y at t, there are many properties (e.g., modal properties) that x and y do not share. You and your body are nonidentical in virtue of being constitutionally related; you and I are nonidentical in virtue of having separate existence. If x and y are constitutionally related at t, there is a unity of x and y at t – a unity without identity. If x and y have separate existence at t, there is no unity. Constitution and separate existence are two ways of being nonidentical.[25]

This refinement of the notion of nonidentity into constitution and separate existence can also apply to the idea of there being "two things." Speaking for myself (and echoing Aristotle), I believe that the "how many" question has no application apart from some sortals: "How many things are in this room?" cannot be answered unless we know the kinds of things we're talking about. However, many philosophers insist on the following: If x and y are nonidentical, then where x and y are, there are two things. Along with Aristotle (see chapter 2), I deny that the inference is valid. In any case, I have carefully defined two ways of being nonidentical. If x and y are constitutionally related, then I would deny that where x and y are, there are two things. x and y are numerically the same; constitution is another species of Aristotle's numerical sameness.

There may still seem to be a difficulty lurking. Kit Fine has pointed out that a statue may be well-made while the piece of alloy (he says simply "an alloy") that constitutes the statue may be not be well-made.[26] Since, by the definition of "the same F," the statue and the constituting piece of the alloy are the same statue, it may seem that we have a contradiction: A statue cannot be both well-made and not well-made. Happily, there is no contradiction. The property of being well-made is a relational property – like the property of being a good student. Jo may be a good student (with respect to her class), but not be a good student (with respect to the national

---

should be analyzed in terms of a sortal.) The phrase should be interpreted in light of the discussion of "the same F": if x and y are the same F but not identical, then x and y are constitutionally related.

[25] Some critics simply do not recognize that there can be two ways of being nonidentical, and hence do not recognize that there is genuine unity without identity. See Sider, "Review of *Persons and Bodies*," in pp. 45–47, and Eric T. Olson, "Review of *Persons and Bodies: A Constitution View*," *Mind* 110 (2001): 427–430. However, Aristotle's notion of "numerical sameness without identity" (chapter 2) clears space for my view.

[26] Kit Fine, "The Non-Identity of a Material Thing and Its Matter," *Mind* 112 (2003): 195–234. Fine remarks, "Although the point is often ignored, it is not a *piece* of alloy but only the *alloy* itself that can properly be said to constitute or make up a statue" (p. 206). My conception of constitution, which I have explored extensively, is different from Fine's.

norm for her grade level). Similarly, the statue may be well-made (with respect to statues) but not well-made (with respect to the alloy in its constituter). So, the problem disappears.

I offer the idea of constitution as a "third way," an intermediate relation between strict identity and separate existence. Let us turn now to criticisms. I'll consider, first, criticisms of the application of the idea of constitution-without-identity to human persons, and then criticisms pointing to defects in my technical apparatus. I'll conclude by giving reasons to accept the Constitution View.

OBJECTIONS AND REPLIES

I want to discuss objections, both to the general idea of constitution and to its application to persons. Since I believe that my amended definition of "constitution" avoids the counterexamples offered by Zimmerman, Sider, Gupta, and Pereboom, I'll not discuss them further. But for other objections, an odd dialectic has developed. There is an almost standard array of objections, which I claim to have answered; but critics remain unconvinced. Indeed, I charge the critics with begging the question, and they demur. I'll summarize the objections, my responses, and the critics' demurral. Then, I'll offer my own diagnosis of the situation.

The almost standard array of objections may be divided into two overlapping groups – one charging that constitution gives rise to problems about counting; the other charging that the Constitution View is really a form of substance dualism.

1. Olson has a number of criticisms about alleged counting problems and overpopulation.[27] Many have the following form: "If my body is 'something numerically different' from me, then there are twice as many Fs (persons, human animals) as we thought there were. But it is absurd to suppose that there are two Fs in the circumstances. Therefore, the Constitution View is absurd."

This line of argument has an obviously question-begging premise – namely, that x and y are numerically the same only if they are identical. I have gone to some lengths to show that objects constitutionally related to each other are numerically the same. Looked at the other way, the term "nonidentity" (or "numerical difference") subsumes two different relations – constitution and separate existence. Where there is the "separate

---

[27] Olson, "Review of *Persons and Bodies.*"

existence" variety of nonidentity, then there are twice as many Fs. But where there is the constitution variety of nonidentity, then there are not twice as many Fs as we thought. Since this is my view (like it or not), an argument that depends on an inference from the nonidentity of x (that is F) and y (that is F), where x constitutes y, to there being two Fs just rests on the prior assumption that the view is false.

I'll give two examples of this question-begging line. (i) Olson takes as a *premise* in an argument against the Constitution View that if x is a person and y is a person and x and y are nonidentical, then there are two persons. In *Persons and Bodies*, I explicitly argue *against* the claim that if x is a person and y is a person and x and y are nonidentical, then there are two persons.[28] Even if my argument there is unsuccessful (and no one has ever nonquestion-beggingly shown that it is), it is clearly not legitimate to argue against me by taking as a *premise* (without further argument) a thesis that I explicitly deny.

Olson takes the Constitution View to give rise to the nonsensical question, "How do I know which of the two numerically different people who share my location I am?" I have shown that, on my view, there are two ways to be "numerically different." If we take "numerically different" in such a way as to imply that there is another person, separate from me, sharing my location now, then my view does not imply that there are two numerically different people where I am. If we take "numerically different" in the other way that allows for constitution, then the question does not arise: I am the (nonderivative) person nonderivatively writing this now. The nonsensical question gets its punch by question-beggingly presupposing that my body is a another person in addition to me. Again: no argument that *assumes* or stipulates that there is no "third way" between identity and separate existence can non-question-beggingly be used against the Constitution View.

(ii) There is a suspicion that a single occurrence of the word "I" has two referents on the Constitution View: the person who is speaking and her body. On my view, the word "I" always nonderivatively refers to the person – the person constituted by the body. Suppose that I entertain the thought, "I am happy." The word "I" nonderivatively refers to myself (the nonderivative person who is constituted by this nonderivative body). Since my (nonderivative) body has no first-person perspective independently of me, it cannot make any nonderivative first-person reference. It

---

[28] *Persons and Bodies*, p. 98.

can only have the property of thinking "I am happy" derivatively. The oddness of attributing thought to a body, even derivatively, is relieved by an analogy to Aristotle's cases of *proshen homonymy* – the phenomenon of words (e.g., "healthy") that get their meaning by reference to a central paradigm case (e.g., "healthy organism").[29] We may speak of healthy food, healthy complexion, and healthy urine, but to understand these locutions, we must understand "healthy organism." Similarly, to understand "S's body is a person," we must understand "S is a person." This dependence of the derivative exemplification of personhood on the nonderivative exemplification of personhood prevents there being two persons where S is.

Just as there are not two thoughts, "I am happy," one by me and one by my body, there are not two references of "I," one to me and one to my body. The reference to me already "takes in," as it were, the body that constitutes me. It is a caricature to suggest that I refer to myself, the (nonderivative) person, and my body refers to itself, the (nonderivative) body, and each of us attributes to itself the property of being happy. Rather, I refer nonderivatively to this nonderivative person; my body refers derivatively to this same nonderivative person. The word "I" has a single referent here – this nonderivative person, myself-constituted-by-my-body – whether we consider the thought as entertained nonderivatively by me or derivatively by my body. Similarly, when someone thinks, "I am happy," there are not two thinkers of the thought. There is only one thinker of that thought nonderivatively: the person constituted by the body.

In my response to the second group of objections, I'll argue that from the fact that there is only one thinker of the thought, Substance Dualism does not follow.

2. Is the Constitution View of human persons really Substance Dualism? To claim that the Constitution View is a form of Substance Dualism counts as an objection since I hold that the Constitution View is materialistic in that all entities in the natural world are ultimately constituted by physical particles.[30] (Substance Dualists who press this objection should just welcome me to their ranks – even if I am unwilling to join them.) This objection has been forcefully pressed by both Dean Zimmerman and Eric Olson.

---

[29] William G. Lycan, Jr., suggested an analogy with Aristotle here. Gareth B. Matthews identified the analogy as Aristotle's *proshen homonymy*.

[30] Others may have more stringent views of materialism than this. E.g., Eric Olson says, "Whatever it [the Constitution View of persons] is, it's not materialism." "Review of *Persons and Bodies*," p. 429.

Consider Olson's objection: "Baker's claim is that we have no material properties except in a derivative way."[31] Olson insists that a "materialist needs to say that we have material properties in ourselves." But of course I do say that "we have material properties in ourselves." Again: Human persons have material properties in exactly the same way that marble statues have them.

I interpreted the notion of "having a property derivatively" in a non-reductive way. I take "having a property" as we use it ordinarily to be a primitive, and then I take (G) – If x has a property F at t, then x has F nonderivatively or x has F derivatively – to be a substantive axiom. So, it is simply not the case that to have a property derivatively is not to have it at all. If you take the constitution-relation seriously as a unity-relation, then to have a property derivatively is not just to have it by courtesy.

I suspect that Olson's belief that to have a property derivatively is not to have it at all stems from what I take to be a metaphysical prejudice: the only properties that something *really* has are intrinsic to it, where "intrinsic" is understood to preclude properties that depend on constitution-relations. As we have seen, there are two ways that things can be nonidentical ("not numerically identical" is Olson's favored locution), there are two corresponding ways to interpret the term "relational." I would prefer to reserve the term "relational" for properties whose relata are separately existing things. In that case, derivative properties are not relational. If you insist on calling "relational" any properties whose relata are nonidentical, then, since I have shown that y-constituted-by-x is a genuine unity, the way in which derivative properties could be "relational" is benign. To think otherwise is to fail to distinguish constitution from separate existence, a distinction that I have tried to make quite clear. In any case, since I have argued that many things have relational properties essentially, I consider it question-begging to criticize the view by assuming that to have a property in virtue of constitution-relations is not really to have it.

Now consider an objection by Zimmerman.[32] The charge takes the form of a dilemma: When a person thinks, "I hope that I'll be happy," there is either one thinker of the thought or two. If there are two, then there are too many thinkers. But if there is only one real bearer of the thought, the critic claims, the Constitution View is indistinguishable from

[31] Ibid.
[32] I interpret Zimmerman's "Critique" to propose a dilemma for the Constitution View: either there are too many thinkers or the Constitution View is just Substance Dualism.

Substance Dualism of the sort that holds that immaterial souls are located in bodies that have mental states in virtue of their relations to souls. If there is only one thinker of the thought, then there are two substances (person and animal), distinguished by the fact that one of them is the thinker and the other one is not. I have already agreed that there is only one thinker of the thought nonderivatively, the person-constituted-by-the-animal. Of course, the person is the thinker nonderivatively, and the body is the thinker of the thought derivatively. And by (G), person and body each is a thinker of the thought. But by (sameF), they are the *same thinker* of the thought. Hence, Substance Dualism does not follow from the fact that person and body is each thinker of the thought – person nonderivatively and body derivatively. This result does not depend on accepting the Constitution View. The point is that the Constitution View, whether correct or not, is not a version of Substance Dualism.

Zimmerman has suggested that the Constitution View of persons is just a terminological variant on Hasker's Emergent Substance Dualism. Both the Constitution View and Emergent Substance Dualism recognize that, in the first instance, the bearer of certain mental properties is the whole person, not any proper part like a brain. But there the similarities end. Whereas Hasker holds that a soul – a distinct spiritual substance that has libertarian free will and that "modifies and directs the functioning of the brain" – emerges from a body, I do not. Let me enumerate some differences between my view and Hasker's: (i) I think that it is implausible to suppose that there are immaterial substances in the natural world. (ii) On Hasker's view, the soul is a proper part of the person; on my view, there are no souls, and hence persons do not have souls as proper parts. (iii) On Hasker's view, the soul directs the functioning of the brain; on my view, the brain functions according to natural processes. (iv) On Hasker's view, the soul has libertarian free will; on my view, there is no libertarian free will.[33] (v) On Hasker's view, the relation between the soul and the body is unlike any other relation that we know of; on my view, the relation between a person and her body is an instance of a very general relation common to all macrophysical objects.[34] I take (i)–(v) to distinguish the Constitution View from Hasker's Emergent Substance Dualism.[35]

---

[33] See my "Moral Responsibility Without Libertarianism," *Noûs* 40 (2006): 307–330.
[34] William Hasker, *The Emergent Self* (Ithaca, NY: Cornell University Press, 1999): 188–195.
[35] This answers Zimmerman's question, What distinguishes the Constitution View from Hasker's Emergent Substance Dualism? See Zimmerman, "Critique."

More generally, there are several substantial ways in which the Constitution View differs from Substance Dualism: On the Constitution View, (1) There are not just two kinds of substances – mental and physical – but many, many kinds of substances. Each primary kind is ontologically special. (This is important because there is not just one big divide in nature between two disparate realms – mental and physical.) (2) The constitution relation itself is comprehensive, and is exemplified independently of any mental properties. So, in contrast to Substance Dualism, there is no special pleading for persons. (3) The derivative/nonderivative distinction is likewise comprehensive, and is exemplified independently of any mental properties.[36]

Indeed, one of the advantages of the Constitution View is that it can avail itself of many of the fruits of Substance Dualism, without endorsing immaterial entities in the natural world. A proponent of the Constitution View, as well as a Substance Dualist, can endorse the following: (i) a person is not identical to a body; (ii) a human person can survive a (gradual) change of body; (iii) a person has causal powers that an animal would not have it did not constitute a person; (iv) concerns about my survival are concerns about myself in the future, not just concerns about someone psychologically similar to me; (v) my survival does not depend on the nonexistence of someone else who fits a particular description (like "is psychologically continuous with me now"); there is a fact of the matter (perhaps not ascertainable by us) as to whether or not a particular person in the future is I. Despite such similarities with Substance Dualism, the Constitution View remains stoutly materialistic.

Moreover, it is noteworthy that the Constitution View does solve or avoid problems that beset mind–body dualism. The insurmountable problem for mind–body dualism is that the relation between mind and body is inexplicable: there is just a mysterious union between mind and body. The Constitution View of human persons, by contrast, has a well-worked out account of the relation between person and human organism (body). The relation is constitution – which is not peculiar to human persons but is the

---

[36] Substance Dualists countenance only one-way borrowing: the body borrows mental properties from the soul. Zimmerman supposes that the "emergent dualist will surely regard [two-way borrowing] as simply a question of semantics." Ibid., p. 316. He does not say why the Substance Dualist's one-way borrowing of mental properties from the soul by the body should not likewise be considered a question of semantics. I suspect that dualists regard soul-to-body borrowing to be not merely semantic; if so, then it is arbitrary to hold that body-to-soul borrowing is just semantic.

metaphysical glue, so to speak, of the material world. The intractability of the relation between mind and body, for Substance Dualism, stemmed from conceiving the relation as a causal one. On the Constitution View, on the other hand, the relation between person and body is not causal. The Constitution View offers significant advantages over traditional Substance Dualism: I can say how person and body are related; the relation is a material one, of a kind that obtains throughout the material world; and the relation is noncausal. Moreover, as I argued in *Persons and Bodies*, the Constitution View of human persons delivers much of what mind–body dualists want – in particular the possibility that you could exist with a different body from the one that you have now.[37]

Zimmerman (and perhaps others) are not convinced by the arguments that I just gave. For example, concerning my charge that the counting problems are question-begging, Zimmerman says:

> Granted, Baker is able to define a relation that ought to be compatible with non-identity, that entails massive property sharing, and that is sometimes close enough for us to count nonidentical things so related as one for many purposes; and, granted, it makes sense to call this a kind of "nonseparateness." But it still needs to be shown that there are not two thinkers or two pains when there are two things thinking or in pain but nonseparate in her sense. And it cannot be shown simply by *calling* the relation "nonseparateness" and insisting that it is part of one's theory that nonseparate things in pain do not add more pain to the world than a single thing in the same sort of pain.[38]

I have a reply. First, pain is an extremely complex matter for persons. Our attitudes and expectations affect our pain; moreover, independently of our attitudes and expectations, pain waxes and wanes without discernible cause. In order to deal with the objection, we must put aside the actual facts about pain and pretend that it is a simple phenomenon.

So: The nonderivative bearer of the property *pain* at t is either y-constituted-by-x (if y is in pain nonderivatively) or x-constituting-y (if x is in pain nonderivatively). If the pain, like the pain of a broken leg, is such that it could be borne by a nonhuman animal (without a first-person perspective), then the human body bears it at t nonderivatively; and the person-constituted-by-the-body bears it at t derivatively. If the pain, like the pain caused by the expectation of being hanged in two weeks, is such

---

[37] *Persons and Bodies.* Think of all the nonorganic replacements of bodily parts (hip, knee, cornea, heart, etc.) currently available. I believe that the body that I have now is essentially organic, and that with enough nonorganic replacements, I would have a different body.

[38] Zimmerman, "Critique," p. 327.

that it could be borne only by a being with a first-person perspective, then the person bears it at t nonderivatively, and the body-constituting-the-person bears it at t derivatively. In either case, we might say that a single instantiation of F at t is shared by x and y.

The amount of pain there is in a single instantiation is not altered by the fact the pain is borne by x derivatively and by y nonderivatively. The fact that x has the pain derivatively and y nonderivatively is the reason that there is no doubling of the pain, for the same reason that there is no doubling of the weight when x constitutes y, and x weighs 200 lbs nonderivatively and y weighs 200 lbs derivatively: x and y share the instantiation of the property "weighs 200 lbs." Similarly, my body and I are the same thinker. When I think a thought – that I wish that I were out in the sun now – there is only one thought token. I have it nonderivatively and my body has it derivatively; my body gets in on the thought because it constitutes me, and constitution is a kind of unity. I have tried to be clear about the ways in which constitution is like identity without actually being identity.

Zimmerman suggests that I do not have the right to use such expressions as "y-constituted-by-x" since (he thinks) they suggest that "there is a further thing composed of *all* the coincident entities."[39] But Zimmerman, *unlike* me, takes constitution to be a mereological relation. He thinks that the relation of constituters to what they constitute is one of parts to wholes. As my definitions show, that is not how I construe constitution. (In chapter 9, I spell out the relationship between constitution and mereology.) My view is that y-constituted-by-x is a single thing, a unity, whose primary kind is determined by y's primary kind. What an entity most fundamentally is is determined by its highest primary kind. (I present a nonmereological view of ontological levels in chapter 11.)

Zimmerman and I seem to be at loggerheads. However, I think that our being at loggerheads raises an important methodological question for metaphysics. Zimmerman says that my claim that there are not really two thinkers "cannot be shown simply by *calling* the relation 'nonseparateness' and insisting that it is part of one's theory that nonseparate things in pain do not add more pain to the world than a single thing in the same sort of pain." In the context of metaphysics, I do not think that this is correct: Zimmerman grants that it "makes sense" to define a relation and call it "nonseparateness." The definitions are clear and coherent. I claim that they apply to certain empirical things. How does one show this? How does

---

[39] Zimmerman, "Critique," pp. 327–328.

one test a metaphysical theory? I don't know of any tests of a coherent metaphysical theory – mine or anyone else's – other than pragmatic ones. I think that the Constitution View illuminates what it aims to illuminate better than any other metaphysical theory. I don't see what more can be asked. And I don't see that any other metaphysician offers more "proof" than I have. (In chapters 1 and 2, I give further reasons to accept the idea of constitution without identity.)

When Plato distinguished two ways in which we can say, "the same," what proof did he offer? Plato has the Eleatic Stranger say that motion (kinesis) is both the same and not the same.[40] It is the same as itself and it is not identical with "the same," i.e., with sameness. I want to say something analogous about "a person and her body are the same and not the same." I want to say that a person is not identical with her body, and so the person and her body are not the same. But the person and her body are the same in that, for example, when the person has a pain, her body not only has a pain, it also has the very same pain. When later philosophers distinguish additionally the "is" of constitution, again, one just sees that, yes, the "is" of constitution expresses a different relation from the "is" of predication and the "is" of identity. I have tried to show what relation the "is" of constitution expresses.

---

[40] *Sophist* 256a10–b4. I am grateful to Gareth B. Matthews both for the reference and for the comments that I make in the text.

9

Mereology and constitution

Material constitution, as I have construed it, is not a mereological relation: It is not defined in terms of a relation of parts to wholes.[1] However, there are many philosophers who suppose that ordinary material objects must be understood in terms of a single, comprehensive relation of parts to wholes. Philosophers who look to mereology to understand objects often simply eschew an ontological account of ordinary objects in favor of a "conceptual" account, according to which there is nothing ontological that makes a person a person or a painting a painting. Ontologically, there are just little items that compose sums, some of which we choose to call persons and others of which we choose to call paintings.[2]

Since the aim of this book is to provide an *ontological* basis for the familiar objects that we encounter – including people, artworks, artifacts, and ID objects generally – I do not take constitution to be a mereological relation: A piece of paper is not part (proper or improper) of the dollar bill that it constitutes. Constituted objects are not identical to any sums. Nevertheless, I want to show here that, although constitution itself is not a mereological relation, the Constitution View has a place for mereology. Sums are the ultimate constituters.

My goal in this chapter is not so much to defeat opponents as to show that the Constitution View can give an ontological account of our ordinary talk about parts. Here, again, are some of my basic presuppositions: I assume (and will defend in chapter 10) three-dimensionalism, together

---

[1] Several philosophers have urged me to define constitution as a mereological relation; I have resisted. I take it to be a metaphysical error to look at ordinary objects through the lens of parts and wholes. Moreover, I believe that (C*) as amended avoids all the counterexamples that insist on adding a mereological clause to the definition of "constitution." In each putative counterexample, either x and y fail to be of different primary kinds (Zimmerman), or the (new) second clause of (2) is violated (Sider), or the amended (6) is violated (Gupta).

[2] E.g., see David Lewis, Theodore Sider, and many others.

with the thesis of the necessity of identity, according to which if x = y, then necessarily x = y. So, if x exists in the actual world, then x – that very object – exists in some other possible worlds.[3] Thus, I disavow counterparts in different worlds.[4]

With these presuppositions, I believe that the Constitution View has a place for mereological notions. Let me begin with a disclaimer: I believe that the word "part" in ordinary language is used in quite different ways from the word "part" in mereological theories.[5] In ordinary talk, there is no such relation as "*the* part-whole relation." The relation of the planet Venus to a sum of Venus and Buckingham Palace is a different relation from the relation of the racehorse Barbaro's rear right leg to Barbaro.

SUMS AND CONSTITUTION

To see how the Constitution View can make use of mereology, let us begin with some differences between sums and ordinary objects: (1) Sums have their parts essentially, but ordinary objects often undergo change of parts. (2) Sums are ontologically innocent in that sums come into existence automatically when their parts do, but ordinary objects do not. (3) Sums are related to their parts differently from the way ordinary objects are related to their parts. Let me explain.

The standard identity condition for sums is simple. Same parts, same sum: x and y are the same mereological sum if and only if x and y have all the same parts.[6] Sums have different persistence conditions from those of

---

[3] I am not a realist about nonactual possible worlds; but I am using the vocabulary of possible worlds because it is so familiar.

[4] Another presupposition – one that I think follows from the above – is that Humean supervenience is false. Since I cannot argue for this assumption here, I'll just state it baldly: A full and accurate description of the actual world cannot be given without appeal to possibility and necessity. This is obviously so in important cases like causation and moral responsibility.

[5] See David H. Sanford, "Fusion Confusion," *Analysis* 63 (2003): 1–4; and David H. Sanford, "The Problem of the Many, Many Composition Questions, and Naive Mereology," *Noûs* 27 (1993): 219–233.

[6] In "Can Mereological Sums Change Their Parts?" (*The Journal of Philosophy*, forthcoming), Peter van Inwagen proposes a different identity condition: x is the same mereological sum as y if and only if x = y. This definition seems to me to have the following consequence: if x is the sum of your cells when you were two years old, and y is the sum of your cells when you are forty years old, then – despite the fact that at forty you have none of the cells you had at two – the sums are identical. This is so since you are identical to yourself. So, if

ordinary objects of the kinds that we encounter in daily life. Consider the sum of atoms in a crystal vase.[7] When the vase is dropped and breaks into pieces, the vase no longer exists but the atoms (and thus their sum) still do exist. Since the vase and the sum of the atoms in it have different persistence conditions, I want to distinguish between sums and constituted objects, ordinary objects. Let me make explicit two assumptions about sums that I need to make the distinction between sums and ordinary objects.

(A) The first assumption about sums is mereological essentialism. Like any aggregate – see chapter 3 – a sum cannot change parts. So, same sum, same parts. Assuming three-dimensionalism, the necessity of identity, and a rejection of counterparts, a sum has its parts essentially. The mereology of Chisholm and Whitehead takes mereological essentialism as an axiom, "a basic tenet of the theory of part and whole."[8] So, the slogan "same sum, same parts" should not be understood as "De facto, same sum, same parts" but rather as "Necessarily, same sum, same parts."

(B) The second assumption about sums, also from Chisholm, is that the parts of sums are three-dimensional objects. (I shall put aside four-dimensionalism until chapter 10.) Throughout this section, by "parts" I mean what I later call "mereological parts." In the next section, I distinguish between mereological parts (parts of sums) and ordinary parts (parts of constituted objects).

With these two Chisholmian assumptions, I can accept the three axioms that Lewis identifies as the "basic axioms of mereology":

I understand van Inwagen's mereology, some sums are identical without having any parts in common. In any case, van Inwagen's definition of "same mereological sum as" would rule out the Constitution View from the outset.

[7] I am assuming that vases exist. Peter van Inwagen, who holds that everything is either a simple or a sum, takes the only sums to be organisms. The simples shaped vase-wise have no sum, on his view. Hence, he would deny that there are vases (in any weighty ontological sense). When your great aunt says, "There are vases," she expresses a truth, but not the proposition that there are vases. Since he takes organisms to be sums (temporally indexed), van Inwagen does not consider sums to be mere aggregates, as I do. (Unlike van Inwagen, I do not believe that everything is either a simple or a sum. Constituted objects are neither.) See Peter van Inwagen, *Material Beings* (Ithaca, NY: Cornell University Press, 1990).

[8] Roderick Chisholm, *Person and Object* (LaSalle, IL: Open Court Publishing Company, 1976), p. 151.

(i) Transitivity: If x is part of some part of y, then x is part of y.
(ii) Unrestricted Composition: Whenever there are some things, then there exists a fusion [sum] of those things.
(iii) Uniqueness of Composition: It never happens that the same things have two different fusions [sums].[9]

Let me make a quick comment on each:

(i) Transitivity: "Parts" in this axiom refers to the undefined relation of a part to a sum, not the defined relation of a part to an ordinary object. (I shall define the latter relation in the next section, "A Constitution View of Parts.")

(ii) Unrestricted composition: This axiom makes sums cheap: For any ys, there is a unique sum of the ys.[10] According to unrestricted composition or universalism, for any objects, there is a sum or fusion of those objects; the objects "in" the sum are the parts of the sum.[11] Sums are thus simply aggregates of things.[12] There is nothing more to a sum than its parts: the spatial arrangement of the parts is irrelevant to the existence of their sum. Summation is aggregation. The sum exists as long as its parts exist. A sum is none other than its parts taken all together; no structure is assumed. The notion of a sum provides a way to refer to a collection of perhaps disparate items by a singular term, a way to get one thing out of many.

A sum is simply an aggregate of items – regardless of their relations to each other or to anything else. The sum of things comes into existence "automatically" when the things come into existence, and the sum lasts as long as the things exist. (In the un-Lewisian context of three-dimensionalism and rejection of counterparts, this is tantamount to mereological essentialism.) It is obvious that no ordinary object is a sum: No ordinary object is simply an aggregate of items.

---

[9] David K. Lewis, *Parts of Classes* (Oxford: Basil Blackwell, 1991), p. 74.
[10] Lewis and Sider endorse this view of sums; van Inwagen, who calls this axiom "universalism," does not. Van Inwagen himself eschews universalism, and puts restrictions on sums: roughly, the y's do not have a sum unless they make up an organism. See Lewis, *Parts of Classes*; van Inwagen, *Material Beings*; Theodore Sider, *Four-Dimensionalism* (Oxford: Clarendon Press, 2001).
[11] I am deliberately avoiding the common term "composition" for the relation between things and their sum. Many philosophers take "composition" and "constitution" to be synonymous. I use "constitution" as a technical term defined by (C*), and I do not want the relation of constitution to be confused with the mereological relation of composition governed by the axioms of standard mereology.
[12] In contrast to the sums that I shall discuss, van Inwagen recognizes what I would call "restricted sums." Items have a sum only if their activity makes up a life. So, strictly speaking, there are no inanimate objects. Since I cannot think of a noncircular way to restrict sums in a way that includes just the objects that (I think) ought to be recognized by ontology, I focus on universalism.

(iii) Uniqueness of Composition: Things have only one sum. On my view, sums are aggregates that constitute ordinary objects.[13] What van Inwagen calls "an aggregate" is a sum on classical mereological theories. On the Constitution View, a sum (or aggregate) may constitute an ordinary object, as we shall see later.

With use of this Chisholm–Lewis mereological theory, the Constitution View has a place for sums.[14] Sums are not identical to ordinary objects, but they *constitute* ordinary objects at various times. According to the Constitution View, constitution is a temporal relation between x (of one primary kind) and y (of another primary kind) at t. So, in order to get a single constituter out of many diverse elements (e.g. atoms), we need to consider the sum of the elements and its primary kind. Since the identity of sums is determined by their parts (as the identity of sets is determined by their members), the primary-kind property of a sum is the property of having parts of such-and-such primary kinds. A sum of the parts that constitutes a complicated machine will be of a very complicated primary kind (viz., the property of having parts of all the kinds in the machine); a sum of gold atoms that constitutes a ring will be of a simple primary kind (viz., the property of having gold parts).[15]

Sums are the ultimate constituters: Some constituters are themselves constituted objects (as is a piece of cloth that constitutes a flag); but all constituted objects are ultimately constituted by sums of physical particles.[16] At any time the flag exists, there is a sum of atoms that constitutes it at that time. Sums are just aggregates that, in various circumstances, constitute objects. Medium-sized objects – both artifactual and natural – are ultimately constituted by mere aggregates. But since constitution is not just aggregation, medium-sized objects are not identical to the sums (aggregates) that ultimately constitute them.[17] So, although constitution is not itself a mereological relation, a constitutionalist need not abjure mereology altogether.

---

[13] Thus, I reject Peter van Inwagen's suggestion that on the Constitution View, things may have two sums, one an aggregate and the other an ordinary object. See Peter van Inwagen, "Review of *Persons and Bodies*," *Philosophical Review* 111 (2002): 138–141.

[14] Neither Chisholm nor Lewis, I think, would approve of this use of his ideas.

[15] If a sum has parts of different primary kinds – say atoms of elements X, Y, and Z – then the primary kind of the sum is a hybrid X/Y/Z. (This suggests the artificiality of sums.)

[16] Later I'll consider plural quantification as a way to eliminate sums as constituters.

[17] There may or may not be a fundamental level, a stopping point. See Jonathan Schaffer, "Is There a Fundamental Level?" *Noûs* (2003) 37: 498–517. Since the Constitution View is not reductionistic, it is indifferent to whether there is a fundamental level or not.

The Constitution View, then, can make peace with mereology by taking ordinary objects to be ultimately constituted by sums.[18] Sums are "ontologically innocent" – requiring no further commitment than to their parts. As David Lewis put it, "In general, if you are already committed to some things, you incur no further commitment when you affirm the existence of their sum."[19] However, if I am right, your commitment to, say, persons or credit cards or even to lakes, is a further commitment than simply to their parts or to the sum(s) of their parts. A world with water molecules that were all spatially separated would be a world in which no lakes existed, but all the parts of lakes, and sums of those parts, would exist. So, by a version of Leibniz's Law,[20] lakes are not identical to sums of water molecules. The relation between sums of water molecules and lakes is, instead, constitution: A lake is constituted at t by the sum of water molecules; and that sum of water molecules is constituted at t by a certain sum of hydrogen atoms and oxygen atoms. Sums are ontologically innocent, but what they constitute – people, credit cards, and lakes – are not.[21]

If, as the Constitution View holds, ordinary objects cannot be identified with sums, how should a proponent of the Constitution View regard the term "composition"? Is constitution just what other philosophers call "composition"? I think that that is just a terminological matter. We may say that constitution is composition, but there are two kinds of composition – mereological and nonmereological – and constitution is nonmereological composition. Alternatively (and preferably, in my opinion), we may say that constitution is not composition; composition is a mereological relation, and constitution is not. Either way – and this is the important point – the relation of the ys to their sum is not the same relation as the relation of the ys to some ordinary object that the sum of the ys makes up.

In short, the Constitution View has a place for mereological sums – not as ordinary objects, but as ultimate *constituters* of ordinary objects: Ordinary objects are ultimately constituted by mereological sums. However, on the

---

[18] There are other ways to reconcile constitution with mereology. E.g., one may take atoms to have two sums at one time. See van Inwagen's "Review of *Persons and Bodies*." (This suggestion is as implausible to me as it is to van Inwagen.)

[19] Lewis, *Parts of Classes*, pp. 81–82.

[20] I am still assuming the necessity of identity (and no counterparts).

[21] Combining the idea of constitution with mereological ideas yields an analogue of the venerable distinction between aggregates and "substances" (fully-fledged objects) that philosophers like Aristotle and Leibniz insisted upon, and that David Lewis and others have no ontological room for.

Constitution View, mereology has a diminished role to play. The upshot is that constitution cannot be understood as mereological composition.

A CONSTITUTION VIEW OF PARTS

The Constitution View has a consequence that can be stated in terms of classical mereology: Every constituted object is a *mereological atom*. That is, no constituted object has any of what mereologists call "parts."

"But wait!" I can hear you say. "Tables are constituted objects and tables obviously have parts; so your view is false." I reply: I said that no constituted object has any parts, as "parts" is used in mereology. Of course, tables have parts, as "parts" is used in English. I shall give an analysis of "x is part of y at t" that applies to parts of ordinary objects. If this analysis is correct, it shows that when mereologists utter what sounds like the English word "part," they are not referring to parts of ordinary things. The analysis makes use both of constitution and of mereology. I'll use the term "mereological part" to refer to a reflexive, nonsymmetrical, and transitive relation, and I'll argue that mereological parts are not parts of ordinary objects. Here is the standard mereological definition of "sum":

(S) x is a sum of the ys $=_{df}$ every y is a mereological part of x, and every mereological part of x overlaps some y,[22]

where "overlap" is understood as "x overlaps y iff x and y share a mereological part." My claim is that the relation between sums and their mereological parts, as defined by (S), is distinct from the relation between ordinary objects and their ordinary parts.

On the Constitution View, ordinary objects are not (identical to) sums; parts of ordinary objects are not mereological parts. Every sum is a mereological part of itself; no ordinary object is part of itself. Although mereological parts are not ordinary parts, we can use classical mereology in defining the parthood relation for ordinary things at times. Let "x < y" stand for "x is a mereological part of y" and let "Czyt" stand for "z constitutes y at t." Then:

(P) x is part of y at t $=_{df} \exists z(x \neq z \ \& \ x < z \ \& \ Czyt)$

(P) defines "x is part of y at t" in such a way that the parts of an ordinary object at t are products of what mereologists call "proper parthood" and

---

[22] More formally: x is a sum of the ys $=_{df} \forall z(z$ is one of the ys $\to z$ is a part of x) & $\forall z[(z$ is part of x $\to \exists w(w$ is one of the ys and z overlaps w)]

constitution: x is part of y at t if and only if x is a proper mereological part of a sum that constitutes y at t.[23] Given (P), if x constitutes y at t, then x is not part of y at t; and if y is a sum of the x's, then the x's are not parts of y. (If y is a sum of the x's, then the x's are mereological parts of y, but not ordinary parts of y as defined by (P)). (P) defines parts of ordinary objects, which are constituted objects. According to (P), mereological parts – in terms of which sums are defined – are not genuine parts.

My aim is not to do ordinary-language philosophy or conceptual analysis. Rather, by defining temporally-qualified parthood in terms of (P), I am saying what genuine parts of ordinary objects really are. (P) leads to a metaphysical account of parthood that applies to ordinary objects like tables, wildflowers, and people.[24] The relation between the Eiffel Tower and the sum of the Eiffel Tower, your left ear and President Lula of Brazil is a different relation from the relation of your car's brake pads to your car, or of your right hand to you. It is only the latter relation that is parthood, and it is that relation that, I believe, (P) captures.

(P) is perfectly general. An atom A is part of my table at noon if A is a mereological part of a sum that constitutes my table at noon. Suppose that someone scratches my table, removing some of the atoms that include A, at 12:30; then A is not part of my table at 1:00. But, of course, A is still mereological part of the sum that did constitute my table at noon. The sum that did constitute my table at noon still exists at 1:00, but it does not constitute my table at 1:00. So, A was part of my table at noon, but not at 1:00. This can be made more precise:

Atom A is part of my table at noon but not at 1:00 $=_{df.}$ (i) There is a sum S such that S constitutes my table at noon and A is a proper mereological part of S; and (ii) there is no sum S' such that S' constitutes my table at 1:00 and A is a proper mereological part of S'.

Let me give two more examples. The first example illustrates the point that if a sum has constituted parts, then parts of the constituted parts – in contrast to parts of mereological parts – may change without affecting the identity of the sum of constituted parts. Here's the example: My table

---

[23] Notice that (P) defines ordinary parthood in terms of constitution. So, the property of having a part p at t may not be had derivatively. The property of having a part p at t is among those excluded from being had derivatively. (See chapter 8.)

[24] Since "part" is used in many ways – "part of the problem," "part of the curriculum," "part of being a girl" – (P) is not a complete definition of "part." Notice, however, that "part" is never used in English to denote "improper part"; the word "part" is always used in contrast to some whole.

has its top as a part at t in virtue of being constituted at t by the sum of the top and the four legs (suppose that the four legs were machined to screw directly into the top). If the top is scratched at t, it is still the same top at t′ (table tops survive scratching), and the same sum of the top and the four legs still constitutes the table at t′. However, the scratched top that had been constituted by one sum of atoms at t is constituted at t′ by a different sum of atoms.

The second example illustrates the constitution of one object by another constituted object, rather than by a sum: Suppose that Person A is constituted by Body B at t, and Body B is constituted at t by a sum of organs that includes tonsils. Body B and Person A both have tonsils as parts at t. The constituting sum of organs has tonsils as mereological parts. After Person A has her tonsils taken out before t′, she is still constituted by the same Body B at t′ (human body can survive loss of tonsils); but she (Person A) as well as Body B is constituted by a different sum of organs at t′ (a sum that does not have tonsils as parts).

Many philosophers insist that if x constitutes y at t, then (at some level) x and y have all and only the same (mereological) parts.[25] They want to define constitution as a mereological notion. Of course, I do not. However, (P) does imply that all and only the atoms contained in my table are also contained in the sum of the top and four legs. But it is a *consequence* of constitution that if x constitutes y at t, then x and y have all their atoms in common at t. If x and y (say, the flag and the piece of cloth) are nonidentical but have the same parts at t, it is *because x and y stand in the constitution relation at t*; it is not the case that x and y stand in the constitution relation at t because x and y have the same parts at t. This dependence of sameness of parts on constitution indicates why I resist putting a clause into the definition of "x constitutes y at t" that says that x and y have the same parts at t:[26] Constitution *explains* sameness of parts. Therefore, it would be a mistake to make sameness of parts a condition of constitution.

Although (P) is not transitive, there is a route from the table to the atoms contained in it as parts. Each of the legs and the top is constituted by a sum of atoms. The table is constituted by the sum of all those sums of atoms that

[25] See Dean W. Zimmerman, "The Constitution of Persons by Bodies: A Critique of Lynne Rudder Baker's Theory of Material Constitution," *Philosophical Topics* 30 (2002): 295–338.
[26] Dean Zimmerman has pressed hard for me to make sameness of parts at some level of decomposition a condition of constitution. See Dean W. Zimmerman, "Critique," especially p. 297. See also Zimmerman's "Persons and Bodies: Constitution Without Mereology?" *Philosophy and Phenomenological Research* 64 (2002): 599–606, especially p. 604.

constitute the legs and the top. In general, an object with parts is constituted by the sums of all the sums that constitute the parts of the object.

Even though my table and the sum of its top and four legs share all their atoms at t, strictly speaking, we can't say that x and y have all their parts in common without equivocation: the relation that an atom bears to a sum of which it is a mereological part is a different relation from the relation that the same atom bears to a constituted object. This is a general point about the difference between mereological parts and genuine or ordinary parts: The relation that your brain bears to the sum of your brain and Mount Everest is surely different from the relation that your brain bears to your body. Sums have only what I have been calling "mereological parts," and, as we have seen, what I have been calling "mereological parts" are not genuine parts. Since an ordinary object has parts defined by (P), but no mereological parts, an ordinary thing may be understood as a mereological atom.

To conclude, let me just list some virtues of this account of parthood in terms of (P):

(1) The conception given by (P) is faithful to the ways that we ordinarily think of parts. Here are some examples: (i) Not only do ordinary things survive change of parts, but they also survive change of parts of parts. The foot of a leg of a table may be replaced without affecting the identity of the table. (ii) A table is not part of itself. (iii) The top, along with each of the four legs, is a part of the table.[27]

(2) Since, given (P), constituted things are mereological atoms, it is natural to include them in the ontology as I urge.

(3) Relatedly, given (P), there's no question about reducing an ordinary thing to its parts.

ARE PARTS MORE BASIC THAN WHOLES?

Let us say that

x is more basic than y if and only if: (i) there is a world w in which x exists and y does not exist and (ii) there is no world w′ in which y exists and x does not exist.

Are parts more basic than wholes? This question does not have a simple answer. (Indeed, I think that it is intuitively right that there is no simple answer; there's no simple relation between parts and wholes.)

On the one hand, a mereological part of a sum is more basic than the sum of which it is a mereological part. Let x be a mereological part of a sum and y

---

[27] But, again, the sum of the top and four legs that constitutes the table is not part of the table, according to (P).

be a sum of which x is part. Now both (i) and (ii) are satisfied: (i) There is a world in which x exists but y does not. Consider a world in which some other part of y (not x) failed to exist; in that world y would not exist, but x would still exist. (ii) There's no world in which x fails to exist but y still exists. It follows from mereological essentialism that in any world in which any of y's parts fail to exist, y fails to exist. Sums (and only sums) have mereological parts, and mereological parts are more basic than the wholes of which they are parts.

On the other hand, a part of an ordinary object – the leg of a chair, say – is not more basic than the chair of which it is a part. Letting "c" be the chair, and "l" be its leg,[28] we see that clause (i) of the definition of "more basic than" is satisfied by l and c: there is a world in which l exists and c doesn't – e.g., a world in which c is smashed but l stays intact. But clause (ii) fails to be satisfied: There is also a world in which c exists but l does not – e.g., a world in which l has been replaced by l', and l has been used for firewood. So, parts of ordinary objects are not more basic than the wholes of which they are parts.

To sum up: Parts of an ordinary object are not more basic than the ordinary object, nor (by the same reasoning) is the ordinary object more basic than its parts. A sum is not more basic than its mereological parts, but its parts *are* more basic than their sum. This result leads to the question of the ontological status of sums.

THE ONTOLOGICAL STATUS OF SUMS

I have endorsed mereological universalism: for any two or more objects whatever, there is an object that is their sum and that exists as long as the two original objects exist. If universalism is correct, then there is an object that has as its parts Buckingham Palace and the Hope diamond. Many philosophers find this implausible. I too find it uncongenial; however, I am willing to endorse universalism (as I endorse essentialism) because my reflection on the everyday world leads to a theoretical need for arbitrary objects as constituters.[29] In this section, I want to try to diminish the implausibility of universalism.[30]

---

[28] For simplicity, I'm omitting times again since they do not matter to the current point.

[29] However, I could avoid universalism by complicating the theory, perhaps, like this: There is a fusion (sum) of things at t if and only if the things exist at t and there is something that they constitute at t. Universalism, unpalatable as it is, is simpler and more straightforward than such restricted and timebound composition.

[30] See Michael C. Rea, "In Defense of Mereological Universalism," *Philosophy and Phenomenological Research* 58 (1998): 347–360, for an argument that the existence of artifacts leads us to embrace universalism.

Ontologically, sums are like objects in some ways and unlike them in other ways. We can count sums and quantify over sums. But sums are not themselves fully-fledged concrete particulars; they are more like collections or aggregates. (Of course, we can quantify over collections or aggregates as well as over fully-fledged concrete particulars.) Some sums have parts that are fully-fledged concrete particulars – e.g., the sum of the chairs in the room or the sum of your appendix and my wallet or the sum of a tabletop and four legs – but the sum *is* just those parts, whatever their arrangement or relations to each other. Sums come into existence automatically when their parts come into existence: there is a sum whose parts are your left eyebrow and Tony Blair's favorite shirt, simply in virtue of the existence of your left eyebrow and Tony Blair's favorite shirt. In this way, sums are ontological free-riders.

But genuine objects, constituted objects, like computers, people, and stars, are not ontological free-riders. Sums (usually) exist before they come to constitute anything. When a sum does come to constitute something, then a new individual that did not exist before comes into existence. Sums are numerous (too numerous to count) but negligible – except when they play a role in constituting objects like atoms, rocks, trees, animals, people, and passports. Except during the brief periods that they constitute objects, sums make no difference to reality. (Whether you affirm or deny that there is a sum of your keys and my wallet has no important consequences.)

Recall Lewis's words:

> [G]iven a prior commitment to cats, say, a commitment to cat-fusions is not a *further* commitment. The fusion is nothing over and above the cats that compose it. It just *is* them. They just *are* it. Take them together or take them separately, the cats are the same portion of Reality either way.[31]

So, mereological sums or fusions are nothing but their parts. Since mereological objects come into existence automatically by their parts' coming into existence, they do not add anything to reality. (I think the fact that sums can be replaced by plural quantification further brings out the ontological impotence of sums.) Sums are nothing on their own, but an

---

[31] Lewis, *Parts of Classes*, p. 81. According to Phillip Bricker, Lewis is as ontologically committed to sums (as individuals) as to their parts. "Ontological innocence," as Lewis embraces it, just implies that sums do not have to be mentioned separately in ontology: "If I am ontologically committed to A and to B, then I am thereby ontologically committed to A + B. For that reason I don't need to list A + B as a separate item in my ontology. But it is a separate item in this sense: it is not identical to any of the other items in my ontology. It really (literally, altogether) exists." (Phillip Bricker, personal correspondence.)

assortment of parts that clearly *are* objects. Lewis again: "it would be double counting to list the cats and then also list their sum. In general, if you are already committed to some things, you incur no further commitment when you affirm the existence of their sum. The new commitment is redundant, given the old one."[32] Or again: "Mereology is innocent in a different way [from plural quantification]: we have many things, we do mention one thing that is the many taken together, but *this one thing is nothing different from the many*."[33]

So, are sums objects or not? Although I have countenanced sums as ultimate constituters, the fact that they are sums – rather than just pluralities – makes no difference except to the question of how many objects there are. Since I have endorsed universalism, I must (hold my nose and) say that sums are objects. However, the unpalatability of commitment to arbitrary sums is mitigated by the fact that the ontological difference that sums make is negligible: the only ontological effect of holding that sums are objects is to increase the number of existing objects. The parts of sums carry the entire ontological load. The Practical Realist would say, If the theory that best explains the everyday world is tidier with the assumption that there are sums, then there are sums.

I put aside here the question of whether the theoretical purpose that sums serve could be equally well served by plural quantification. If so, we could recast the Constitution View in favor of "the x's constitute y at t," where y and the x's are of such-and-such primary kinds. The Constitution View could be reformulated to hold that the ultimate constituters are the x's, instead of the sum of the x's.[34] In that case, we could construe talk of the sum of the x's in terms of a linguistic device of using a singular term to refer to a plurality. If our talk of sums were shown to be a mere convenience that can be eliminated, then I would be happy to eliminate them in favor of pluralities. I leave that task for another person.

The important ontological fact of the matter is this: Material objects are three-dimensional constituted objects, whether the ultimate constituters are considered either singly as sums (à la universalism) or severally as the items that allegedly make up the sums (à la plural quantification). In this chapter, I have opted for universalism – with the caveat that sums are

---

[32] Lewis, *Parts of Classes*, pp. 81–82.

[33] Ibid., p. 87. Emphasis mine. In the end, I believe that Lewis does not accept composition as identity as any more than an analogy.

[34] Another alternative is to say that the x's have a sum at t if and only if there is some y such that the x's constitute y at t.

tantamount to ontological free riders. As a Practical Realist, I care more about whether the view illuminates the world we encounter than about whether ultimate constituters are the x's or sums of the x's.

SOME PHILOSOPHICAL PUZZLES

Why, you may ask, do we need constitution at all when we have mereology? The short answer is that I am interested in an ontological account of ordinary objects that gain and lose parts – stars, trees, automobiles, statues, people, and passports. The persistence conditions of ordinary things differ from the persistence conditions of mereological sums. On the one hand, ordinary things of many kinds survive change of parts; mereological sums cannot survive change of parts. On the other hand, mereological sums continue to exist as long as their parts continue to exist; ordinary things do not continue to exist as long as their parts continue to exist. (Again: Smash the porcelain figure to smithereens, and the porcelain figure exists no more; but the sum that constituted it right before it was smashed still exists.) Since the persistence conditions of ordinary objects differ from the persistence conditions of mereological sums, ordinary objects cannot simply be (identical to) mereological sums. The ontological gap between mereological sums and ordinary objects is filled by the notion of constitution.

The Constitution View has a second type of pay-off. Not only does it provide a unified ontological account of all the material objects that we encounter in everyday life, but it also helps solve certain philosophical puzzles. In this section, I shall show how the Constitution View can handle some puzzles.[35]

Tibbles the cat   One puzzle is this:[36] At t1, Tibbles was an ordinary cat on a mat. Suppose that at t1, someone distinguished an entity that was Tibbles minus his tail and called this "peculiar animate entity" "Tib." So, since Tibbles has a tail at t1, but Tib does not, Tibbles ≠ Tib. At t1, both Tibbles and Tib were on the mat. At t2, an accident befalls Tibbles, who – still on

---

[35] I do not deny that there are other solutions (e.g., four-dimensionalist solutions), but I want to show that the Constitution View has some solutions, which, I believe, are the most natural solutions. For another three-dimensionalist solution, see "The Doctrine of Arbitrary Undetached Parts," in Peter van Inwagen, *Ontology, Identity and Modality* (Cambridge: Cambridge University Press, 2001): 75–94.

[36] The puzzle traces back through Peter Geach to William of Sherwood. The version given here comes from David Wiggins, "On Being in the Same Place at the Same Time," *Philosophical Review* 77 (1968): 90–95. Reprinted in Michael Rea, ed., *Material Constitution: A Reader* (Lanham, MD: Rowman and Littlefield Publishers, Inc., 1997), pp. 3–9.

the mat – loses his tail. At t3, Tibbles still has not left the mat. Now, at t3, there's a cat without a tail on the mat. Tailless Tib sits there; but so does Tibbles, who has lost his tail but survived. Are there one or two catlike objects on the mat at t3? Since Tib ≠ Tibbles, it seems that at t3, there are two catlike entities on the mat. Unhappy result!

The Constitution View has an easy way to avoid the unfortunate conclusion that at t3, there are two cats on the mat. At t1, Tibbles is constituted, say, by the sum of a head, torso, four legs, and tail. At t1, there is nothing that is *constituted* by the sum of the same head, the same torso, the same four legs (and no tail). So, at t1, there is no "peculiar animate entity" to name "Tib." The only cat on the mat at t1 is Tibbles; it is false to say, "At t1, both Tibbles and Tib were on the mat." There is no tailless cat on the mat at t1. But at t3, after his unfortunate accident, Tibbles, still on the mat, is constituted by the sum of the same head, the same torso, the same four legs, and no tail. Tibbles is constituted by different sums at different times. There never were two catlike entities on the mat. Tibbles remained alone on the mat throughout the interval from t1 to t3 – at t1 constituted by the sum of head, torso, legs and tail; at t3, tailless. The putative puzzle simply disappears if we look to constitution.[37]

Trunk/tree   Consider a tree that has one branch: On Monday, the tree consists of a trunk and a single branch. Then on Tuesday, someone cuts off the branch, leaving nothing of the tree but the trunk. What's the relation between tree and trunk? To some philosophers, there seems to be a puzzle here.[38] It seems that someone reasonably may make the following three assertions on Tuesday:

(a) This tree is identical with (is one and the same object as) this trunk.
(b) This tree was bigger yesterday.
(c) This trunk was not bigger yesterday.

But (a)–(c) are logically inconsistent: they cannot all be true. There are several ways to remove the inconsistency. The Constitution View rejects

---

[37] Someone may object: Why isn't Tib a distinct cat at t1? Surely, cat-favorable circumstances hold for Tib at t1 as well as for Tibbles at t3. No. Although I cannot provide a full account of cat-favorable circumstances, we may be fairly sure that they rule out a cat's having proper parts that are cats or a cat's being a proper part of another cat.

[38] The example and the following triad come from Eli Hirsch, *The Concept of Identity* (New York: Oxford University Press, 1982), p. 57.

(a): the trunk is not identical to the tree since the trunk and tree have different persistence conditions.[39]

According to the Constitution View, on Monday, the tree is constituted by the sum of branch and trunk. On Tuesday, the tree is constituted, not by a sum, but by the trunk. The relation of the sum of the branch and trunk to the tree on Monday is the same as the relation of the trunk alone to the tree on Tuesday. And that relation is the same relation as the relation of the lump to the statue. The difference between the trunk/tree case and the lump/statue case is that the lump existed before the statue existed, but the trunk did not exist before the tree existed. But in both cases, the persistence conditions of the constituted object differ from those of the constituting object.

Puzzles of vagueness   In chapter 6, we saw how there can be vagueness in the world. Granted, for any indeterminacy in the world, there is determinacy. The three kinds of vagueness in the world all depend on the distinction between sums and ordinary objects.

First, vagueness of temporal boundaries is indeterminacy of existence at a time. As we saw earlier, the sun has vague (or blurred) temporal boundaries: there is no exact moment at which it came into existence. But if there are some times t at which it is indeterminate that the sun exists then, then there must be other times t' at which it is determinate that the sun exists then (at t'). Only something that exists determinately at some time t' could exist indeterminately at some other time t. And the indeterminate existence of the sun is explained by indeterminacy of constitution. To say that the sun exists indeterminately at t is to say that: for some sums, (i) it is indeterminate whether any of those sums constitute anything at t, and (ii) those sums are causally continuous with sums that determinately constitute the sun at t'.

Second, vagueness of spatial boundaries is indeterminacy of existence at a place. Your dog Fido has vague (or blurred) spatial boundaries: there is no exact boundary between Fido and not-Fido. There are places near the surface of Fido where it is indeterminate that Fido exists there. But if there are some places p at which it is indeterminate that the dog exists there, then there must be other places p' at which it is determinate that Fido exists there (at t'). Only something that exists determinately at some place p' could exist indeterminately at some other place p. To say that at t Fido

---

[39]   Hirsch, whose puzzle this is, also rejects (a) and introduces a relation that he calls "constitutive identity."

exists indeterminately at p is to say that: for some sums, such that place p is occupied in some but not in others, (i) it is indeterminate which of those sums constitutes Fido at t, and (ii) in each of those sums place p' is occupied and Fido determinately exists at p'.

Third, vagueness of parts is a generalization of vagueness of spatial boundaries (i.e., vagueness of spatial boundaries may be thought of as a case of vagueness of parts). An organism has vagueness of parts: a semi-detached umbilical cord is such that it is indeterminate whether it is part of the organism at t. But if there is something x such that it is indeterminate that x is part of an organism at t, then there must be other things y such that it is determinate that y is part of the organism at t. To say of some x that an organism indeterminately has x as a part at t is to say that: for some sums, some of which contain x and others of which do not, (i) it is indeterminate which of those sums constitutes the organism at t, and (ii) each of those sums contains y such that y is determinately a part of the organism at t.

Ordinary objects, but not sums, may have indeterminate parts. Sums as well as ordinary objects may have indeterminate temporal and spatial boundaries; e.g., the sum of my dining room chairs has indeterminate temporal and spatial boundaries in virtue of the fact that the chairs have indeterminate temporal and spatial boundaries. Distinguishing between sums and ordinary objects gives us a way to solve some of the puzzles of vagueness. Moreover, it gives us an ontological explanation of each of these kinds of vagueness – vagueness of parts and of temporal and spatial boundaries. Language and thought are not the only sources of vagueness. There is vagueness in the world.

So, the distinction between sums and ordinary objects confers a number of advantages on the Constitution View: it explains how ordinary objects can have vague spatial boundaries, vague temporal boundaries, and vague parts, without courting vague identity.[40]

CONCLUSION

To conclude this chapter, let us turn to the main pay-off of the Constitution View: The Constitution View provides a unified ontological

---

[40] See the discussion in chapter 11 of the relation between x's being in the ontology and x's existing at t. See the discussion in chapter 6 of the dependence of an object's spatial and temporal boundaries on the object's *determinate* existence. See also chapter 10, "Count Indeterminacy?"

account of all the kinds of material objects that we encounter in everyday life, from car keys to kittens to people. We can acknowledge that what makes a person a person or an automobile an automobile is an ontological matter, not just a matter of how we use our concepts. By holding that, in addition to the relation of aggregation, there is a distinct metaphysical relation – constitution – we can acknowledge that ordinary things are in the ontology. The many kinds of ordinary objects typically overlooked by philosophers – e.g., artworks and artifacts – receive the same kind of treatment as water molecules and planets. An intention-dependent or ID object (e.g., Cellini's *Perseus*) is constituted by something (a piece of bronze), which in turn is constituted by a sum of atoms of copper and tin bonded in a certain way in a certain shape. It's constitution all the way down to sums of physical particles.

Many philosophers look to mereological theories of various sorts to understand material objects. If one is concerned with the everyday world – populated with objects that are intention-dependent and objects that are not – mereology does not offer a comprehensive approach to the disparate kinds of objects that we interact with. The Constitution View, whether allied to a mereological view or not, does. Unlike mereological views taken alone, the Constitution View is an ontological account of all kinds of everyday objects.[41]

---

[41] I wrote this chapter as a concession to mereology, but I can do without mereology and appeal to aggregates, instead of sums, as I did in chapter 3. In "Can Mereological Sums Change Their Parts?," Peter van Inwagen holds that philosophers who take mereological sums to have their parts essentially "have failed to grasp an essential feature of the concept 'mereological sum'." Anyone who agrees with him should substitute "aggregates" for "mereological sums" in the context of the Constitution View.

10

Three-dimensionalism defended

So far, I have simply assumed that we live in a three-dimensional world that endures over time. But three-dimensionalism is not uncontested. Indeed, the greatest challenge to the Constitution View is four-dimensionalism. In this chapter, I first want to show that the challenges from four-dimensionalism do not unseat the intuitively satisfactory three-dimensionalism of ordinary life. I shall argue that three-dimensionalism is not ruled out by Theodore Sider's technical argument from vagueness for four-dimensionalism. Then, I shall show that, despite the fact that constitution is a vague relation, the Constitution View does not imply that the number of objects in ontology is indeterminate. Next, I shall argue that the so-called "paradoxes of coincidence" are no reason to favor four-dimensionalism over three-dimensionalism. I'll conclude with reasons to prefer three-dimensionalism over four-dimensionalism.

THREE-DIMENSIONALISM VS. FOUR-DIMENSIONALISM

Three- and four-dimensionalism differ with respect to whether or not objects have temporal parts in addition to their spatial parts. Four-dimensionalism is the view that "every object, x, has a temporal part at every moment, t, at which it exists."[1] A temporal part may be thought of as a temporal slice or a temporal segment of a physical object. Four-dimensionalism implies that if a baseball, say, exists from, say, t1 to t2, the baseball has a temporal part at every time in the interval between t1 and t2, and – here's the kicker – at each time t of its existence, it has a temporal part that exists at t and at no other time. That is, if x exists at t, then x has a temporal part that exists at t and only at t. As Theodore Sider puts it, four-dimensionalism may be formulated "as the claim that, necessarily, each spatiotemporal object has a temporal part at every

---

[1] Theodore Sider, *Four-Dimensionalism* (Oxford: Clarendon Press, 2001), p. 138.

moment at which it exists."[2] What the three-dimensionalist and the four-dimensionalist disagree about, then, is the following thesis:

> (T) If x exists from t1 until t5, then there is something (a temporal part of x) that exists at t3 and *only* at t3.

The three-dimensionalist and the four-dimensionalist disagree about how many objects there are. According to the four-dimensionalist, "Any filled region of spacetime is the total career of some object."[3] So, each of the tiniest spacetime regions – disconnected or not – that is filled with anything is a whole object. The three-dimensionalists, from Aristotle on, have more intuitive (and robust) notions of what it takes to be an object.

Of course, a three-dimensionalist also can speak of temporal parts, but for the three-dimensionalist, temporal parts are not themselves objects. If x exists from t1 until t5, a three-dimensionalist can speak of x's temporal part at t3; but for the three-dimensionalist, the temporal part is, perhaps, an ordered pair of x and t3, not a concrete object. Sider calls temporal parts understood as ordered pairs of enduring objects and times, "ersatz temporal parts."

The three-dimensionalist and four-dimensionalist views differ on the nature of persistence. Suppose that a kitten is born at t1 and lives until t4. According to the three-dimensionalist view, a cat, whole and entire, comes into existence at some time – say, t1 – and the whole cat *endures* until some later time, say, t4: the whole cat exists between t1 and t4.[4] According to the four-dimensionalist view, the whole cat never exists at any one time; only part of the cat exists at any time between t1 and t4. The cat not only has spatial parts, but it also has temporal parts; and at t2, say, the temporal part of the cat at t3 does not exist. So, on four-dimensionalism, only part of the cat is present at any time since it has temporal parts at other times; the whole cat is never present at any one time. The cat persists by having temporal parts at later times.

According to four-dimensionalism, objects perdure; according to three-dimensionalism, objects endure. Sider put the contrast picturesquely: "A perduring object is 'spread out' over a region of spacetime, whereas an enduring object 'sweeps through' a region of spacetime, the whole of the object occupying the region's subregions at different times."[5] (When a

---

[2] Ibid., p. 59.   [3] Ibid., p. 120.

[4] Since I do not believe that cats (or anything else) come into existence instantaneously, "t1," etc., should be thought of as designating intervals (with vague boundaries).

[5] Sider, *Four-Dimensionalism*, p. 3.

weary colleague says, "I'm not all here today," the four-dimensionalist may sincerely and literally assert, "You're not all here on any day.")

There are two varieties of four-dimensionalism: the worm view and the stage view. On the worm view, objects are four-dimensional worms, spread out in spacetime. On the stage view, objects are instantaneous stages. On the usual four-dimensionalist views, everyday terms refer to worms; on Sider's four-dimensionalist view (a stage view), everyday terms refer to instantaneous objects. Other four-dimensionalists (e.g., Mark Heller) suppose that everyday terms do not ever refer to the objects of the (true) four-dimensional ontology.[6]

THE ARGUMENT FROM VAGUENESS

Sider has an industrial-strength metaphysical argument for four-dimensionalism: the argument from vagueness. Although the premises of the argument from vagueness are based on assumptions that I do not hold, I do not want press that point here. Rather, I want to propose a version of the three-dimensionalist Constitution View given in chapter 8 as a view that both avoids Sider's argument from vagueness and gives a robust account of ordinary objects as genuine objects that gain and lose parts.

Sider's argument for four-dimensionalism is analogous to Lewis's argument for unrestricted composition. Since I have already accepted (at least provisionally) unrestricted composition or universalism in chapter 9, it will be no surprise that my response to Sider's argument does not reject Lewis's argument for unrestricted composition. My tack, as we shall see, is somewhat different.

In order not to beg the question against the three-dimensionalist, Sider formulates his argument in terms of temporal mereology. Take the notion of (mereological) parthood-at-t to be primitive. Then, say that two things "overlap-at-t" if and only if something is (a mereological) part of each of them at t. Now, define "fusion-at-t": "x is a fusion-at-t of class S iff (1) every member of S is part of x at t, and (2) every part of x at t overlaps-at-t some member of S."[7]

There are three crucial terms in Sider's argument: an "assignment," a "D-fusion," and a "minimal D-fusion." An assignment is a function: An

---

[6] Ibid., pp. 60–61.
[7] Ibid., p. 58. I am following Sider in using "fusion" instead of "sum"; "fusion" and "sum" are interchangeable.

assignment is "any (possibly partial) function that takes one or more times as arguments and assigns non-empty classes of objects that exist at those times as values."[8] A D-fusion is a diachronic sum: An object x is a D-fusion of an assignment f if and only if "for every t in f's domain, x is a fusion-at-t of f(t)." A D-fusion of the assignment that exists only at times in the assignment's domain is a *minimal* D-fusion.[9]

Sider elaborates: Consider two times at which I exist. Let f be a function with just those two times in its domain that assigns to each the class of subatomic particles that are part of me then. "I am a D-fusion of f, since at each of the two times I am a fusion of the corresponding class of subatomic particles." However, I'm not a *minimal* D-fusion of f, since I also exist at other times. A minimal D-fusion of me is one that, for each of the times at which I exist, assigns the class of subatomic particles that are part of me then. A "minimal D-fusion of some objects at various times consists of those objects at those times and nothing more." A *minimal* D-fusion is an object that exists only at the times specified in the domain of a given assignment.

The argument from vagueness has two parts: first, an argument that establishes (U):

(U) Every assignment has a minimal D-fusion.

The second part is the claim that (U) entails four-dimensionalism. For example, consider an assignment that has only one instant t its domain, to which it assigns an object. If every assignment has a minimal D-fusion, then the assignment that has only a single instant t in its domain, to which it assigns an object o, has a minimal D-fusion: the object o exists at t and *only* at t. If there are objects that exist only instantaneously, then (Sider argues) there are temporal parts. An object that exists only at t is an instantaneous temporal part.[10] Hence, (U) entails four-dimensionalism.

But what is the argument for (U)? It is the argument from vagueness that relies on the claim that, if not every assignment has a minimal D-fusion, then there must be a sharp cut-off in a continuous series of pairwise similar cases in whether or not a minimal D-fusion occurs. But, Sider claims, it is implausible to suppose that there is a sharp cut-off between very similar cases in whether or not a minimal D-fusion occurs. The argument is this:[11]

---

[8] Ibid., p. 133.   [9] Ibid.   [10] Ibid., pp. 138–139.
[11] Theodore Sider, "Against Vague Existence," *Philosophical Studies* 114 (2003): 135–146.

1. Some assignments fail to have minimal D-fusions – i.e., minimal diachronic fusions do not always exist. (premise for reductio)

Then,

2. There is a sorites connecting a case where no minimal D-fusion exists to a case there it does.
3. It's never vague whether a minimal D-fusion exists. (premise)

So,

4. There's a sharp cut-off in the sorites.

But

5. 4 is implausible.

So,

6. Every assignment has a minimal D-fusion – i.e., minimal diachronic fusions always exist – and thus (U) is true.

However, this argument from vagueness is not invulnerable. As Sider notes in *Four-Dimensionalism*, there is an exception to premise 5: there is a three-dimensionalist view that countenances a sharp cut-off that is not implausible. I'll quote Sider at length:

There is, however, a three-dimensionalist ontology that would secure such a cut-off: a version of mereological essentialism according to which, intuitively, nothing exists but mereological sums, which have their parts permanently, and exist as long as those parts exist. Minimal D-fusions could be restricted nonvaguely: *an assignment has a minimal D-fusion, roughly, when and only when it is the temporally longest assignment for a given fixed class of objects.* The idea is that mereological fusions of objects "automatically" come into existence when their parts do, automatically retain those same parts, and automatically go out of existence when any of those parts go out of existence.[12]

Sider observes that mereological essentialism – the view that objects have their parts essentially – is a three-dimensionalist view that escapes his argument from vagueness for four-dimensionalism.[13] However, mereological-essentialist views (like Chisholm's) have the consequence that ordinary objects are not genuine objects; what we call "tables" and "chairs" are only fictions or ontological parasites, *entia successiva*. When we speak of the persistence of ordinary objects, we are speaking in a "loose and popular"

---

[12] Sider, *Four-Dimensionalism*, p. 135, emphasis added.   [13] Ibid., p. 180.

way about *entia successiva*. On Chisholm's view, genuine concrete objects have their parts essentially. There are true statements about ordinary objects like tables and chairs, but such statements must be translatable into statements about objects that have their parts essentially.

Sider admits that Chisholm's mereological essentialism escapes his (Sider's) argument from vagueness, but Chisholm's view has the drawback of not recognizing ordinary objects that change their parts as genuine objects. They are only fictions or logical constructions, *entia successiva*. Now, a theory according to which there really are no tables or other ordinary objects is not as good as one that recognizes tables and other ordinary objects as genuine objects. With this in mind, I suggest the following as a three-dimensionalist possibility that both avoids Sider's argument from vagueness for four-dimensionalism and at the same time has a robust conception of ordinary objects that gain and lose parts. It is, unsurprisingly, the Constitution View that takes sums (fusions) as constituters.

Let me summarize the idea that I want to formulate: Start with Chisholm's universe, populated by three-dimensional objects that have their parts essentially. Call such objects "Chisholm objects." Then to the Chisholm objects, add ordinary objects, like tables and chairs, that survive changes in their parts. Then consider the relation between Chisholm objects and ordinary objects. The relation is constitution at a time. So, Chisholm objects are the sums employed as constituters in chapter 9. And since Chisholm objects have their parts essentially, there is a sharp cut-off in a sorites of Chisholm objects. So, Chisholm objects falsify line 5 – there is a sharp cut-off in the sorites that is not implausible.

The three-dimensionalist view that I shall propose is similar to the view that Sider calls the "Nothing but three-dimensionalist sums" view – but without the "Nothing but": "if x is ever composed of the ys, then: at any time at which each of the ys exist, x exists and is composed of them; and at any time at which x exists, it is composed of the ys."[14] Call any x that satisfies this definition a fusion. (These are the three-dimensionalist fusions/sums of chapter 9.) The "Nothing but three-dimensionalist sums" view gives a picture: "the world consists exclusively of three-dimensional objects that are individuated by, and whose persistence conditions are given by, their parts."[15]

---

[14] Ibid., p. 181.   [15] Ibid.

On the view that I propose, there are such three-dimensionalist fusions, which have their parts essentially; but three-dimensionalist fusions are not the exclusive occupants of the world. Ordinary objects are objects but are not three-dimensionalist sums: Chisholm objects are those fusions that are ultimately constituters of ordinary objects. Ordinary objects are ultimately constituted by different three-dimensionalist fusions – by different Chisholm objects – at different times. So, the view to be considered is a hybrid that appeals both to Chisholm objects (objects that have their parts necessarily) and ordinary objects (that survive change of parts).

Typically, constituted objects can gain and lose parts. A flag tattered in battle is still the same flag that it was before the battle. A human body, which undergoes complete change of parts every several years, is an obvious example of an object's surviving change of parts. So, I am not suggesting mereological essentialism with respect to ordinary objects. But I am suggesting, *pace* Chisholm, that ordinary material objects are not ontologically inferior to objects that do not gain and lose parts. No, I think that medium-sized objects, including persons, are "mereologically inconstant," and that they are genuine objects. Although ordinary objects may change parts, they are ultimately constituted by Chisholm objects that do not change parts.

Let's return to mereology. Chisholm objects are fusions (i.e., sums), and as I have already mentioned, I suppose that for any things – call them "the ys" – there is a unique fusion of the ys at all times that the ys exist. As we saw in chapter 9, fusions come into existence "automatically" with the coming into existence of the things that are its parts and remain in existence as long as its parts do. So, Chisholm objects – fusions – are characterized by mereological essentialism.

There are several properties of fusions of special interest for Chisholm objects: (i) For any ys that exist at t, there is a unique fusion at t of the ys. (ii) That fusion exists as long as its parts (the ys) exist – regardless of the arrangement or spatial locations of the ys. So, if the ys exist from t1 to t3, there is a fusion of them at each time from t1 to t3; and their fusion at t1 = their fusion at t2 = their fusion at t3. (iii) A fusion has its parts essentially. (By contrast, ordinary objects – stars, trees, people, automobiles, statues, credit cards – gain and lose parts during the periods of time that they exist.)

Now we can see why Chisholm objects falsify (U). Consider a Chisholm object that lasts from t1 until t4. An assignment that has in its domain all the times from t1 until, say, t2 and that assigns to each of those times the Chisholm object does not have a minimal D-fusion. The D-fusion of that assignment is not minimal, because the Chisholm object exists at times other than those in the domain – e.g., at t3. The assignment is not "the temporally longest assignment for a given fixed class of objects," and hence does not have a minimal D-fusion.[16]

In light of the Chisholm objects, not every assignment has a minimal D-fusion. The Chisholm part of the three-dimensionalist view that I am suggesting is immune to the argument from vagueness. A Chisholm object will be a minimal D-fusion of an assignment whose domain is the set of all the times at which that object exists, and which assigns to each time in its domain the unit set of the object itself; but on the view that I'm proposing, there will be many assignments that do not have minimal D-fusions – namely, assignments whose domains are proper subsets of the times at which the Chisholm objects exist.

The point here is that the mereological essentialism of Chisholm objects allows nonvague restrictions on minimal D-fusions (i.e., allows there to be sharp cut-offs in whether a minimal D-fusion occurs in a continuous series). So, Sider's conclusion that every assignment has a minimal D-fusion is avoided – without implying that there is any vagueness about whether a minimal D-fusion occurs. I can agree with Sider that "in any case of minimal D-fusion, either minimal D-fusion definitely occurs or minimal D-fusion definitely does not occur."[17]

As we saw in chapter 9, although fusions are not ordinary objects, there is nonetheless a role for fusions in an account of ordinary objects: the fusions that are Chisholm objects are the ultimate constituters of ordinary objects. At t, a fusion may have its parts arranged in a certain way ("chairwise"), and it may constitute a chair at t. When the arrangement of its parts changes – say, they fly to flinders – the same fusion that constituted a chair at t ceases to constitute a chair. The chair ceases to exist, but the fusion does not.

Many fusions constitute nothing at all. There is a fusion now of the particles that now constitute the fish that I'll have for dinner and the particles that now constitute your backscratcher, but such a fusion is not a would-be constituter of an ordinary object. Such fusions do not constitute anything. Although it is not the case that all fusions constitute something, the converse does hold: all constituted objects are ultimately constituted by fusions. Chisholm objects are the fusions that are ultimate constituters.

---

[16] Ibid., p. 135.　　[17] Ibid., p. 134.

Consider, for example, a table made up at t of four legs and a table top. Suppose again that the legs are attached to the top by being screwed into holes in the top. The table is constituted at t by the Chisholm object consisting of the particles in the five parts arranged in a certain way at t. That Chisholm object began to exist when the particles that make up the five parts came into existence, and it existed a very long time before it came to constitute the table. The same Chisholm object may constitute a table at one time, and a bridge at another time – depending on the arrangement of its parts and the circumstances it is in. It constitutes a table only when it is in table-favorable circumstances (determined partly by the arrangement of parts and partly by human activities). The table has different modal properties from those of the Chisholm object – e.g., the table could not survive too much rearrangement of its parts, but the Chisholm object could. The table is constituted at t by a Chisholm object. Chisholm objects are not constituted by anything.

The view that I just proposed eliminates vagueness with respect to the domain of Chisholm objects, but not with respect to the domain of ordinary objects. So, Sider may say that I have not met his challenge. But I think that there's a better way to understand the dialectic of the situation.

I have just argued that Chisholm objects falsify (U) – the thesis that every assignment has a minimal D-fusion. But the "objects" that are the D-fusions are not ordinary objects; they are ... well, fusions, mere mereological objects. They are constituters of ordinary objects; D-fusions are the objects postulated to play a theoretical role in understanding ordinary objects.

With respect to D-fusions, a three-dimensionalist can agree that there is no vagueness. But it does not follow that there is no vagueness in genuine objects of the various primary kinds. Similarly, we can agree with Lewis that "In any case of composition, either composition definitely occurs, or composition definitely does not occur," without supposing that composition is the only object-making relation. My own view, as we have seen in chapters 6 and 9, is that the constitution relation is vague. There may be no fact of the matter at t about whether such-and-such Chisholm object constitutes at t a table. I think that a sorites argument shows this. But from the fact that constitution is vague, all that follows is vagueness with respect to the existence of ordinary objects at specified times. In chapter 11, I discuss the relation between existing simpliciter and existing at t. As we have seen in chapter 6, there is indeterminacy about existing at t only for objects that (determinately) exist simpliciter. So, the vagueness of constitution (and the threat of sorites with respect to when a fusion constitutes an object) does not make ordinary objects fictions or logical constructions.[18]

Sider holds that it cannot be vague how many things exist in a world with only finitely many objects. It may seem as if the Constitution View denies this. As I argued in chapter 6, all the things that we encounter come into existence gradually. So, it may be thought that, on the Constitution View, it is vague whether such objects exist or not. Not so. What is vague is whether an ordinary object – a house, say, or an organism – exists *at some time*. What Sider thinks is impossible is "count indeterminacy" – "indeterminacy in how many objects *there are*, not merely in how many objects *exist at* some specified time."[19]

I am not committed to indeterminacy in how many objects *there are*. What is indeterminate, on my view, is whether x exists at some particular time. But, as I said in chapter 6, it cannot be indeterminate whether x exists at t unless it is determinate that x exists simpliciter.

Both spatial and temporal indeterminacy presuppose determinate existence. The domain of the unrestricted existential quantifier includes everything that exists (ever), and there is no indeterminacy in that domain.[20] In chapter 11, there is a full discussion of the difference between existing simpliciter (i.e., being in the domain of the unrestricted existential quantifier) and existing-at-a-time. The point here is that the Constitution View does not court count indeterminacy.

Therefore, I propose this "split-level" account of material objects as a three-dimensionalist view that both accommodates realism about ordinary objects, and escapes Sider's argument from vagueness.[21] So, I see no pressure to give up three-dimensionalism for four-dimensionalism.

A final challenge by the four-dimensionalist is that spatial coincidence is paradoxical on three-dimensionalist views, and not on four-dimensionalist

---

[18] See chapters 6 and 11.   [19] Sider, *Four-Dimensionalism*, p. 136.
[20] I do not believe that possible objects – like the grandchildren that I could have had – exist. There are no such beings, though there might have been. But that is another story.
[21] I presented a predecessor of these arguments at a book symposium on Theodore Sider's *Four-Dimensionalism*, at the Central APA, March, 2003. I'd like to thank Ed Gettier for ongoing discussion of these issues. Of course, he is not to blame for my errors.

views. I put "paradoxes of coincidence" in scare-quotes because, according to the Constitution View, there is no paradox about the spatial coincidence of a constituted thing and what constitutes it.[22] The idea of constitution is complex and well defined: it is much more than a claim that there happen to be two things at the same place at the same time. However, many philosophers regard the idea of spatial coincidence as puzzling, and they think that four-dimensionalism can "solve" the puzzles.[23] I want to show that four-dimensionalism has nothing on the Constitution View with respect to matters of spatial coincidence.

To see what the standard four-dimensionalist takes to be paradoxical, consider a well-worn case: Suppose that a sculptor molds a lump into a statue. Say that distinct objects coincide when they exist at the same place at the same time and have all the same subatomic particles. There are at least two putative puzzles of coincidence – one temporal and one modal. The temporal puzzle is to show how the statue and the lump can be distinct and yet coincide at times – during part of the lump's existence, say. The modal puzzle is to show how the lump and the statue can be distinct and yet differ only in their modal properties – e.g., the lump could have existed in a world without statues, but the statue could not have. Begin with the putative temporal puzzle.

The putative temporal puzzle is to explain how a lump and a statue can be distinct, yet coincide across time. Sider credits the worm theory for its treatment of the putative temporal puzzle of coincidence: the worm theory admits coincidence and explains how it's possible. The explanation is a simple analogy: Coincidence is no more objectionable than roads that overlap. The statue and the lump simply have a shared temporal part. There are two possible cases; either the lump and the statue share some, but not all, their temporal parts, or they share all their temporal parts. If the lump and the statue share some, but not all, temporal parts, then they are

---

[22] For example, Trenton Merrick denies that two distinct objects can be "co-located" because he defines co-location as a mereological relation. Unsurprisingly, I do not accept his definition. (Indeed, I take his remarks to be another reason to distinguish constitution from a mereological notion like composition.) See Trenton Merricks, *Objects and Persons* (Oxford: Clarendon Press, 2001), p. 39.

[23] The spatial coincidence of objects is a straightforward part of the Constitution View. I have never seen anything paradoxical in spatial coincidence. I see my task as giving an account of constitution (that results in "coincidence"), never as trying to eliminate coincidence. What Sider and others find repulsive, I find attractive. So, when Sider speaks of "the threat of co-location" or "the merit of doing away with coincidence" (*Four-Dimensionalism*, p. 163), I am nonplussed.

distinct. Everyone agrees that if a (e.g., the lump) lasts longer than b (e.g., the statue), then a ≠ b. So, the worm view offers no "solution" to the putative puzzle of coincidence in the case where the lump and the statue have some different temporal parts; it simply agrees with the Constitution View in this case – the lump and the statue are nonidentical.

But, still assuming the worm view, what if the lump and the statue share *all* their temporal, as well as spatial parts? What if the lump and the statue came into existence at exactly the same time and went out of existence at exactly the same time? (This would happen if the statue came into existence by removing parts of a large lump until a small lump came into existence at the same time as the statue; and the statue and lump went out of existence by further removing pieces of the small lump.) This raises the modal puzzle, in which the lump and the statue share all their spatial and temporal parts (i.e., they come into existence at the same time and go out of existence at the same time, and are spatially coincident during the entire time that they exist).

The worm view has absolutely nothing to say about any modal puzzle of coincidence – e.g., that the lump and the statue could have had different temporal extensions if, say, the statue had been squashed although the lump continued to exist. Although the lump and the statue are wholly coincident, they might not have been. Typically, four-dimensionalists analyze statements about what could have happened to the statue as statements not about the statue per se, but about *counterparts* of the statue in other possible worlds.[24] What seems to be coincidence of nonidentical objects is simply a matter of our concepts: "lump" and "statue" have different counterparts in different possible worlds. In the actual world, there is just a single four-dimensional worm to which we apply our concepts "lump" and "statue."

So, the worm view must treat the temporal and modal cases differently: Whether the lump and the statue are distinct depends on whether the lump happens to outlast the statue (or vice versa). In the case where the lump outlasts the statue, the worm view must say that there is an ontological difference between the lump and the statue since they have some different temporal parts. In the case where the lump and the statue come into existence and go out of existence at the same time, the worm view must deny that there is an ontological difference between the lump and statue since they have all the same temporal (as well as spatial) parts. So, the worm version of

---

[24] See David Lewis, *On the Plurality of Worlds* (Oxford: Basil Blackwell, 1986).

four-dimensionalism treats the putative paradoxes of coincidence in a disjointed way: The lump and statue are distinct in one case but not in the other.

By contrast, the Constitution View treats the two cases in the same way: The lump and statue are distinct in both cases. In both temporal and modal cases, there is an ontological difference between the lump and the statue: the lump constitutes the statue without being identical to it. What makes the statue the thing that it is (a statue) is different from what makes the lump the thing that it is (a lump). The distinctness of the lump and the statue is guaranteed by the fact that they differ in their persistence conditions, whether they actually coincide or not. In neither the temporal nor the modal case, according to the Constitution View, is the difference between the lump and the statue merely "conceptual."

Indeed, although the lump and the statue have all the same subatomic parts, the lump and the statue do not supervene on the same "base facts," to use Sider's term.[25] (It is crucial to distinguish constitution from supervenience.) On the Constitution View, a lump is a lump in virtue of the arrangement of atoms in the lump, but it is not the case that a statue is a statue in virtue of the arrangement of atoms in the statue. To be a statue is not just to be atoms arranged "statuesquely." Atoms arranged statuesquely are not (and do not constitute) a statue in a world lacking artists and the conventions of art. A meteor that looks like a statue is not a statue. The difference between a statue and a statue-looking meteor is not just that one has a property that the other lacks; statue and meteor are fundamentally different kinds of things. A world with statues is ontologically different from a world with only meteors. If the lump and statue do not supervene on the same "base facts," then by Leibniz's Law, they are not identical. So, there's no puzzle: What makes the lump a lump is different from what makes a statue a statue. So it is no surprise that they are nonidentical. (Perhaps allegiance to Humean supervenience – which, of course, I don't share – prevents philosophers from recognizing this.) The modal puzzle disappears on the Constitution View.

The appearance of the modal puzzle stems from the false thesis that the nature of a thing is determined by its subatomic parts and their relations to each other.[26] If one holds that mereological view, then it is a puzzle how there can be two distinct things that have the same subatomic parts related to each other in the same way. But the thesis that the nature of a thing is determined by its subatomic parts and their relations to each other is false

---

[25] Sider, *Four-Dimensionalism*, p. 158.   [26] Ibid., p. 141.

anyway – regardless of issues of coincidence. (What makes something a statue [or any other ID object] is not determined by its microstructure.) So, it seems to me that the solution to the putative modal puzzle of coincidence is simple: give up a false belief.

Sider holds a variant on the standard "worm" approach to four-dimensionalism. Sider's preferred four-dimensional theory is the stage view, according to which continuants (i.e., "the objects that we typically discuss, name, quantify over and discuss, whatever those objects turn out to be") are stages, rather than temporally extended spacetime worms. On the stage view, since "the names for the continuants involved [in referring to the lump and statue] name the shared stage rather than the distinct worms, the stage theorist does away with distinct coinciding continuants."[27] I think that the effect of this approach is to explain the appearance of coinciding entities by saying that there is just a single entity – a stage – with two names – a lump-name and a statue-name. This shared stage has different sets of temporal and modal counterparts, depending on whether the counterparts are lump-counterparts or statue-counterparts.

Although the stage view does eliminate the phenomenon of coinciding entities, it does so at the cost of eliminating entities that are recognizable altogether. Indeed, it does so at the cost of eliminating noninstantaneous entities altogether. In a "strict and philosophical sense," no entity lasts even a nanosecond; all entities are instantaneous.[28] That's a high cost, especially when you ask what is supposed to be so objectionable about coinciding entities anyway? Sider finds two things objectionable about coinciding entities. (i) We don't usually assume that ordinary objects are capable of co-location; and (ii) "the objects in question share all the same microscopic parts."[29] Neither of these complaints seems very serious. The former is just an intuition that you may or may not have; I don't have it, for example. The latter poses no problem for those who do not take the identity and existence of ordinary objects to be determined by their microscopic parts. And the latter poses no problem for those who recognize as genuine, ordinary objects (like artifacts and artworks) that have relational properties essentially. Yes, the Constitution View is committed to coinciding entities – but this is a small price to pay for a global metaphysics that leaves the world as we encounter it intact.

---

[27] Ibid., p. 191.
[28] Temporal parts get refigured as temporal counterparts. See Sider, *Four-Dimensionalism*, p. 193.
[29] Ibid., p. 141.

So, four-dimensionalism does not offer a compelling alternative to the Constitution View. Indeed, since four-dimensionalists consider parts to be objects, they seem equally committed to co-location of distinct entities when they countenance complete overlap of parts of two worms. Moreover, the stage view does violence to deeply held beliefs about persistence. On the stage view, nothing literally persists. Nothing that exists at t1 is identical to anything that exists at t2. (As Sider put it, "A 'stage' is instantaneous and so will not exist tomorrow."[30]) Sider responds to the objection that instantaneous stages cannot have the features that ordinary things have – e.g., beliefs. "Beliefs take time," he says. His response is that having a belief is a matter of having certain relations to temporal counterparts.[31] So, there is no single bearer of any belief. I suspect that psychologists and neuroscientists would scoff at such a construal of belief. Consequences like these are serious drawbacks to the stage view – too serious, in my opinion, to swallow in order to solve putative puzzle cases that arguably are not puzzles in the first place. So, the Constitution theorist need not quake at four-dimensionalists' treatment of spatial coincidence.

REASONS TO PREFER THREE-DIMENSIONALISM

I suspect that whether one prefers three- or four-dimensionalism depends partly on one's conception of metaphysics. In general, metaphysics is to expose and explain the most comprehensive features of reality. There are, I believe, two pictures of (what we might call) the arena of metaphysical inquiry – the *explananda* for metaphysical explanation. On the traditional picture, philosophers have given accounts of reality that explain why things seem the way that they do: Plato explained the world of sights and sounds in terms of the Forms; Aristotle explained organisms in terms of matter and form. The goal was to explain the observed world. Today's metaphysicians, by contrast, seem to care less about the world as encountered, and more about (admittedly fascinating) philosophical puzzles – like the problem of the heap or puzzles arising from the supposition that "Ted splits into Ed and Fred."[32] If one seeks a metaphysical account of the world that we encounter and interact with, there is every reason to prefer three-dimensionalism. (Indeed, some proponents of four-dimensionalism explicitly disavow any

---

[30] Ibid., p. 201.   [31] Ibid., pp. 197–198.   [32] Ibid., p. 165.

interest in the world of ordinary things.[33]) Rather than tarry on metaphysics in general, or on the many arguments against four-dimensionalism, let us turn to a particular consequence of four-dimensionalism.

The consequence on which I want to focus is the standard four-dimensionalist conception of material objects as series of spatiotemporal parts. According to four-dimensionalism, all four-dimensional worms are ontologically on a par. The differences among mountains, cats, rocks, microscopes, and people do not show up in basic ontology. Moreover, objects of these disparate kinds are on an ontological par with a four-dimensional worm that has as (mereological) parts the eruption of Mount Vesuvius at t, houses in Pompeii at t', and rubble at t'', or a worm that has as (mereological) parts Galileo's recanting in Rome in 1633, a cat's scratching itself in the next room a moment later, and the air between Galileo and the cat in the interval between the recantation and the scratching. Worse, all the above – from mountains and microscopes to arbitrary sums of four-dimensional objects – are on an ontological par with any collection of spatiotemporal particles.

There are uncountably many four-dimensional worms, each of which is an object. Only a tiny fraction of worms are salient to us, but there are no ontological differences among them. Sider and other four-dimensionalists don't count cats, or people, or Fs of any sort; they count "objects." What is an object? Sider says, "Any filled region of spacetime is the total career of some object."[34]

Four-dimensionalists need not deny that ordinary things like cats, rocks, microscopes, and people exist. What they deny is this: that they are *fundamentally* different kinds of things from each other, and that they are *fundamentally* different from arbitrary sums (like sum of the Statue of Liberty at t1, my husband's eyebrows at t2, and the Pentagon at t3). The ontology is one of filled spacetime regions, period. As Sider holds, *any* filled region of spacetime (however disconnected spatially or temporally) contains at least one real object, and there are no fundamental differences among filled regions of spacetime.[35]

Thus, there is no ontological distinction in four-dimensionalism between genuine objects and mere aggregations of spatiotemporal parts.

---

[33] I would count Heller here.   [34] Sider, *Four-Dimensionalism*, p. 120.

[35] Sider's own view is a stage version (not a worm version), according to which "the objects that we typically discuss, name, quantify over, and discuss. . . . are stages" (*Four-Dimensionalism*, pp. 190–191). Whereas worms are temporally extended, stages are instantaneous. (Since it took Nixon a second to say, "I am not a crook," during which there were nondenumerably

This has the unhappy consequence, mentioned in chapter 2, that when we say that the World Trade Center Towers went out of existence when they collapsed, we are saying no more, ontologically speaking, than we say when we say that the one-minute temporal part of the Towers thirty-minutes before the collapse went out of existence twenty-nine minutes before the collapse. After the collapse, the Towers had no more temporal parts; but the sum of particles with which four-dimensionalists identify the Towers continued to have temporal parts. We just stopped calling the continued temporal parts of the sum of particles "towers." I believe that when we say that the Towers went out of existence, we mean something more robust than four-dimensionalism can deliver.

This is even more obvious when we speak of the going out of existence of people. Consider a person who was blown to bits by a car bomb. On a four-dimensionalist view, what happened to her was no more ontologically significant than, say, the end of her temporal part that lasted all day on her thirteenth birthday. What made the bomb victim's temporal part her last temporal part was simply a matter of our concept "person." Ontologically speaking, there is no difference between the end of her last temporal part and the end of any other temporal part. (The redistribution of qualities resulting from the bomb is not an ontological difference.)

In short, I do not believe that four-dimensionalism can do justice to the ontological significance of going out of existence. Not only is there not a fundamental ontological difference between the bomb-victim's existing and not existing (or the Towers' existing and not existing), but also there is no ontological difference between spatiotemporal parts that are what we call "person" or "tower" and just a random assortment of spatiotemporal parts. Any arrangement of matter in any region of spacetime, no matter how disconnected, is an object.

A related question arises from the availability of too many worms. Suppose that you have a cat, one you chose out of a litter. If four-dimensionalism is true, then there is no fact of the matter, independent of language, about how many cats you have. There are uncountably many four-dimensional objects in the vicinity of your cat. We may truly *say* that there is exactly one cat in the room. But there are infinitely many equally good four-dimensional

---

many instantaneous stages, what did his use of "I" refer to?) The stages that make you up are temporal counterparts. Since the worm view is more prevalent, I shall not discuss the stage view in detail.

cat-candidates in the room that overlap each other almost completely. What is to make it true to say that there is exactly one cat in the room – despite the existence of the infinite number of "almost identical" cat-candidates in the room – is that the word "cat" is vague. Four-dimensionalists who are super-valuationists insist that "cat" has many "precisifications" (i.e., there are many ways of making the word "cat" precise.)[36] On any precisification, there is exactly one cat in the room. Alternatively, since the infinite number of cat-candidates overlap each other to such a degree, there is "near-identity," which we may take as one.[37] So, a four-dimensionalist may use a linguistic theory of vagueness to license *saying* that there is exactly one cat in the room, even though, if there were no language, there is *no fact of the matter* that there is exactly one cat in the room.

By contrast, consider how the Constitution View treats the case of there being exactly one cat. On the Constitution View, apart from language, there is plainly a fact of the matter that there is exactly one cat in the room. Whether or not there is exactly one cat in the room has nothing to do with our language.[38] That there is exactly one cat in the room is a state of affairs that definitely obtains. Whether there is exactly one cat in the room is straightforwardly a matter of biological fact of a sort that does not depend on language.

In sum, by construing any filled region of spacetime as an object, four-dimensionalism has an anemic conception of ordinary material objects. Four-dimensionalism countenances too many objects – since time is dense, too many infinities of objects. The four-dimensionalist conception of an object is not robust enough to make sense of our ordinary distinctions between an object's existing and not existing, and it is not robust enough to make sense of there being exactly one cat in the room as a biological fact, whether there are any languages or not. Four-dimensionalists are very canny, and they have plenty to say about these matters. But my point is that four-dimensionalism gives us no ontological purchase on ordinary objects.

---

[36] See chapter 6 for a discussion of supervaluationism.

[37] David K. Lewis, "Many, But Almost One," in *Papers in Metaphysics and Epistemology* (Cambridge: Cambridge University Press, 1999), pp. 164–182.

[38] Except in the way that every expressible fact depends on language: If we used "cat" to refer to dogs, then we could not express the fact that there is exactly one cat in the room by means of the words "There is exactly one cat in the room." But the fact that there is one cat in the room would remain, however we expressed it.

CONCLUSION

In contrast to four-dimensionalist views, the three-dimensionalist Constitution View gives theoretical backing to what I take to be the natural way to understand reality – viz., that there exist enduring objects that come into existence and go out of existence, and that familiar objects are much as we think they are. In general, the three-dimensionalist view is much more illuminating about ordinary objects than is the four-dimensionalist view. That is prima facie reason to prefer three-dimensionalism. The fact that the three-dimensionalist Constitution View can evade four-dimensionalist arguments clinches the case for three-dimensionalism.

11

Five ontological issues

The familiar things that we interact with daily have ontological significance in their own right: they are not *really* something else. Persons, microscopes, cats, and all the other inhabitants in the everyday world are of real kinds whose appearance in the world makes an ontological difference: "Person," for example, is not just a phase-sortal like "child"; nor does it designate a property or abstract entity; nor does it refer to a logical construction of nonpersonal elements. Similarly for other familiar objects: something that is a microscope could not have existed without being a microscope. Ordinary objects are nonredundant, in that they cannot be omitted from ontology without rendering ontology deficient. An inventory of what exists is incomplete if it leaves out persons, screwdrivers, houses, cats, or the other kinds of things that we routinely interact with. (Or so I have argued for the past ten chapters.) In this chapter, I want to discuss five of the ontological issues in the background of this view of ordinary things: Ontological Significance, Time and Existence, Ontological Novelty, Ontological Levels, and Emergence.

AN ACCOUNT OF ONTOLOGICAL SIGNIFICANCE

I have said several times that ordinary things have ontological significance. How should we understand what ontological significance is? Intuitively, to say that Fs (tigers, chairs, anything) have ontological significance is to say that the addition of a (nonderivative)[1] F is not just a change in something that already exists, but the coming-into-being of a new thing. The primary

---

[1] A nonderivative F is a thing that is an F nonderivatively. The reason for the qualification "nonderivative" is that a derivative F may lose the property of being F without thereby going out of existence. E.g., my body is a person derivatively, but if I went out of existence while my body remained, my body would cease to be a person without ceasing to exist altogether. So, the ontological significance of a property is determined only by those things that have the property nonderivatively.

bearers of ontological significance are properties. An ontologically significant property is a property that partly or wholly determines its (nonderivative) bearer's persistence conditions – the conditions under which it
would continue to exist or to cease existing.[2] For example, being a
billionaire is not an ontologically significant property since someone
could cease to be a billionaire without ceasing to exist. But being a person
is an ontologically significant property since nothing could cease to be a
person without ceasing to exist. Being a person is not only an essential
property of (nonderivative) persons, but also helps determine the persistence conditions of (nonderivative) persons. (See chapter 4.) So,

(OS1) The property of being an F has ontological significance if and only if for any
x, if x has the property of being an F (nonderivatively), then x's persistence
conditions are partly or wholly determined by being an F.

Not only are properties ontologically significant, but so also are their
(nonderivative) bearers: A (nonderivative) F has ontological significance in
virtue of being an F if and only if the property of being an F has ontological
significance.

(OS2) A (nonderivative) F has ontological significance in virtue of being an F if and
only if the property of being an F has ontological significance.

I'll use "Fs have ontological significance" to abbreviate "(nonderivative)
Fs have ontological significance in virtue of being an Fs."[3] (OS1) and
(OS2) aim to explicate the basic idea of ontological significance: Being an
F is an ontologically significant property if and only if the addition of a
(nonderivative) F adds to the stock of what there is.[4]

Now it is easy to see that on the Constitution View, persons[5] and the
other objects we interact with, identified by their primary-kind properties,
have ontological significance, given (OS1) and (OS2). Indeed, since
every primary-kind property determines the persistence conditions of its
(nonderivative) bearers, every primary-kind property has ontological

---

[2] In "Why Constitution is Not Identity," *Journal of Philosophy* 94, 1997: 599–621, I argued
that everything that can go out of existence altogether has persistence conditions.

[3] That is, "Fs have ontological significance" is short for: 'For all x, if x is a nonderivative F,
then x has ontological significance in virtue of being an F."

[4] Although I avoid the "qua" locution, the way that I have elucidated "Fs have ontological
significance" suggests that an alternative to that expression might be "Fs-qua-Fs have
ontological significance."

[5] That is, nonderivative persons. In general, I'll drop the qualification when it seems clear that
I am talking about nonderivative Fs.

significance – being a person, being a human animal, being a statue, being a piece of marble. So, on the Constitution View, persons, microscopes, houses, cats, and so on all have ontological significance. Persons have ontological significance in virtue of being persons, even when they are constituted by human animals; houses have ontological significance in virtue of being houses, even when they are constituted by aggregates of disparate objects. So, primary-kind properties determine persistence conditions and hence confer ontological significance on their (nonderivative) bearers.[6]

So, the Nobel Peace Prize winner for 2004 has ontological significance in virtue of being a person (her primary-kind property), not in virtue of winning the prize or being a woman or being an African.[7] My screwdriver has ontological significance in virtue of being a screwdriver, not in virtue of being a lifter-of-tops-of-paint-cans. Being a screwdriver entails being a tool, being an artifact, and being a material object. Of all the properties that a thing has, it is only its essential properties – a thing's primary-kind property and properties entailed by the primary-kind property – that have (and confer on the thing) ontological significance.

The reason that the properties that determine persistence conditions are ontologically significant is that the persistence conditions apply to an object per se, not just to an object designated in a certain way.[8] Persistence conditions so conceived are *de re persistence conditions*. De re persistence conditions of x are the conditions under which x would cease to exist altogether (and not just cease to be a G – a wife, a teacher, or an avid reader), and conditions under which x would persist (and not just continue to be a G). And the reason that objects have de re persistence conditions is that objects do not last forever: they go out of existence altogether. Here is a simple argument for de re persistence conditions:

> (I) If x exists at t and is not eternal, then x can cease to exist altogether (and not just cease to be an F).[9]

---

[6] The question is not: Which comes first – primary kinds or persistence conditions? Everything is of some primary kind, and every primary kind has associated persistence conditions.

[7] The 2004 Nobel Peace Prize winner was Wangari Maathai of Kenya.

[8] For arguments against the Lewisian view to the contrary that de re modal predicates are ambiguous, see below, and see my "Why Constitution is Not Identity."

[9] Of course, if being an F is an essential property of x, then x's ceasing to be an F is sufficient for x's ceasing to exist altogether.

(II) If x can cease to exist altogether (and not just cease to be an F), then there are conditions under which x would cease to exist (and not just cease to be an F), and conditions under which x would persist (and not just continue to be an F).

(III) If there are conditions under which x would cease to exist (and not just cease to be an F), and conditions under which x would persist (and not just continue to be an F), then x has de re persistence conditions.

∴ (IV) If x exists at t and is not eternal, then x has de re persistence conditions.

There is a prominent line of thought that aims to cast doubt on the idea of a thing's having de re modal properties, such as a thing's having a property essentially, or of having de re persistence conditions. Since on the Constitution View, things have their primary-kind-properties essentially and they have de re persistence conditions, I need to counter those who deny that there are de re modal properties.

There are two closely related versions of the line of thought that aims to cast doubt on the idea that a thing, independently of the way that it is referred to, has a property essentially.[10] One argues that concrete things have no modal properties, like having F essentially; the other argues that modal predicates are ambiguous and attribute different properties to a thing, depending on how the thing is referred to. Since I hold that things have their primary-kind properties essentially, I need to rebut both versions of the line of thought that casts doubt on the idea of a thing's having a property essentially, regardless of how it is referred to.

Consider a specimen argument – call it "the statue argument" – against which either of the lines of argument may be directed:

(a) *David* is essentially a statue.
(b) Piece (the piece of marble that makes up *David*) is not essentially a statue.
So, (c) *David* ≠ Piece.

The first argument that I need to rebut is adapted from Alan Gibbard, who argues that concrete things have no modal properties:[11]

(1) "Modal expressions do not apply to concrete things independently of the way that they are designated."
(2) "A property, if it is to be a property, must apply or not apply to a thing independently of the way that it is designated."
∴ (3) "Expressions constructed with modal operators. . .simply do not give properties of concrete things."[12]

---

[10] My discussion of these two versions comes from my "Why Constitution is Not Identity."
[11] Alan Gibbard, "Contingent Identity," *Journal of Philosophical Logic* 4 (1975): 187–221.
[12] Ibid., p. 201.

This argument (1)–(3) may be deployed against premise (a) that attributes a de re modal property to *David* or against premise (I) that attributes the possibility of a thing's going out of existence altogether and not just ceasing to be an F.

Gibbard's argument is obviously valid, but, I think unsound. Premise (1) is subject to counterexamples; for modal expressions include not only predicates like "is essentially a statue," but also many other kinds of predicates. Suppose that a surgeon removes a bullet from a wounded soldier's shoulder, and later presents the bullet to the injured soldier and declares, "This thing could have killed you." Then it seems true of that particular bullet, independently of the way that it is designated, that it could have killed the soldier. In general, predicates ascribing abilities and powers to concrete things, independently of the way that they are designated, entail that modal expressions apply to concrete things. (For example, Alice can swim the English Channel.) Many predicates which are not overtly modal expressions and which apply to concrete things presuppose that modal expressions apply to those concrete things. Predicates that attribute to concrete things dispositions ("is courageous", "is even-tempered"), attitudes ("is afraid of flying", "believes that Winters are long in Vermont"), probabilities ("has a probability of 0.5 of turning up heads") or causal powers ("is lethal") all apply to concrete things only if modal expressions apply to those things independently of the ways that they are designated. So the truth of ordinary statements in which modal expressions apply to concrete things just does not, in general, depend on how those things are designated.

Furthermore, statements containing ineliminable modal expressions that apply to concrete things independently of the ways that they are designated seem to play a role in the sciences. For example, Mars (that very object) could have been a site where multicellular life developed. Or suppose that an electron gun in a double-slit experiment is slightly disturbed and fires an electron off-target, so to speak. It is true of that particular electron that it could have hit the target, or that it could have had a slightly different velocity. To say that the truth of such statements depends on how things are designated would be to say that truth in the physical sciences can depend on how things are designated. In that case, anyone who assumes that realism requires truth independently of the way things are designated would face the specter of irrealism in the physical sciences. If this is not what philosophers want to say, then they should deny (a).

The difficulty with both (1) and (2) is that each is formulated as a general principle, without restriction to essential properties. The argument (1)–(3) could be recast in a more restricted version that would avoid the counter-examples. For example, (1)–(3) could be replaced by (1′)–(3′):

(1′) Modal expressions that purport to attribute essential properties do not apply to concrete things independently of the way that they are designated.

(2′) An essential property, if it is to be an essential property, must apply or not apply to a thing independently of the way that it is designated.

∴ (3′) Modal expressions that purport to attribute essential properties . . . simply do not give essential properties of concrete things.

The strength of the original (1)–(3) was its generality: it begged no questions against the statue argument. Of course, the downside of that generality were the counterexamples to (1). Now the problem with (1′)–(3′) is the reverse. (1′)–(3′) would avoid the counterexamples, but at the cost of begging the question against the statue argument; a proponent of the statue argument would denounce (1′) right off the bat. So if (1′)–(3′) is to be used without begging the question against the statue argument, (1′) requires independent argument. Whether such an argument will be forthcoming for (1′) which does not beg the question against the statue argument remains to be seen.[13] (Note that a proponent of the statue argument need not deny (2′); for an essentialist may well claim that *David* is essentially a statue independently of the way that it is designated.)

The upshot of the discussion of Gibbard's argument is this: its controversial premise – that concrete things have no modal properties – is supported by an argument (1)–(3) that is unsound. Replacement of the false premise, as in (1′)–(3′), results in an argument that begs the question against the statue argument. So, Gibbard's argument does not establish the premise that there are no modal properties of concrete things. Now turn to

---

[13] One might suppose that (1′) could be motivated by examples like W. V. Quine's "mathematical cyclist" – see *Word and Object* (Cambridge, MA: MIT Press, 1960), p. 199. As an argument against essentialism, this case has been thoroughly dissected in the literature and found wanting. For example, see Ruth Barcan Marcus, "Essential Attribution," in *Modalities: Philosophical Essays* (New York: Oxford University Press, 1993), p. 54. Marcus also refers the reader to other writers as well (Terence Parsons, Alvin Plantinga, and Richard Cartwright). I have also heard Max Cresswell and Phillip Bricker discuss Quine's example. Moreover, Cresswell pointed out to me that Quine actually took rejection of essentialism as a premise rather than a conclusion, as evidenced by Quine's attempting to discredit quantified modal logic by claiming that it led to "the metaphysical jungle of Aristotelian essentialism." ("Three Grades of Modal Involvement," in *The Ways of Paradox and Other Essays* [New York: Random House, 1966], p. 174.)

the second line of argument that aims to cast doubt on a thing's having properties essentially, independently of how it is described.

The second line of thought that aims to cast doubt on a thing's having modal properties (independent of how it is specified) claims that modal predicates are ambiguous.[14] For example, some claim that de re modal predicates are "predicates whose reference is affected by the subject term to which they are attached."[15] Harold Noonan calls such predicates "Abelardian predicates" – predicates "whose reference is determined by a component of the sense of the subject-expression to which they are attached."[16] On this view, predicates of the form "is essentially F" attribute different properties to a thing, depending how it is referred to. The predicate "is essentially F" does not attribute a single property in all linguistic contexts.

Here is a Noonan-style argument against the statue argument: The property denoted by "is essentially a statue" in premise (a) is not the same property as the property denoted by "is essentially a statue" in premise (b). So, there is not a single property that *David* has but Piece lacks, in which case (a) and (b) do not entail (c); the argument is invalid.

Here is my reply: The first premise of the Noonan-style argument depends on the claim that the property denoted by "is essentially a statue" depends on the meaning of the subject term to which it is attached. I believe that this key claim is false. My argument here is extremely simple: expressions denoting persistence conditions have the same status as expressions denoting essential properties, with respect to dependence on the meanings of the subject terms to which they are attached. In that case:

(d) (The meaning of a predicate of the form "is essentially F" depends on the meaning of the subject term to which it is attached) if and only if (the meaning of a predicate expressing persistence conditions depends on the meaning of the subject term to which it is attached).

(e) It is false that the meaning of a predicate expressing persistence conditions depends on the meaning of the subject term to which it is attached.

---

[14] David Lewis is perhaps the most prominent proponent of the view that de re modal predicates are ambiguous. See his "Survival and Identity," in Amelie O. Rorty, ed., *The Identities of Persons* (Berkeley: University of California Press, 1976), pp. 17–40, and his "Counterparts of Persons and Their Bodies," *Journal of Philosophy* 68 (1971): 203–211. My argument against Noonan-style arguments also applies to Lewis.

[15] Harold Noonan, "Indeterminate Identity, Contingent Identity and Abelardian Predicates," *Philosophical Quarterly* 41 (1991): 183–193; here, p. 188.

[16] Ibid., pp. 189–190.

∴ (f) It is false that the meaning of a predicate of the form "is essentially F" depends on the meaning of the subject term to which it is attached.

If this argument is sound, then there is no difficulty in holding that objects have their primary-kind properties essentially, independently of the way they are designated, and that they have de re persistence conditions. And there is no threat to the account of ontological significance that I gave. Is the argument (d)–(f) sound?

The first premise seems straightforward and uncontroversial. It follows from the argument (I)–(IV) above that objects have de re persistence conditions, which apply to the object per se, and not to the object as designated in a certain way. But if an object has de re persistence conditions, there is no motivation for the view that the meaning of a predicate expressing persistence conditions depends on the meaning of the subject term to which it is attached. Indeed, it would be altogether implausible to combine the *semantic* view that the meaning of a predicate expressing persistence conditions depends on the meaning of the subject term to which it is attached with the *metaphysical* view that the object has de re persistence conditions. Hence, in light of the argument for de re persistence conditions, we should accept (f), and with it, the refutation of the Noonan-style argument.

My conclusion here assumes acceptance of the metaphysical argument for de re persistence conditions given earlier in (I)–(IV). Anyone who rejects my conclusion there – (IV) – must reject one of the premises of that argument. The only premise that seems to me a candidate for rejection is premise (I): If x exists at t and is not eternal, then x can cease to exist (and not just cease to be an F). Since "exists at t and is not eternal" just means "can cease to exist," the only way to reject premise (I) is to hold that all existing objects are eternal. That is, to reject premise (I) is to hold that no object can cease to exist altogether; it can only lose or change properties, but never go out of existence. As I said at the end of chapter 10, four-dimensionalists cannot properly handle the phenomenon of going out of existence. In any case, it is utterly implausible to hold that all objects are eternal.

But I grant that if you did hold that all objects are eternal, you could reject my argument and accept the Lewis/Noonan view that modal predicates are ambiguous. To do so, however, would be to give up on an ontological account of even the microphysical world as far as we know about it. (For one thing, in light of phenomena like radioactive decay, it seems empirically false that particles are eternal.) I shall leave this section with a conditional: If it is not the case that all objects are eternal, then the account of ontological significance given here undergirds my ontological account of ordinary objects presented in part I.

In the next section, I shall first assume – on the basis of what is known about the everyday world – that not all objects are eternal and show that such an assumption presents no problems for logic. If it is not the case that all objects are eternal, we must consider the relation between time and existence.

TIME AND EXISTENCE

To understand the relation between existing-at-a-time and existing *simpliciter*, the discussion rightly focuses on the domain of the unrestricted existential quantifier – the domain of the wide open ∃, not restricted in any way, the most inclusive domain that includes everything that exists.[17] I'll call the domain of the unrestricted existential quantifier "the Domain," and I'll use "x is in the Domain" and "x exists simpliciter" interchangeably. The Domain is simply the collection of all the objects that exist. Period.

My aim is to show that although the Domain is not subject to change (as Eternalists agree), the world is ontologically different at different times (as Presentists agree): the world does not come "ready-made."[18] My strategy is to construe certain objects as essentially existing at times ("in time"), but to construe being in the Domain as atemporal (in that "∃t(x is in the Domain at t)" is meaningless). I shall argue that the world – though not the Domain of the unrestricted existential quantifier – is ontologically different at different times. I'll sketch a picture of how the Domain, which is subject to no temporal qualification whatever, can include objects that exist only in time.

Let's begin with the atemporality of being in the Domain. To be in the Domain is to be within the scope of the logician's "∃." What does the Domain include? The Domain includes everything; it is the complete ontology. Since it is the complete ontology, nothing can be added to the

---

[17] I am agreeing here with Sider that there are meaningful disagreements about what exists. (Sider, "Introduction," *Four Dimensionalism: an Ontology of Persistence and Time* [Oxford: Clarendon Press, 2001]). Sider cites Peter van Inwagen, "The Number of Things," in Ernest Sosa, ed., *Philosophical Issues 12: Realism and Relativism* (Oxford: Blackwell, 2002), pp. 176–196, but van Inwagen makes much stronger claims than the one I am agreeing to here.

[18] This term comes from Sider, who is an eternalist. See, *Four-Dimensionalism*, p. xxii. See chapter 7 for discussion of Eternalism and Presentism.

Domain and nothing can be taken away from it. "Everything" includes both abstract objects – like times and numbers – for which it meaningless to say that they exist at a time at all, and concrete objects – like Socrates – that exist at times.

There are two distinct ways of existing – in time (like you, me, and Socrates) and not in time (like numbers). To exist simpliciter or to be in the Domain is either to exist in time or to exist not in time. I call this "the Bimodal View" because it recognizes two fundamental modes of existence: temporal and nontemporal. "The Domain" is just the name for all the temporal and nontemporal objects.

The Domain is atemporal: it is not subject to any temporal qualifications whatever. I am using "nontemporal" for abstract objects, about which it makes sense to say that there is no time at which they exist: Abstract objects exist simpliciter, but do not exist at a time. And I am using "atemporal" for the Domain, about which it does not make sense even to say that there is no time at which it exists. Since the unrestricted existential quantifier is univocal and since the (atemporal) Domain includes nontemporal objects as well as temporal objects, our English rendering of existential quantification as "There exists" is not a present-tense occurrence of "exists"; "exists" is tenseless.[19]

We can see the atemporality of being in the Domain of "∃" as follows: For any object in the Domain, whether it is a temporal object or not, it makes no sense to say that there is some time at which it is in the Domain, and it equally makes no sense to say that there is some time at which it is not in the Domain. It makes no sense to say that an object is *already* in the Domain, or is *always* in the Domain, or is *not yet* in the Domain. Temporal qualifications just do not apply to being in the Domain. When I say that the Domain itself is atemporal, I do not mean that all the objects in the Domain are nontemporal. (Socrates is not nontemporal.) Rather, I mean that for any object in the Domain (whether temporal or nontemporal), its being in the Domain – like 2's being less than 3 or red's being a color – is not in time at all.

In short, the atemporal Domain is nothing but all the temporal objects (that exist in time) and all the nontemporal objects (that exist but not in

---

[19] As every beginning logic student learns, the logician's "∃" is tenseless. Why not paraphrase the logician's "∃" as "there exists in the past, present or future"? (Peter van Inwagen and Patricia Blanchette raised this question.) Not only is the standard reading tenseless, but also it is possible that there exist numbers in a world without time. In such a world, there is not temporal reading of "∃." (Marian David supplied the latter answer.)

time). The Domain is not itself an object of any sort – neither concrete (existing at some time) nor abstract (existing simpliciter, but not at a time). The Domain is simply everything.[20]

Although there are two kinds of objects atemporally in the Domain – temporal objects and nontemporal objects – there are not two senses of "exist."[21] There are, rather, two modes or ways of existing. Some kinds of things – abstract objects like the number 9 – are nontemporal and hence do not exist at times. Other kinds of things – finite concrete objects like Socrates – are in the Domain because they exist at times. So, I do not regard existing-at-t (expressed by the two-place predicate "Ext") to be just a matter of temporal location; rather, existing-at-t is a basic mode of existing. Existing at a time does *not contrast* with existing simpliciter. Rather existing at a time is one of two ways to exist simpliciter.

Concrete particulars exist at times and hence are temporal objects.[22] Existing-at-t is a fundamental mode of existence, irreducible to any other mode of existing. The things that we encounter in the world exist at times. If Socrates, for example, exists at all, he exists at some time. In fact, Socrates exists (or existed – tenses don't matter here) from 470–399 BCE and *only* from 470–399 BCE. He came into existence in 470 and went out of existence at 399.[23] He is not an eternal or pre-existing object that simply acquired a temporal location at 470. When Socrates began to exist, a completely new entity came into being. Objects like Socrates exist by being in time: They come into existence at some time and cease to exist at some later time. They cannot exist otherwise than at times. (Although Socrates is essentially in time, it is not essential that he exist from 470 to 399 – he might have been executed in 404.) Existence at a time, which may be symbolized by a predicate "Ext," is a property. Existing at some time or other is a property that Socrates has essentially; existing at 400 BCE is a distinct property that Socrates has contingently.

---

[20] There are logical puzzles here. If the Domain were the set of all things that exist simpliciter, then the Domain would be another thing, and hence would be a member of itself. But the solution to Russell's Paradox precludes a set's being a member of itself.

[21] See Gareth B. Matthews, "Senses and Kinds," *Journal of Philosophy* 69 (1972): 149–157, and "Dualism and Solecism," *Philosophical Review* 80 (1971): 85–95.

[22] Temporal objects are concrete particulars, not events. Following Kim, I take events to be objects' having properties at times; I do not take events to be particulars.

[23] I am assuming that Socrates' thoughts about an afterlife were mistaken.

Since Socrates is a temporal object, the condition for Socrates' being in the Domain (or his existing simpliciter) is that there be some time t such that he exists at t:

$$\exists x(x = s) \text{ if and only if } \exists t(Est)$$

So, Socrates is in the Domain (since there's a time at which he exists), but it makes no sense to say that he is in the Domain in 400 BCE or in 2007 CE or at any other time. This is not to say that Socrates is in the Domain or exists simpliciter even when he doesn't exist. Since it makes no sense to say that there is a time t such that Socrates is in the Domain at t, it makes no sense to say that there is a time t such that: both Socrates is in the Domain at t and Socrates does not exist at t.

But what is nontemporally expressed by "$\exists x(x = s)$" does implicate time – since the condition of Socrates' being in the Domain is that there be a time such that Socrates exists at that time ($\exists t(Est)$). Socrates's being in the Domain of the existential quantifier "$\exists$" is not some nontemporal way of existing; rather, it is none other than there being a time at which Socrates exists. His existing occurs at some particular time and his existing at that time is what makes the existential generalization true. That is, his existing at 400 BCE, or at any other time makes it true that $\exists t(Est)$, and hence makes it true that Socrates is in the (atemporal) Domain. So, Socrates' being in the Domain depends on his existing at some time, and not vice versa. To put it another way: Socrates is in the Domain *in virtue of the fact that* there is a time at which he exists. Socrates is in the Domain as a (logical) *consequence* of his existing at some time, not as a precondition of his existing in time.

In short, the relation between a temporal object's existing simpliciter and its existing at a particular time is the relation between an existential generalization and a true instantiation of the existential generalization. For a temporal object, its existing-at-particular-times is its *only* mode of existence; a temporal object is in the Domain only in virtue of there being a time at which it exists. Socrates comes into existence at the earliest time t at which there is a true instance of the existential generalization "$\exists t(Est)$." Different objects come into existence at different times. Therefore, *the world* – the flesh-and-blood temporal world that includes us in the twenty-first century CE, and included Socrates between 470 and 399 BCE – is ontologically different at different times. So, let us relativize the ontology of the world to time and say:

the ontology of the world at t = all abstract objects and all objects x such that Ext.

Nevertheless, the Domain of the unrestricted existential quantifier remains atemporal:

the Domain = all abstract objects and all objects x such that ∃t Ext.[24]

The Bimodal View accepts this distinction between the atemporal Domain (that includes both all the nontemporal and all the temporal objects that exist at any time) and the temporal ontology of the world at t (that includes both all the nontemporal objects and all the objects that exist at t).[25] Since different objects exist at different times, the world exhibits ontological diversity.

Let me sum up the Bimodal View, according to which the Domain is atemporal, but the world exhibits ontological diversity:

1. Objects (both temporal and nontemporal) are in the Domain. "Being in the Domain" is not subject to temporal qualification of any kind. Some things (like numbers) are nontemporal (they do not exist at times); other things (like Socrates) are essentially temporal (they exist only at times). Socrates exists only from 470 until 399 BCE – the times that satisfy "Est." Since ∃t(Est), Socrates is in the Domain.
2. The reason that we can quantify over any object at any time is that for a temporal object to be in the Domain is for there to be some time at which it exists.[26]

"Does Socrates exist?" you may ask. – That's an incomplete question. Socrates is a temporal object, who exists at some times but not at others. (And it makes no sense to say that he exists simpliciter at all times or at any time; to say that Socrates exists simpliciter is to say that ∃x(x = s).) We can complete the question, "Does Socrates exist?" in any of several ways: "Does Socrates exist in 400 BCE?" (yes) "Does Socrates exist in 2007 CE?" (no) "Does Socrates exist now?" (no) "Does Socrates exist simpliciter?" (yes) – This is not to say that Socrates exists in two ways – atemporally in the Domain and temporally in

---

[24] I am here ignoring the possibility that there is an eternal deity that exists at no time.

[25] We could go further and define the *complete* temporal ontology of the world at t to include all the objects that came into existence at any time earlier than t.

[26] Am I saying that we can existentially quantify over an object when it does not exist? Yes. We can quantify over any object in the Domain. Existential quantification does not entail that a temporal object *exists at the time* that it is quantified over; it entails, rather, that it *exists at some time or other* (i.e., that it is in the Domain, that it exists simpliciter).

the world in time. He exists in one way: temporally, in time, in the world, and because of this he – the temporal Socrates – is in the Domain.[27]

3. Existing-at-a-time is a basic mode of existing, the mode we are most familiar with. Satisfaction of the open sentence "x exists at t" is the necessary and sufficient condition for a temporal object to be in the Domain or to exist simpliciter. "x exists at t" has ontological import. It does not merely give a temporal location for something that "already exists" in the Domain; there is no such thing as "already existing" in the Domain.

4. For temporal objects, existing-at-t is metaphysically prior to being in the Domain in that it is only in virtue of existing at a particular time that a temporal object exists simpliciter or is in the Domain. Socrates is in the Domain only because he existed in time. The Domain is just the collection of objects nontemporal and temporal.

5. Temporal objects – all those that we encounter, those that do not exist perpetually – come into existence at some time t. To say that x comes into existence at t is to say: "Ext & $\sim\exists t'(t' < t$ & Ext$')$." If x comes into existence at t,[28] then x does not exist before t. So, there is ontological novelty in the world.

The Bimodal View here may at first resemble a Growing-Universe View, but the "growth" is in the world; there is no room for "growth" in the complete ontology. And unlike the Growing-Universe views, my view does not imply that objects that begin in the future do not exist; it only implies – what is surely right – that they do not exist now.

The Bimodal View tries to take what is intuitively right about Eternalism and Presentism, and leave behind what seems wrong with each. (See chapter 7.) Neither Presentism nor Eternalism distinguishes between the ontology of the world at a time and the collection of all the objects that make up the Domain. According to Presentism, both the Domain and the ontology of the world are relativized to the present and both change over time. According to Eternalism, neither the Domain nor the ontology of the world changes over time. According to the Bimodal View, the ontology of the world changes over time, but the Domain does

---

[27] That is, Socrates' being in the Domain is an atemporal fact. Are all atemporal facts necessary? No. If there had not been a time at which Socrates existed, he would not have been in the domain.

[28] Since, as I argued in chapters 2 and 6, concrete things come into existence gradually, this is an idealization. There is no exact first moment in which a concrete thing begins to exist.

not.[29] So, the Bimodal View leaves behind the Presentist's constantly changing domain of the unrestricted existential quantifier.

The Bimodal View shares with Eternalism the claim that the domain of the unrestricted existential quantifier is fixed; it is not subject to change. Nevertheless, the Bimodal View differs from Eternalism in several respects.

The first way in which the Bimodal View differs from Eternalism is that on the Bimodal View, the ontology of the world is in time and is different at different times. On Eternalism, it is not. On the Eternalist view (as I understand it), the ontology of the world at any time is just the collection of objects that make up the Domain.[30]

The second way in which the Bimodal View differs from Eternalism concerns the status of temporal existence (expressed by "x exists at t"). According to the Bimodal View, there are two basic ways of existing: temporally and nontemporally. Eternalists (I think) construe all existence, understood ontologically, to be nontemporal: they do not consider existing in time to be a different mode of existence from existing nontemporally. According to the Bimodal View, not all existence is nontemporal. For some objects (temporal objects) existence is a matter of existing at some time or other; their being in the Domain depends on existing-at-a-time. I disagree with Theodore Sider, an Eternalist, when he says, "'Exists-at' is analogous to the spatial predicate 'is located at', not the logician's '∃'."[31] According to the Bimodal View, "exists at t" is intimately connected with the "∃." Existing-at-t is one of two basic modes of existence.

The third way in which the Bimodal View differs from Eternalism concerns the metaphysical priority of Socrates' existing-at-a-particular time to Socrates' being in the Domain. His being in the Domain depends on there being a time at which he exists; and this in turn depends on his existing-at-a-particular time. When Sider says that "the world comes 'ready-made' with a single domain D of objects: the class of all the objects there are,"[32] it sounds as if he is taking the Domain to constrain what exists at particular times. The Bimodal View takes the order of priority to be the reverse: What exists in the world at particular times determines what is in

---

[29] Since the Domain is atemporal (subject to no temporal qualifications at all), it is meaningless to say that an object is in the Domain only when it exists.

[30] An eternalist may agree that, if he were to accept my definition of the "ontology of the world at t," he would agree that the ontology of the world changes; however, I think it highly unlikely that he would accept my definition. I admit that this may be merely a semantic difference between the Bimodal View and Eternalism.

[31] Sider, *Four-Dimensionalism*, p. 59.   [32] Ibid., p. xxii.

the Domain (or rather determines what is in the temporal part of the Domain).

The fourth way in which the Bimodal View differs from Eternalism is that only the Bimodal View is compatible with the BA theory of time. (See chapter 7.) Eternalism has no place for an ongoing now in its account of reality. Nor does Eternalism have resources to show how temporal reality, conceived of wholly in terms of the B-series could give rise to the appearance of an ongoing now, as opposed to successions of simultaneous events. If all there is to time is the B-series, how could our lives be so bound up in the passage of time? On the other hand, the Bimodal View is neutral with respect to the BA theory.

The obvious benefit of the BA theory over the pure B-theory is that it includes temporal distinctions that matter to us. For example, think about your best friend, who, let us suppose for the sake of convenience of pronouns, is a woman. She exists in 2007. That is an important (B-series) fact about her. But equally important is the (A-series) fact that she exists now. She did not die last night – an A-series fact. On the B-theory alone, your friend's existing now has no metaphysical significance whatever; indeed, it is not a different fact from her existing at 4:00 on December 30, 2007. By contrast, the BA theory, when wedded to the Bimodal View, gives a metaphysical (not just semantic or "conceptual") account of things' being in the past, present, and future: being now is a transient relation between times and self-conscious beings. Granted, the BA account is in terms of self-conscious beings; but, as I have noted, self-conscious beings are as much a part of reality as rocks and trees. Combining the B- and A-series into a metaphysical account of time further distinguishes the Bimodal View from Eternalism.

In short, the Bimodal View differs from Eternalism in several ways: (1) the Bimodal View distinguishes two basic ways of existing, temporal and nontemporal; (2) it recognizes the ontology of the world at t to be distinct from the Domain; (3) it welcomes the BA theory of time, and (4) it takes temporal language to be nonsensical if applied to the Domain.

In this section on Time and Existence, I have argued that there is no conflict between the commonsense view that the world exhibits ontological novelty and the metaphysical view that the domain of the unrestricted existential quantifier is atemporal. *The world* changes ontologically over time as new objects like Socrates and new kinds like dinosaurs come into existence. Nevertheless, *the Domain* of the unrestricted existential quantifier is not subject to change (because it is not temporal at all).

ONTOLOGICAL NOVELTY

The account just given of the coming-into-existence of new entities in the world can be extended to the coming-into-existence of new kinds of entities – new primary kinds. (See chapter 2.) Indeed, anyone who believes in the evolution of the universe or in the evolution of biological species must either countenance novel primary kinds or else deny that objects of apparently novel primary kinds (e.g., stars, horses) are real objects. We can understand ontological novelty as the evolution or introduction at some time or other of objects of new primary kinds – e.g., the first organisms or Galileo's first telescope. Say that a primary kind K is more complex than a primary kind K' if objects of kind K' can constitute objects of kind K.[33] Then the comparative ontological richness of the world at different times may be understood as follows:

> (OR) The world at t' is *ontologically richer* than the world at t iff there are objects of more complex primary kinds at t' than at t.

A new primary kind (natural or artifactual) is a genuine novelty whose evolution or introduction makes the world ontologically richer. This view, again, allows for ontological novelty in the world, but not in the Domain of the unrestricted existential quantifier, not in the complete ontology.

ONTOLOGICAL LEVELS

It is natural to think of reality as having levels of some kind: There is a familiar picture of subatomic particles, atoms, molecules, cells, and finally organisms as forming a chain. Subatomic particles are parts of atoms, which are parts of molecules, which are parts of cells, which are parts of organisms.

The standard conception of levels is mereological: The objects at Level $L+1$ are mereological sums of the objects at level L.[34] Given this

---

[33] Unfortunately, this is only a sufficient condition.
[34] See, for example, Jaegwon Kim, "The Nonreductivist's Troubles with Mental Causation," in *Supervenience and Mind* (Cambridge: Cambridge University Press, 1993), pp. 336–357. Originally published in John Heil and Alfred Mele, eds., *Mental Causation* (Oxford: Clarendon Press, 1992), pp. 189–210; Jaegwon Kim, "Making Sense of Downward Causation," in Peter Bogh Andersen, Claus Emmeche, Niels Ole Finnemann, and Peder Voetmann, eds., *Downward Causation* (Aarhus, Denmark: Aarhus University Press, 2000), pp. 305–321; Brian P. McLaughlin, "The Rise and Fall of British Emergentism," in Angsar Beckesmann, Hans Flohr, and Jaegwon Kim, eds., *Emergence or Reduction? Essays on the Prospects of Nonreductive Physicalism* (Berlin: Walter de Gruyter, 1992), pp. 49–93.

interpretation of levels, cells are sums or fusions of molecules, which are sums of atoms, and so on.

This mereological conception inexorably leads to the conclusion that there really are no different ontological levels of reality. A sum and its parts are on the same ontological level. E.g., the sum of your two eyes is on the same ontological level as either of your two eyes. This is so despite the fact that the sum of your left eye and your right eye is not identical to your left eye and not identical to your right eye. Generalizing, the sum of x and y is not on a higher level than x or y. Sums are mere aggregates; and ontologically, an aggregate is on no higher level than its parts.

The upshot of the mereological conception of levels is that there is only one level of reality: the bottom, if there is one.[35] If there is no fundamental level, then every object has parts, and there are parts of parts of parts with no stopping place. So, whether or not there's a fundamental level of reality at the "bottom," the mereological interpretation of levels – the interpretation that reduces objects at one (apparent) level to its parts at the next lowest level – does not provide a basis for multiple ontological levels.

However, on the mereological view, there are still (nonontological) "levels," determined by descriptions. On a mereological conception, multiple levels should be thought of, not as levels of reality, but as levels of description. Of course, I agree that there are levels of description, but from the fact that there are levels of description, it does not follow that there are no ontological levels. The levels of description may well reflect ontological levels. And from the fact that objects and their mereological sums are on the same ontological level, it does not follow that there are no ontological levels. It only follows that mereology cannot account for them.

Constitution offers an alternative way to understand levels – a way not based on mereology. On the Constitution View, sums of molecules constitute people, but sums of molecules are fundamentally different kinds of things from people. So, the difference in level between molecule-talk and people-talk is not just a difference in level of description; it is a difference in what is being talked about. The idea of constitution makes sense of this ontological difference between molecules and people. Given the Constitution View, it is easy to give a sufficient condition for "higher-level primary-kind property."

---

[35] See Jonathan Schaffer, "Is There a Fundamental Level?", *Noûs* 37 (2003): 498–517.

G is a higher-level primary-kind property than F if: there are some x, y, t such that:

> (i) x's primary-kind property is F and y's primary-kind property is G, and
> (ii) x constitutes y at t.

This gives us a sufficient condition for different levels: If G is a higher-level primary-kind property than F, then there are levels, such that F is on one level and G is on a higher level.

Levels so defined are ontological: they are levels of reality, not levels of explanation or of description. The existence of levels, so defined, does not imply that all of material reality is well-ordered by level. (It is not the case that for *any* properties P_1 and P_2, either P_1 is a higher-level property than P_2, or P_2 is a higher-level property than P_1, or P_1 and P_2 are on the same level.) There is no single hierarchy of levels. There is no answer to the question, Are robots on a higher level than sea slugs? And as we saw in chapter 8, there may be branching. So, the ordering of levels is only partial.

Objects also are on different ontological levels: atoms (and aggregations of atoms) are on a lower level than are credit cards or passports. The notion of P's being a higher-level primary-kind property than Q leads right away to a sufficient condition for some entity's being on a higher level than some other entity:

> y is a higher-level entity than x if: There are primary-kind properties, F and G, such that:
>
> > (i) x has F as its primary-kind property and y has G as its primary-kind property and
> > (ii) G is a higher-level primary kind property than F.

Now we can give a general sufficient condition for one property (whether a primary-kind property or not) to be a higher-level property than another. Omitting reference to times again:

> Property Q is a higher-level property than property P if: There is a y such that:
>
> > (i) y nonderivatively has Q and
> > (ii) for any x, if y is a higher-level entity than x, then it is *not* the case that x nonderivatively has Q, and
> > (iii) there is some z such that: y is a higher-level entity than z & z non derivatively has P.

For example, making a promise is a higher-level property than sneezing: There is an x (you, say) who (i) nonderivatively makes a promise; (ii) none of your lower-level constituters nonderivatively makes a promise; (iii) one of your lower-level constituters (your body) nonderivatively sneezes.

To sum up the account of ontological levels: The notion of constitution leads immediately to a sufficient condition for one primary-kind property's being a higher-level property than another primary-kind property. The difference in level of primary-kind properties leads to a sufficient condition for one entity's being a higher-level entity than another entity. Finally, the difference in level of entities leads to a sufficient condition for one property's being a higher-level property than another – whether the properties are primary-kind properties or not.[36]

EMERGENCE

The idea of constitution provides a natural way to understand evolution and the emergence of new kinds of individuals. We have just seen how the Constitution View provides for an account of levels of reality. If we add the plausible hypothesis that higher-level primary kinds come into being over time, we get an ontologically robust kind of emergence.

There is an enormous literature on emergence. The term "emergent property" is used in each of two ways in the literature: (1) as a (reducible) "network property" that consists in some organizational feature of the elements of the bearer's substrate; and (2) as a novel property that is irreducible to other properties.[37] The first use is found mostly in the scientific literature; the second use is the one that concerns us here.

Almost all the characterizations of emergence are mereological. For example, the "naked emergent intuition" is that an emergent property is a property of a whole that "transcends" in some way the properties of its parts.[38] Emergent properties of a whole are distinct from the properties of their parts, and cannot be explained or predicted on the basis of the properties of their parts ("their microstructures").[39]

---

[36] Notice that this construal of levels presupposes the Constitution View of objects. Hence, I could not use the idea of ontological levels in formulating the Constitution View of objects. However, I could use the idea of ontological levels – as I did in chapter 5 – to define property(instance)-constitution, "x's having F at t constitutes x's having G at t." Levels are independently secured by the Constitution View of objects.

[37] See Paul M. Churchland, "Reduction, Qualia, and the Direct Introspection of Brain States," in *A Neurocomputational Perspective* (Cambridge, MA: MIT/ Bradford Press, 1989), pp. 47–66 (p. 51).

[38] Paul Teller, "A Contemporary Look At Emergence," in Beckermann, Flohr and Kim, eds., *Emergence or Reduction?* pp. 139–153 (quote is on p. 139).

[39] See Jaegwon Kim, "Making Sense of Emergence," *Philosophical Studies* 95 (1999): 3–36, and Louise Antony, "Making Room for the Mental: Comments on Kim's 'Making Sense of Emergence'," *Philosophical Studies* 95 (1999): 37–44.

According to Jaegwon Kim, the core idea of emergence is this: "[A]s systems acquire increasingly higher degrees of organizational complexity, they begin to exhibit novel properties that in some sense transcend the properties of their constituent parts, and behave in ways that cannot be predicted on the basis of the laws governing simpler systems."[40] If this is the core idea, then it seems to me clear that there are emergent properties. Any ID property provides an obvious example: The property of committing perjury, for example, is a property that transcends the properties of the perjuror's parts, and is a new kind of behavior that cannot be predicted on the basis of the laws governing the parts of the perjuror or of any simpler system.

Kim also characterizes emergentists like this:

> For them everything that exists is constituted by matter, or basic material particles, there being no "insertion" of alien entities or forces from the outside. It is only that complex systems aggregated out of these material particles begin to exhibit genuinely novel properties that are irreducible to, and neither predictable nor explainable in terms of the properties of their constituents.[41]

On all these characterizations of emergence, if we add constitution as a relation distinct from aggregation, there are many, many emergent properties. Indeed, all ID properties are emergent. Although Kim does not (appear to) recognize ID properties as genuine properties, ID properties do satisfy his criterion for being real. Kim endorses "Alexander's Dictum," according to which "to be real is to have causal powers."[42] As we saw in chapter 3, artifactual properties are ID properties, and artifactual properties – e.g., the property of being an assault weapon – have effects. The property of being an assault weapon has different effects in different circumstances: something's being an assault weapon in your carry-on as you try to go through airport security has the effect of your being detained; something's being an assault weapon may trigger a minimum–sentence rule that lengthens a felon's time in prison. These are real effects, no less real for being ID properties. Being an assault weapon, being detained, adding extra years to a prison term are all ID properties.[43]

---

[40] Kim, "Making Sense of Emergence," p. 3.   [41] Ibid., p. 4.

[42] Kim, "The Nonreductivist's Troubles With Mental Causation," p. 348.

[43] For detailed arguments, see my "Nonreductive Materialism," in Brian McLaughlin and Ansgar Beckermann, eds., *The Oxford Handbook for the Philosophy of Mind* (Oxford: Oxford University Press, forthcoming).

Kim does not believe that complex systems aggregated out of material particles do exhibit such novel properties. But as I have argued throughout this book, there is another basic relation besides aggregation – constitution – and an entity is the kind of thing that it is, not in virtue of the aggregation of particles, but in virtue of constitution. (Put an aggregate of molecules in certain circumstances, and a new entity, a micro-organism, comes into being.) If complex systems are *constituted* by aggregates to which they are not identical, then emergent properties seem inevitable.

ID properties, on any noneliminativist theory of them, are emergent properties on the standard characterizations. What the Constitution View contributes is a theoretical explanation of how constituted entities can be nonderivative bearers of ID and nonID properties that are ontologically distinct from the properties of the entities' parts and that cannot be explained or predicted on the basis of the properties of the entities' parts.[44]

CONCLUSION

After presenting an account of ontological significance in terms of primary kinds and de re persistence conditions, I defended the account against philosophers who deny that there are modal properties that objects have independently of the ways that they are designated. I argued that anything that exists at t and is not eternal has de re persistence conditions (under which it would cease to exist altogether); and anything with de re persistence conditions has modal properties independently of the way that it is designated. In addition, I rebutted two arguments that, if successful, would undercut my view.

Then, I showed how the existence of temporally contingent objects raised no problems for an atemporal construal of the domain of the unrestricted existential quantifier. An atemporal construal of the domain of the unrestricted existential quantifier allows that the world is a temporal world, and is ontologically different at different times: The world today is very different from the world centuries ago. There is genuine novelty in the world. Not only do new individuals come into existence, but also new kinds of things crop up too.

---

[44] In her "Making Room for the Mental," Louise Antony distinguishes between two types of nonreductive materialists along these lines. She is sanguine about the possibility of explaining, say, mental properties in terms of more basic properties, but she also takes them to be ontologically distinct from basic properties.

The novelty is not only provided by us. The evolution of the universe from the Big Bang until the appearance of *Homo sapiens* also displays novelty. A world containing only the particles coming out of the Big Bang is ontologically different from a world with stars; a world without organisms is ontologically different from a world with organisms; a world without passports is ontologically different from a world with passports; and so on. There are many different primary kinds of things; and at different times, things of new primary kinds come into existence. After a discussion of ontological novelty, I gave a (nonmereological) account of ontological levels. I ended by showing how the Constitution View supports an old-fashioned view of emergence.

Let me conclude with a brief personal remark about Practical-Realist metaphysics. It is time to get on the table an alternative to the dominant metaphysical theories that accord no ontological significance to things that everyone cares about – not only concrete objects like one's car keys, or the *Mona Lisa*, but also commonplace states of affairs like being employed next year, or having enough money for retirement. I believe that such ordinary phenomena are the stuff of reality, and I have tried to offer a metaphysics that has room in its ontology for the ordinary things that people value. It is not enough to have familiar sentences turn out to be true when paraphrased in unfamiliar ways. I do not want to relegate what really matters to mere concepts or semantics, or to distribution of microscopic qualities over spacetime. My aim is to see the metaphysical significance of the world as we encounter and interact with it – all day, every day. As the American pragmatist Charles Sanders Peirce wisely urged, "Let us not pretend to doubt in philosophy what we do not doubt in our hearts."[45]

---

[45] Charles Sanders Peirce, "Some Consequences of the Four Incapacities," in Philip P. Wiener, ed., *Charles Sanders Peirce: Selected Writings* (New York: Dover Publications, 1958), p. 40.

Select bibliography

Anscombe, G. E. M. (1981). "Causality and Determination," in *Metaphysics and the Philosophy of Mind, Collected Philosophical Papers, Volume II* (Minneapolis: University of Minnesota Press), pp. 133–147.

(1985). "Were You a Zygote?" in A. Phillips Griffiths, ed., *Philosophy and Practice* (Cambridge: Cambridge University Press), pp. 111–115.

Antony, Louise (1999). "Making Room for the Mental: Comments on Kim's 'Making Sense of Emergence'," *Philosophical Studies* 95: 37–44.

Antony, Louise and Joseph Levine (1997). "Reduction With Autonomy," in James E. Tomberlin, ed., *Mind, Causation and World (Philosophical Perspectives 11)* (Malden, MA: Blackwell), pp. 83–106.

Armstrong, David M. (1997). *A World of States of Affairs* (Cambridge: Cambridge University Press).

Austin, J. L. (1961). "A Plea for Excuses," *Philosophical Papers* (Oxford: Oxford University Press), pp. 123–152.

(1962). *Sense and Sensibilia* (Oxford: Oxford University Press).

Baker, Lynne Rudder (1974–75). "Temporal Becoming: The Argument From Physics," *Philosophical Forum* 6: 218–236.

(1979). "On the Mind-Dependence of Temporal Becoming," *Philosophy and Phenomenological Research* 39: 341–357.

(1982). "Underprivileged Access," *Noûs* 16: 227–241.

(1993). "Metaphysics and Mental Causation," in John Heil and Alfred Mele, eds., *Mental Causation* (Oxford: Clarendon Press), pp. 75–96.

(1995). *Explaining Attitudes: A Practical Approach to the Mind* (Cambridge: Cambridge University Press).

(1997). "Why Constitution is Not Identity," *Journal of Philosophy* 94: 599–621.

(1999). "Unity Without Identity: A New Look at Material Constitution," in Peter A. French and Howard K. Wettstein, eds., *New Directions in Philosophy: Midwest Studies in Philosophy*, Volume 23 (Malden, MA: Blackwell Publishers), pp. 144–165.

(2000). *Persons and Bodies: A Constitution View* (Cambridge: Cambridge University Press).

(2001). "Philosophy *in Mediis Rebus*," *Metaphilosophy* 32: 378–394.

(2002). "On Making Things Up: Constitution and its Critics," *Philosophical Topics: Identity and Individuation* 30: 31–51.

(2002). "The Ontological Status of Persons," *Philosophy and Phenomenological Research* 65: 370–388.

(2003). "The Difference that Self-Consciousness Makes," in Klaus Petrus, ed., *On Human Persons* (Frankfurt: Ontos Verlag), pp. 23–39.

(2004). "The Ontology of Artifacts," *Philosophical Explorations* 7: 99–111.

(2005). "When Does a Person Begin?", *Social Philosophy and Policy* 22: 25–48.

(2006). "Moral Responsibility Without Libertarianism," *Noûs* 40: 307–330.

(forthcoming). "The Metaphysics of Malfunction," in Pieter Vermaas and Wybo Houkes, eds., *Artefacts in Philosophy*.

(forthcoming). "Social Externalism and First-Person Authority," *Erkenntnis*.

(forthcoming). "First-Person Externalism," *The Modern Schoolman*.

(forthcoming). "Nonreductive Materialism," in Brian McLaughlin and Ansgar Beckermann, eds., *The Oxford Handbook for the Philosophy of Mind* (Oxford: Oxford University Press).

Baker, Lynne Rudder, Dean Zimmerman, Michael C. Rea, and Derk Pereboom (2002). Book Symposium on *Persons and Bodies*, *Philosophy and Phenomenological Research* 64: 592–635.

Beall, J. C. and Greg Restall (2000). "Logical Pluralism," *Australasian Journal of Philosophy* 78: 475–493.

Bernat, James (1998). "A Defense of the Whole Brain Concept of Death," *Hastings Center Report* 28: 14–24.

Bolton, Robert (1976). "Essentialism and Semantic Theory in Aristotle: Posterior Analytics, II, 7–10," *Philosophical Review* 85: 514–544.

Boyd, Richard (1980). "Materialism Without Reductionism: What Physicalism Does Not Entail," in Ned Block, ed., *Readings in the Philosophy of Psychology, Volume I* (Cambridge, MA: Harvard University Press), pp. 67–106.

Braun, David and Theodore Sider (2007). "Vague, So Untrue," *Noûs* 41: 133–156.

Broad, C. D. (1923). *Scientific Thought* (London: Routledge & Kegan Paul).

Brower, Jeffrey E. Brower and Michael C. Rea (2005). "Material Constitution and the Trinity," *Faith and Philosophy* 22: 57–76.

Burge, Tyler (1982). "Other Bodies," in Andrew Woodfield, ed., *Thought and Object* (Oxford: Oxford University Press), pp. 97–120.

(1993). "Mind-body Causation and Explanatory Practice," in John Heil and Alfred Mele, eds., *Mental Causation* (Oxford: Clarendon Press), pp. 97–120.

Burke, Michael B. (1994). "Preserving the Principle of One Object to a Place: A Novel Account of the Relations Among Objects, Sorts, Sortals and Persistence Conditions," *Philosophy and Phenomenological Research* 54: 591–624.

Castañeda, Hector-Neri (1966). "He: A Study in the Logic of Self-Consciousness," *Ratio* 8: 130–157.

(1967). "Indicators and Quasi-Indicators," *American Philosophical Quarterly* 4: 85–100.

Chisholm, Roderick (1976). *Person and Object* (LaSalle, IL: Open Court Publishing Company).

Churchland, Paul (1989). *A Neurocomputational Perspective: The Nature of Mind and the Structure of Science* (Cambridge, MA: MIT/Bradford).

Clapp, Lenny (2001). "Disjunctive Properties: Multiple Realization," *Journal of Philosophy* 98: 111–136.

Corcoran, Kevin (2001). "Materialism With a Human Face," in Kevin Corcoran, ed., *Body, Soul, and Survival* (Ithaca, NY: Cornell University Press), pp. 159–180.

Crisp, Thomas (2004). "Defining Presentism," in Dean Zimmerman, ed., *Oxford Studies in Metaphysics* (Oxford: Clarendon Press), pp. 15–20.

Crisp, Thomas and Ted Warfield (2001). "Kim's Master Argument," *Noûs* 35: 304–316.

Davidson, Donald (1984). "On the Very Idea of a Conceptual Scheme," in *Inquiries into Truth and Interpretation* (Oxford: Clarendon Press), pp. 183–198.

Dipert, Randall (1993). *Artifacts, Artworks, and Agency* (Philadelphia: Temple University Press).

Doepke, Frederick C. (1982). "Spatially Coinciding Objects," *Ratio* 24: 45–60.

Elder, Crawford L. (1995). "A Different Kind of Natural Kind," *Australasian Journal of Philosophy* 73: 516–531.

(2004). *Real Natures and Familiar Objects* (Cambridge, MA: MIT Press).

Eldredge, Niles (2000). *The Triumph of Evolution* (New York: W. H. Freeman).

Evans, Gareth (1978). "Can There Be Vague Objects?" *Analysis* 38: 208.

Feldman, Fred (1992). *Confrontations with the Reaper* (New York: Oxford University Press).

Ferrari, Michel and Robert J. Sternberg, eds. (1998). *Self-Awareness: Its Nature and Development* (New York: Guilford Press).

Fine, Kit (2003). "The Non-Identity of a Material Thing and Its Matter," *Mind* 112: 195–234.

Ford, Norman M. (1988). *When Did I Begin? Conception of the Human Individual in History, Philosophy and Science* (Cambridge: Cambridge University Press).

(2002). *The Prenatal Person* (Malden, MA: Blackwell Publishing).

Foster, John (1991). *The Immaterial Self: A Defence of the Cartesian Dualist Conception of the Mind* (London: Routledge).

Funder, David C. and B. C. Sneed (1993). "Behavioral Manifestations of Personality: An Ecological Approach to Judgmental Accuracy," *Journal of Personality and Social Psychology* 64: 479–490.

Gale, Richard (1968). *The Language of Time* (New York: Routledge & Kegan Paul).

Gallup, Gordon, Jr. (1977). "Self-Recognition in Primates: A Comparative Approach to Bidirectional Properties of Consciousness," *American Psychologist* 32: 329–338.

Garrett, Brian (1991). "Vague Identity and Vague Objects," *Noûs* 25: 341–351.

Gibbard, Alan (1975). "Contingent Identity," *Journal of Philosophical Logic* 4: 187–221.

Gopnik, Alison, Andrew Meltzoff, and Patricia Kuhl, eds. (1999). *How Babies Think: The Science of Childhood* (London: Weidenfeld & Nicolson).

Graff, Delia and Timothy Williamson, eds. (2002). *Vagueness* (Burlington, VT: Ashgate Publishing Co.).

Grünbaum, Adolf (1968). "The Status of Temporal Becoming," in Richard Gale, ed., *The Philosophy of Time* (London: Macmillan), pp. 322–354.

Hasker, William (1999). *The Emergent Self* (Ithaca, NY: Cornell University Press).

Heil, John and Alfred Mele (1993). *Mental Causation* (Oxford: Clarendon Press).

Hershenov, David (2006). "The Death of a Person," *Journal of Medicine and Philosophy* 31: 107–120.

(forthcoming). "Problems with a Constitution Account of Persons."

Heyes, Cecilia and Anthony Dickinson (1993). "The Intentionality of Animal Action," in Martin Davies and Glyn W. Humphreys, eds., *Consciousness: Psychological and Philosophical Essays* (Oxford: Blackwell), pp. 105–120.

Hilpinen, Risto (1993). "Authors and Artifacts," *Proceedings of the Aristotelian Society* 93: 155–178.

Hirsch, Eli (1982). *The Concept of Identity* (New York: Oxford University Press).

Hoffman, Joshua and Gary S. Rosenkrantz (1997). *Substance: Its Nature and Existence* (London: Routledge).

Houkes, Wybo and Anthonie Meijers (2006). "The Ontology of Artifacts: The Hard Problem," *Studies in the History and Philosophy of Science* 37: 118–131.

Johnston, Mark (1992). "Constitution is Not Identity," *Mind* 101: 89–105.

Kagan, Jerome (1989). *Unstable Ideas* (Cambridge, MA: Harvard University Press).

Kakol, Tomasz (2005). "The SameP-Relation as a Response to Critics of Baker's Theory of Constitution," *Journal of Philosophical Logic* 34: 561–579.

Kaplan, David (1989). "Demonstratives," in J. Almog, J. Perry, and H. Wettstein, eds., *Themes from Kaplan* (New York: Oxford University Press), pp. 481–614.

Keefe, Rosanna and Peter Smith, eds. (1996). *Vagueness: A Reader* (Cambridge, MA: MIT/Bradford).

Kim, Jaegwon (1989). "Mechanism, Purpose, and Explanatory Exclusion," in James E. Tomberlin, ed., *Philosophy of Mind and Action Theory: Philosophical Perspectives 3* (Atascadero, CA: Ridgeview Publishing), pp. 77–108. Reprinted in *Supervenience and Mind* (Cambridge: Cambridge University Press), pp. 237–264.

(1989). "The Myth of Nonreductive Materialism," *Proceedings and Addresses of the American Philosophical Association* 63: 31–47. Reprinted in *Supervenience and Mind* (Cambridge: Cambridge University Press), pp. 265–284.

(1992). "'Downward Causation' in Emergentism and Nonreductive Physicalism," in Ansgar Beckermann, Hans Flohr, and Jaegwon Kim, eds., *Emergence or Reduction? Essays on the Prospects of Nonreductive Physicalism* (Berlin: de Gruyter), pp. 119–138.

(1992). "The Nonreductivist's Troubles with Mental Causation," in John Heil and Alfred Mele, eds., *Mental Causation* (Oxford: Clarendon Press), pp. 189–210. Reprinted in *Supervenience and Mind* (Cambridge: Cambridge University Press, 1993), pp. 3–36.

(1993) *Supervenience and Mind: Selected Philosophical Essays* (Cambridge: Cambridge University Press).

(1993) "Multiple Realization and the Metaphysics of Reduction," in *Supervenience and Mind* (Cambridge: Cambridge University Press), pp. 309–335.

(1993). "The Nonreductivist's Troubles With Mental Causation," in *Supervenience and Mind: Selected Philosophical Essays* (Cambridge: Cambridge University Press, 1993), pp. 336–357.

(1998). *Mind in a Physical World* (Cambridge, MA: MIT Press).

(1999). "Making Sense of Emergence," *Philosophical Studies* 95: 3–36.

(2000). "Making Sense of Downward Causation," in Peter Bogh Andersen, Claus Emmeche, Niels Ole Finnemann, and Peder Voetmann, eds., *Downward Causation* (Aarhus, Denmark: Aarhus University Press), pp. 305–321.

(2002). "The Layered Model: Metaphysical Considerations," *Philosophical Explorations* 5 (2002), pp. 2–20.

(2005). *Physicalism, or Something Near Enough* (Princeton: Princeton University Press).

Kornblith, Hilary (1993). *Inductive Inference and Its Natural Ground: An Essay in Naturalistic Epistemology* (Cambridge, MA: MIT Press).

Koslicki, Kathrin (2003). "The Crooked Path from Vagueness to Four-Dimensionalism," *Philosophical Studies* 114: 107–134.

(2004). "Constitution and Similarity," *Philosophical Studies* 117: 327–364.

Kripke, Saul A. (1972). *Naming and Necessity* (Cambridge, MA: Harvard University Press).

Kroes, Peter and Anthonie Meijers (2006). "The Dual Nature of Technical Artefacts," *Studies in History and Philosophy of Science* 37: 1–4.

LaPorte, Joseph (2000). "Rigidity and Kind," *Philosophical Studies* 97: 293–316.

Lewis, David K. (1971). "Counterparts of Persons and Their Bodies," *Journal of Philosophy* 68: 203–211.

(1976). "Survival and Identity," in Amelie O. Rorty, ed., *The Identities of Persons* (Berkeley: University of California Press), pp. 17–40.

(1986). *On the Plurality of Worlds* (Oxford: Basil Blackwell).

(1991). *Parts of Classes* (Oxford: Basil Blackwell).

(1999). "Many, But Almost One," in *Papers in Metaphysics and Epistemology* (Cambridge: Cambridge University Press), pp. 164–182.

Loewer, Barry (2001). "Review of J. Kim, *Mind in a Physical World*," *Journal of Philosophy* 98: 315–324.

(2002). "Comments on Jaegwon Kim's *Mind in a Physical World*," *Philosophy and Phenomenological Research* 65: 655–662.

Lowe, E. J. (1983). "Instantiation, Identity and Constitution," *Philosophical Studies* 44: 45–59.

(1983). "On the Identity of Artifacts," *Journal of Philosophy* 80: 220–232.

(1993). "The Causal Autonomy of the Mental, *Mind* 102: 629–644.

(1994). "Vague Identity and Quantum Indeterminacy," *Analysis* 54: 110–114.

Marcus, Ruth Barcan (1993). "Essential Attribution," in *Modalities: Philosophical Essays* (New York: Oxford University Press), pp. 53–73.

Markosian, Ned (2004). "In Defense of Presentism," in Dean W. Zimmerman, ed., *Oxford Studies in Metaphysics*, Vol. 1 (Oxford: Clarendon Press), pp. 47–82.

Matthews, Gareth B. (1971). "Dualism and Solecism," *Philosophical Review* 80: 85–95.

(1972). "Senses and Kinds," *Journal of Philosophy* 69: 149–157.

(1982). "Accidental Unities," in Malcolm Schofield and Martha Craven Nussbaum, eds., *Language and Logos: Studies in Ancient Greek Philosophy Presented to G. E. L. Owen* (Cambridge: Cambridge University Press), pp. 223–240.

(1990). "Aristotelian Essentialism," *Philosophy and Phenomenological Research* 50 (Supplement, Fall): 251–262.

(1992). "Aristotle's Theory of Kooky Objects," unpublished manuscript.

McLaughlin, Brian P. (1992). "The Rise and Fall of British Emergentism," in Ansgar Beckermann, Hans Flohr, and Jaegwon Kim, eds., *Emergence or*

Reduction? Essays on the Prospects of Nonreductive Physicalism (Berlin: Walter de Gruyter), pp. 49–93.

McTaggart, J. M. E. (1927). "Time," in *The Nature of Existence*, Vol. 2 (Cambridge: Cambridge University Press): Book V, ch. 33, and in Richard Gale, ed., *The Philosophy of Time* (London: Macmillan, 1968), pp. 86–97.

Mellor, Hugh (1999). "The Time of Our Lives," lecture delivered on October 22, 1999 in London to the Royal Institute of Philosophy. www.dspace.cam.ac.uk/bitstream/1810/753/1/TimeLives.html

Merricks, Trenton (2001). *Objects and Persons* (Oxford: Clarendon Press).

(2001). "Varieties of Vagueness," *Philosophy and Phenomenological Research* 62: 145–157.

Morreau, Michael (2002). "What Vague Objects are Like," *Journal of Philosophy* 99: 333–361.

Noonan, Harold (1991). "Indeterminate Identity, Contingent Identity and Abelardian Predicates," *Philosophical Quarterly* 41: 183–193.

(2004). "Are There Vague Objects?" *Analysis* 64: 131–134.

Noordhof, Paul (1999). "Causation by Content?" *Mind & Language* 14: 291–320.

Oaklander, L. Nathan (2003). "Presentism: A Critique," in Hallvard Lillehammer and Gonzalo Rodriguez-Pereya, eds., *Real Metaphysics* (London: Routledge), pp. 196–211.

Oderberg, David (1996). "Coincidence Under a Sortal," *Philosophical Review* 105: 145–171.

Olson, Eric T. (1997). *The Human Animal* (New York: Oxford University Press).

(2001). "Review of *Persons and Bodies*," *Mind* 110: 427–430.

Parker, Sue Taylor, Robert W. Mitchell, and Marria L. Boccia, eds. (1994). *Self-Awareness in Animals and Humans* (Cambridge: Cambridge University Press).

Pasnau, Robert (2002). *Thomas Aquinas on Human Nature: A Philosophical Study of Summa Theologiae 1a 75–89* (Cambridge: Cambridge University Press).

Peirce, Charles Sanders (1868/1958). "Some Consequences of the Four Incapacities," in Philip P. Wiener, ed., *Charles Sanders Peirce: Selected Writings* (New York: Dover Publications), pp. 39–72.

Pereboom, Derk (2002). "On Baker's *Persons and Bodies*," *Philosophy and Phenomenological Research* 64: 615–622.

(2002). "Robust Nonreductive Physicalism," *Journal of Philosophy* 99: 499–531.

Pereboom, Derk and Hilary Kornblith (1991). "The Metaphysics of Irreducibility," *Philosophical Studies* 63: 125–145.

Perry, John (1970). "The Same F," *Philosophical Review* 79: 181–200.

(1979). "The Problem of the Essential Indexical," *Noûs* 13: 3–21.

Preston, Beth (1998). "Why is a Wing Like a Spoon? A Pluralist Theory of Function," *Journal of Philosophy* 95: 215–254.

Quine, W. V. O. (1960). *Word and Object* (Cambridge, MA: MIT Press).

(1966). "Three Grades of Modal Involvement," in *The Ways of Paradox and Other Essays* (New York: Random House), pp. 156–174.

(1995). "Naturalism; or, Living Within One's Means," *Dialectica* 49: 251–262.

Rea, Michael C. (1998). "In Defense of Mereological Universalism," *Philosophy and Phenomenological Research* 58: 347–360.

(1998). "Sameness Without Identity: An Aristotelian Solution to the Problem of Material Constitution," *Ratio* (new series) 11: 316–328.

(2002). *World Without Design: Ontological Consequences of Naturalism* (Oxford: Clarendon Press).

(2003). "Four-Dimensionalism," in Michael J. Loux and Dean W. Zimmerman, eds., *The Oxford Handbook of Metaphysics* (Oxford: Oxford University Press), pp. 246–280.

Rochat, Philippe, ed. (1995). *The Self in Infancy: Theory and Research* (Amsterdam: North-Holland, Elsevier).

Russell, Bertrand (1923). "Vagueness," *Australasian Journal of Philosophy and Psychology* 1: 84–92.

Salmon, Nathan P. (1982). *Reference and Essence* (Oxford: Blackwell).

Sanford, David H. (1993). "The Problem of the Many, Many Composition Questions, and Naive Mereology," *Noûs* 27: 219–233.

(2003). "Fusion Confusion," *Analysis* 63: 1–4.

Schaffer, Jonathan (2003). "Is There a Fundamental Level?" *Noûs* 37: 498–517.

(2003). "The Metaphysics of Causation," in Edward N. Zalta, ed., *The Stanford Encyclopedia of Philosophy* (Spring 2003 Edition). http://plato.stanford.edu/archives/spr2003/entries/causation-metaphysics/.

Schwartz, Stephen P. (1999)."Why it is Impossible to be Moral," *American Philosophical Quarterly* 36: 351–359.

Segal, Gabriel and Elliott Sober (1991). "The Causal Efficacy of Content," *Philosophical Studies* 63: 1–30.

Shoemaker, Sydney (2003). "Causality and Properties," in *Identity, Cause and Mind*, 2nd ed. (Oxford: Clarendon Press), pp. 206–234.

Sider, Theodore (2001). *Four-Dimensionalism: An Ontology of Persistence and Time* (Oxford: Clarendon Press).

(2002). "Review of *Persons and Bodies: A Constitution View*," *Journal of Philosophy* 99: 45–48.

Simons, Peter (1987). *Parts: A Study in Ontology* (Oxford: Clarendon Press).

Smart, J. J. C. (1963). *Philosophy and Scientific Realism* (London: Routledge & Kegan Paul).

Snowdon, Paul F. (1990). "Persons, Animals and Ourselves," in Christopher Gill, ed., *The Person and the Human Mind* (Oxford: Clarendon Press), pp. 83–107.

Sosa, Ernest (1993). "Putnam's Pragmatic Realism," *Journal of Philosophy* 90: 605–626. Reprinted in Jaegwon Kim and Ernest Sosa, eds., *Metaphysics: An Anthology* (Oxford: Blackwell, 1999), pp. 607–619.

Sosa, Ernest (1997). "Subjects Among Other Things," in Michael C. Rea, ed., *Material Constitution* (Lanham, MD: Rowman and Littlefield), pp. 63–89.

Stalnaker, Robert (1988). "Vague Identity," in David Austin, ed., *Philosophical Analysis* (Dordrecht, Holland: Kluwer Academic Publishers), pp. 349–360.

Stump, Eleonore (1995). "NonCartesian Substance Dualism and Materialism Without Reductionism," *Faith and Philosophy* 12: 505–531.

Stump, Eleonore and Kretzmann, Norman (1981). "Eternity," *Journal of Philosophy* 78: 429–458.

Swinburne, Richard (1997). *The Evolution of the Soul*, rev. ed. (Oxford: Clarendon Press).

Talliaferro, Charles (1994). *Consciousness and the Mind of God* (Cambridge: Cambridge University Press).

Teller, Paul (1992). "A Contemporary Look At Emergence," in Ansgar Beckermann, Hans Flohr, and Jaegwon Kim, eds., *Emergence or Reduction? Essays on the Prospects of Nonreductive Physicalism* (Berlin: Walter de Gruyter), pp. 139–153.

Thomasson, Amie L. (1998). "A Nonreductivist Solution to Mental Causation," *Philosophical Studies* 89: 181–195.

(1999). *Fiction and Metaphysics* (Cambridge: Cambridge University Press).

(2003). "Realism and Human Kinds," *Philosophical and Phenomenological Research* 78: 580–609.

(2007). *Ordinary Objects* (Oxford: Oxford University Press).

Thomson, Judith Jarvis (1998). "The Statue and the Clay," *Noûs* 32: 149–173.

Tooley, Michael (1990). "The Nature of Causation: A Singularist Account," *Canadian Journal of Philosophy* (Supplementary Volume 16, ed. David Copp): 271–322.

(1997). *Time, Tense and Causation* (Oxford: Clarendon Press).

Tye, Michael (1990). "Vague Objects," *Mind* 99: 535–557.

Van Gulick, Robert, "Who's in Charge Here?" (1993) in John Heil and Alfred Mele, eds., *Mental Causation* (Oxford: Clarendon Press), pp. 233–258.

Van Inwagen, Peter (1988). "How to Reason About Vague Objects," *Philosophical Topics* 16: 255–284.

(1990). *Material Beings* (Ithaca, NY: Cornell University Press).

(2001). "The Doctrine of Arbitrary Undetached Parts," in *Ontology, Identity and Modality* (Cambridge: Cambridge University Press), pp. 75–94.

(2002). "The Number of Things," in Ernest Sosa, ed., *Philosophical Issues 12: Realism and Relativism* (Oxford: Blackwell), pp. 176–196.

(2002). "Review of *Persons and Bodies*," *Philosophical Review* 111: 138–141.

(forthcoming). "Can Mereological Sums Change Their Parts?" *Journal of Philosophy*.

Vermaas, Pieter E. and Wybo Houkes (2003). "Ascribing Functions to Technical Artifacts: A Challenge to Etiological Accounts of Functions," *British Journal for the Philosophy of Science* 54: 261–289.

Wasserman, Ryan (2004). "The Constitution Question," *Noûs* 38: 693–710.

White, Nicholas (1986). "Identity, Modal Individuation and Matter in Arisotle," in Peter A. French, Theodore E. Uehling, Jr., and Howard K. Wettstein, eds., *Studies in Essentialism* (Midwest Studies in Philosophy XI) (Minneapolis: University of Minnesota), pp. 475–494.

Wiggins, David (1968). "On Being in the Same Place at the Same Time," *Philosophical Review* 77: 90–95. Reprinted in Michael Rea, ed., *Material Constitution: A Reader* (Lanham, MD: Rowman and Littlefield Publishers, Inc.), pp. 3–9.

(2001). *Sameness and Substance Renewed* (Cambridge: Cambridge University Press).

Williamson, Timothy (1994). *Vagueness* (London: Routledge).

(2003). "Vagueness in Reality," in Michael J. Loux and Dean Zimmerman, eds., *The Oxford Handbook of Metaphysics* (Oxford: Oxford University Press), pp. 690–715.

Wilson, Robert A. (2005). "Persons, Social Agency, and Constitution," *Social Philosophy and Policy* 22: 49–69.

Yablo, Stephen (1987). "Identity, Essence and Indiscernibility," *Philosophical Review* 104: 293–314.

Zemach, Eddy M. (1991). "Vague Objects," *Noûs* 25: 323–340.

Zimmerman, Dean W. (2002). "*Persons and Bodies*: Constitution Without Mereology?" *Philosophy and Phenomenological Research* 64: 599–606.

(2002). "The Constitution of Persons by Bodies: A Critique of Lynne Rudder Baker's Theory of Material Constitution," *Philosophical Topics* 30: 295–338.

Index

animalism, 90–91
Anscombe, G. E. M., 72n, 74n, 97n
Antony, Louise, 108n, 239n
Aristotle, 33, 77
  and artifacts, 60, 61n, 62n
  and numerical sameness, 40–41, 171
  on matter and form, 71
Armstrong, David, 5n, 98n
artifacts, 49–53
  and aggregates, 49–51
  and natural objects, 59–64, 65
  malfunction, 55–59
  ontological status of, 64–65
Austin, J. L., 14n, 125n

Beall, J. C., 123n
Bernat, James, 84n
Blanchette, Patricia, 227n
Bolton, Robert, 61n
Boyd, Richard, 82n
Braun, David, 123n, 140n
Bricker, Phillip, 27n, 192n
Broad, C. D., 142n
Brower, Jeffrey E., 41n
Burge, Tyler, 62n, 104n
Burke, Michael B., 42n

Castañeda, Hector-Neri, 69n
causal powers, 33, 42, 98n, 115,
    116–119
causation
  commonsense causation, 97–99
  nonreductive causation, 111–116
  property-constitution view (PC View),
    111–115
Chisholm, Roderick, 34n, 37, 37n, 183
  and vagueness, 203–204, 205–207
Churchland, Paul, 17n, 237n
Clapp, Lenny, 111n, 114n

co-location, 165–166, 166n, 209n
  "paradoxes of coincidence," 208–213
constitution, relation of, 32
  definition, 161
  "G-favorable circumstances," 160–161
  plausibility of, 39–43
  spatial coincidence, 161
  see also primary kinds
Constitution View, 32–39
  of artifacts, 53–55
  of human persons, 67–82, 92
  of parts at t, 187–189
  of property-instantiations, 112–116
  treatment of metaphysical puzzles,
    194–197
Craig, William Lane, 146n
Crisp, Thomas, 101n, 142n
Curd, Patricia, 71n

Darwinism, 70, 71, 81, 86
David, Marian, 227n
Davidson, Donald, 46n
de Regt, Herman, 75n
de re modality, 221–225
derivative and nonderivative property
    exemplification, 166–170
  see also "having a property derivatively"
Derksen, Ton, 75n
D-fusions, 201–202
Dickinson, Anthony, 77n
Dipert, Randall, 52n
Doepke, Frederick C., 42n

Elder, Crawford L., 5n, 51n, 63n
Eldredge, Niles, 86n
eliminativism, 26, 27n, 27–31
emergence, 237–239
  conceptions of, 237–238
  Constitution View of, 238–239

essential properties, 34n
  see also persistence conditions
  see also primary kinds
Evans, Gareth, 128n
existence,
  Bimodal View of, 227–233
  "the Domain" (of unrestricted
    existential quantifier),
    226–228

Feldman, Fred, 84n
Fine, Gail, 71n
Fine, Kit, 171n
Finnis, John, 73n
first-person perspective, 68–71
  robust vs. rudimentary, 75–81
Ford, Norman M., 72n, 74n
Foster, John, 91n
four-dimensionalism, 27n, 28–29
  argument from vagueness, 201–203
  stage version, 201, 212, 214n
  thesis of, 200
  worm version, 201
Funder, D., 16n

Gale, Richard, 146n
Gallup, Gordon Jr., 70n, 77, 77n, 78n
Garrett, Brian, 127n
Gazzaniga, Michael, 74n, 85n
Gettier, Edmund L., 138n
Gibbard, Alan, 221n, 221–222
Gopnik, Alison, 76, 77n
Grünbaum, Adolf, 145n, 150–153
Gupta, Anil, 162n

Hasker, William, 91n, 176
"having a property derivatively," 37–39,
  166–170
Heller, Mark, 201
Hershenov, David B., 85n, 164n
Heyes, Cecilia, 77n
Hilpinen, Risto, 51n, 52n
Hindriks, Frank, 48n
Hirsch, Eli, 195n
Hoffman, Joshua, 59n
Houkes, Wybo, 51n, 52n, 55n
human organisms, 68
  coming into existence, 72–75

ID Phenomena ("intention-dependent"),
  11–13, 106–110

identity, 33, 35, 170n
  and nonidentity, 170–171

Jauernig, Anja, 151n
Johnston, Mark, 42n

Kagan, Jerome, 77n, 78, 78n
Kąkol, Tomasz, 163n, 164n
Kaplan, David, 147n
Kim, Jaegwon, 5n, 99–120, 165n, 234n,
  237n–238n
  basic principles, 100
  on causation, 99–104, 100n, 102n, 106n
  on emergence, 238–239
  on generalization argument, 104–106
  on micro-based properties, 109n
  on realization, 100, 108–109
  response to Kim on causation, 106–110
Kornblith, Hilary, 17, 17n, 99n, 114n
Koslicki, Kathryn, 42n, 132n
Kripke, Saul, 5n, 42
Kuhl, Patricia, 77n

LaPorte, Joseph, 61n, 63n
levels 112n, 234, 237n
  descriptive, 111, 111n
  mereological conception, 112n, 234–235
  ontological conception, 112, 113, 235–237
Levine, Joseph, 108n
Lewis, David, 5n, 10n, 26n, 30n, 58n, 184n,
  216n, 224n
  on vagueness, 123–124, 124n, 132n
Lewis, Michael, 76n
life and death, 82–85
Loewer, Barry, 101n
Lovley, Derek, 64n
Lowe, E. J., 42n, 118n, 134n
  and artifacts, 52n
Lycan, William G., Jr., 174n

Mallon, Ronald, 48n
Marcus, Ruth Barcan, 223n
Markosian, Ned, 142n
materialism, 93
Matthews, Gareth B., 7n, 11n, 40, 40n, 48n,
  80n, 228n
McTaggart, J. M. E., 143n
Meijers, Anthonie, 52n, 56n, 75n
Meijsing, Monica, 75n
Mellor, Hugh, 152n
Meltzoff, Andrew, 76, 77n

Index

mereology, 32, 32n, 162
  aggregates, 49–51, 161
  Chisholm–Lewis axioms, 183–185
  constitution as a non-mereological
    relation, 181–182
  mereological conception of levels, 113n
  mereological essentialism, 183
  ontological status of sums, 191–194
  sums as ultimate constituters, 185–187
Merricks, Trenton, 30n, 31n, 90n, 123n, 209n
metaphysics, 47, 47n, 213–214, 218–240
  see also Practical Realism
mind-independence/mind-dependence,
    18–20, 64, 153
Morreau, Michael, 127n

Neisser, Ulric, 77, 77n, 78, 78n
nonreductionism, 3–4, 25, 26, 29–32
  "irreducibly real," 4, 5–6, 7–10, 25
  nonreductive materialism, 116–119
  see also eliminativism, reductionism
Noordhof, Paul, 118n
Noonan, Harold, 67n, 127n, 224n, 224–225

Oaklander, L. Nathan, 146n
Oderberg, David, 42n
Olson, Eric T., 90n, 172–175, 174n
ontological novelty, 234
ontological significance, account of, 218–226
ontology, 21
overdetermination, the argument from,
    100–102, 119n

parsimony, the argument from, 10
Pasnau, Robert, 80n
Peirce, Charles Sanders, 240n
Pereboom, Derk, 99n, 101n, 111n, 114n
  on definition of "x constitutes y at t,"
    163n, 163–164, 165
Perry, John, 147n
persistence
  conditions for individuals, 33, 36, 42,
    220–221, 225
  first-personal conditions, 71
  nature of, 200–201
persons
  coming into existence, 75–81
  ontological uniqueness of, 89–90
  see also first-person perspective
plural quantification, 32n, 192–194
Povinelli, Daniel J., 78n

Practical Realism, 15–20
  as approach to metaphysics, 238–239
  grades of empirical involvement, 15–18
  see also mind-independence/mind-
    dependence
Preston, Beth, 51n
Prince, Christopher G, 78, 78n
primary kinds, 33–39, 112, 159

quasi-naturalism, 85–89
  and methodological naturalism, 88
  vs. scientific naturalism, 87
Quine, W. V. O., 88n, 223n

Rea, Michael C., 5n, 41n, 42n, 142n,
    165, 191n
reductionism, 26, 27–31
Restall, Greg, 123n
Rochat, Philippe, 78, 78n
Roman Catholic teaching, 73
Rosenkrantz, Gary S., 59n, 63n
Russell, Bertrand, 121n

Salmon, Nathan P., 133n
Sanford, David H., 182n
Schaffer, Jonathan, 58n, 98n, 101n, 235n
Schartz, Stephen P., 138n
Segal, Gabriel, 118n
Shoemaker, Sydney, 111n
Sider, Theodore, 5n, 9n, 31n, 46n, 46–47,
    164n, 226n
  on constitution, 161–162, 212–213
  on vagueness, 123n, 140n, 184n,
    199n–208n, 201–204
Sie, Maureen, 48n
Simons, Peter, 42n
Slors, Marc, 75n
Smart, J. J. C., 145n
Sneed, C., 16n
Snowdon, Paul F., 90n
Sober, Elliott, 118n
Sonderegger, Katherine, 48n
Sosa, Ernest, 18, 18n, 42n
Stalnaker, Robert, 135n
Stump, Eleonore, 71n
  and Kretzmann, Norman, 82n
Substance Dualism, 91–92, 176–178
supervenience, 100, 108, 116n, 118,
    119, 119n
  Humean, 51n, 52n, 182n
Swinburne, Richard, 91n

Talliaferro, Charles, 91n
Teller, Paul, 237n
"the everyday world," 4
"the same F," 169–170
Thomasson, Amie L., 5n, 12n, 52n,
    63n, 101n
Thomism, 91n
Thomson, Judith Jarvis, 42n
three-dimensionalism, 27–28, 29n
    argument against Sider, 203–208
    arguments for, 213–214
time, 136n
    and existence, 226–233
    A-series and B-series, 143–149
    BA theory of time, 149–152
    eternalism, 142, 155, 231–233
    growing-universe view, 142, 231
    presentism, 142, 154–155, 231–232
Tooley, Michael, 98n, 142n
Tye, Michael, 127n

unity, 166–172

vagueness, 121, 124n
    epistemicism, 122, 136n
    higher-order vagueness, 138
    sorites arguments, 135–140, 136n
    supervaluationism, 122–123, 136n

vagueness in the world, 127–135, 137n,
    181n, 196–197
    arguments for, 123–127
van Inwagen, Peter, 5n, 26, 26n, 30n, 31n, 90n
    and artifacts, 57n
    on mereology, 182n, 183n, 185n, 194n
    on vague objects, 127n, 135n
Vermass, Pieter E., 51n, 55n
von Eckhardt, Barbara, 16n
von Willigenburg, Theo, 48n

Warfield, Ted, 101n
Wasserman, Ryan, 34n
White, Nicholas, 40n
Wiggins, David, 20, 20n, 41n, 42n, 194n
    and artifacts, 60, 60n, 61, 62n
Williamson, Timothy,
    on vagueness, 123n, 128, 128n
Wilson, Robert A., 76n, 80n, 164n
Wittgenstein, Ludwig, 125n

Yablo, Stephen, 42n

Zemach, Eddy M., 127n
Zimmerman, Dean, 43n, 43–46
    on constitution, 162n, 165n, 167n,
        175–180, 177n
    on parts, 181n, 189–190